The Buddha and the Christ

FAITH MEETS FAITH
An Orbis Series in Interreligious Dialogue
Paul F. Knitter, General Editor

In our contemporary world, the many religions and spiritualities stand in need of greater intercommunication and cooperation. More than ever before, they must speak to, learn from, and work with each other, in order to maintain their own identity and vitality and so to contribute to fashioning a better world.

FAITH MEETS FAITH seeks to promote interreligious dialogue by providing an open forum for the exchanges between and among followers of different religious paths. While the series wants to encourage creative and bold responses to the new questions of pluralism confronting religious persons today, it also recognizes the present plurality of perspectives concerning the methods and content of interreligious dialogue.

This series, therefore, does not want to endorse any one school of thought. By making available to both the scholarly community and the general public works that represent a variety of religious and methodological viewpoints, FAITH MEETS FAITH hopes to foster and focus the emerging encounter among the religions of the world.

FAITH MEETS FAITH SERIES

The Buddha and the Christ

Explorations in Buddhist and Christian Dialogue

Leo D. Lefebure

ORBIS BOOKS

Maryknoll, New York 10545

The Catholic Foreign Mission Society of America (Maryknoll) recruits and trains people for overseas missionary service. Through Orbis Books, Maryknoll aims to foster the international dialogue that is essential to mission. The books published, however, reflect the opinions of their authors and are not meant to represent the official position of the society.

Published by Orbis Books, Maryknoll, N.Y. 10545

Grateful acknowledgment is given to the following publishers, who have generously granted permission for reprinting materials in this book.
Darton, Longman and Todd (London) and Doubleday (Garden City, New York), for scripture quotes from *The New Jerusalem Bible*, © copyright 1985.
Shambhala Publications (Boston, Massachusetts) for selections from *The Flower Ornament Scripture,* volume 1, translated by Thomas Cleary, © copyright 1984.
Parallax Press (Berkeley, California) for selections from *The Moon Bamboo* by Thich Nhat Hanh, © copyright 1989.
Bantam Books (New York) for selections from *Peace Is Every Step* by Thich Nhat Hanh, © copyright 1991.

Manufactured in the United States of America

Library of Congress Cataloging-in-Publication Data

Lefebure, Leo D., 1952-
    The Buddha and the Christ : explorations in Buddhist and Christian
dialogue / Leo D. Lefebure.
        p.   cm. — (Faith meets faith series)
    Includes bibliographical references and index.
    ISBN 0-88344-924-2 (paper)
    1. Christianity and other religions—Buddhism. 2. Buddhism
— Relations—Christianity. I. Title. II. Series: Faith meets
faith.
BR128.B8L44   1993
261.2'43—dc20
                                                    93-7972
                                                        CIP

To my Colleagues and Friends
the Faculty and Students
of Mundelein Seminary
University of Saint Mary of the Lake

Contents

III
CONTEMPORARY PATHS
Engaged Buddhism and Theology of Liberation

A Note on Orthography

The problem of rendering non-Western systems of writing into Roman letters for English and other modern European languages is notoriously difficult. Joining many publishers who do not insert diacritical marks for words such as the Sanskrit *Śūnyatā*, this book also omits them.

Scholars and others who know languages such as Sanskrit, Pali, Arabic, or Japanese do not need the diacritical marks to identify words in their original written form. And persons who do not know these languages gain little from having the marks reproduced. We recognize that languages employing different orthographic systems have a richness and distinctiveness that *are* partially conveyed by the orthographics of diacritical marks. And while we do not wish to be part of flattening out the contours of our linguistically plural globe, the high cost of ensuring accuracy in using the diacritical marks does not justify reproducing them here.

Acknowledgments

The generosity, insights and contributions of countless persons have come together to make the writing of this book possible. I would like to thank the many Buddhists in both Asia and the United States who have welcomed me and shared their practice and their perspectives with me. I would like to thank the Association of Theological Schools of the United States and Canada for the opportunity to participate in the Junior Scholars Program in 1988-89 and for a research grant that made the beginning of research on this project possible. I especially thank Professor Masao Abe for graciously serving as mentor to me in this program and for his kind hospitality in Kyoto during the summer of 1989. I owe a great debt both to Professor Abe and also to the numerous other scholars in Japan, both Buddhist and Christian, who discussed this project with me and broadened my understanding of Buddhism and of the issues involved in interreligious dialogue.

I also would like to thank the Association of Theological Schools and the Center for Development in Ministry of the University of Saint Mary of the Lake for co-sponsoring a series of lectures delivered at the Dominican House of Studies in River Forest, Illinois, in the fall of 1989. This work is an expansion and development of ideas presented in those lectures.

I thank the administration of Mundelein Seminary for the research leave to begin this project, and I thank my colleagues at Mundelein Seminary who read and commented on earlier drafts of the manuscript, especially John Shea, Lawrence Hennessey, Louis Cameli, and Eugene LaVerdiere.

The wisdom, the suggestions, and the criticisms of so many persons have contributed to the shaping of this book and to whatever merits it may have. The weaknesses and limitations of this essay are truly my own.

Prologue

Invitation to a Journey

The Prospects of Buddhist-Christian Dialogue

I arrived at the Theravada Buddhist monastery of Wat Rempoeng near Chiang Mai in the north of Thailand on a hot Wednesday afternoon in August. While I knew relatively little about Buddhist monastic life, I was eager to learn, and I was hoping to have some enlightening conversations with the monks I would meet.

My friend and I were given the white clothes worn by those entering meditation and were led to a small concrete-block hut. I went out for a walk and began to chat with some of the monks who spoke English. They were quite friendly and showed me their manual printing press, where they were preparing a new edition of the Buddhist scriptures. One of the monks assured me that all religions are really the same — only the language that we use is different.

universalit]

Later that afternoon a Buddhist nun escorted my companion and me to another building for our first lessons in meditation. Though she spoke excellent English and was delighted that we were there, she had no interest in interreligious dialogue, in discussing beliefs or doctrines. Instead, she proceeded to show us how to meditate with our bodies. We did sitting meditation (sitting cross-legged and attending to our breathing) and walking meditation (walking very slowly and noting the rise and fall of each step). She also taught us a complex series of very slow hand and arm and torso movements — another form of meditation with our bodies.

I had come to learn about Buddhism, but my first lesson was that Buddhism is not a matter of talking, of discussing doctrines and beliefs, of comparing ideas about human existence and the universe. My initiation into the monastic life of Theravada Buddhism was a lesson on sitting and walking, on paying attention to the present moment and acknowledging my movements and thoughts, following my breath at each moment. "Acknowledge, acknowledge" was the constant refrain of my teachers. The point of meditation was not to obtain new thoughts through discussions, but to observe the arising of thoughts and thereby bring the mind to concentration and stillness.

We received no dinner that evening, for Thai Buddhist monks follow the ancient custom of eating no solid food after noon. Our hosts did offer to feed us if we wished, but we declined.

The next morning one of the senior monks who was my meditation teacher instructed me to do eight hours meditation each day, alternating one half-hour sitting meditation and one half-hour walking meditation. I thought to myself, "Well, eight hours a day isn't so bad," and went off to my hut to begin.

After practicing this routine for several hours, I decided to take a break and went outside for a walk. It was a gorgeous late afternoon, and the sounds of evening services filled the air. The voices of monks chanting the Buddhist scriptures from one side of the monastery complex mingled with the voices of nuns chanting back from the other side. I stood for a long time in front of a statue of the Buddha, entranced by the sights and sounds of the moment.

The next morning my meditation teacher told me that he did not want me walking around and looking at statues. He told me that he wanted me to meditate twenty-four hours a day and to increase the periods of sitting and walking by ten minutes each day. From then on, the days seemed interminably long. The pain of sitting and walking for ever longer periods grew greater, and at times I had a sense of doing violence to myself. My mind would become still up to a certain point, and I felt at times as if I were on the verge of a different form of awareness, but then my mind would begin to wander again.

In one sense the initiation was not a success. I did not achieve the concentrated oneness of mind that Buddhists call *samadhi*. Nor did I have the types of conversations I had hoped for. But I did learn something of how one is initiated into Buddhist monastic life in Thailand, and I learned that for the Buddhists who were my hosts, what mattered most was not to dialogue, not to discuss ideas and beliefs and concepts and doctrines, whether Buddhist or Christian, but rather to practice meditation. My hosts were warm and hospitable; they repeatedly urged me to prolong my stay. But dialogue in the Western sense of the term was far from their minds.

I learned that the very practice of interreligious dialogue itself is not to be taken for granted. While many Buddhists, especially in Japan and the United States, are interested in discussing perspectives on human existence with Christians, my first experience in a Buddhist monastery was hardly the type of dialogue that I expected.

I begin with this recollection not only because it was my own introduction to Buddhist monastic life, but also as a caution for all that will follow. One danger for Western Christians who enter into dialogue with Buddhists is to overemphasize the role of talking—especially conversations about the doctrinal and intellectual side of religious life. We sometimes treat Buddhists as if they were one more intellectual position comparable to Western theological or philosophical perspectives. Aloysius Pieris, a Sri Lankan Jesuit theologian, warns us: "It is common knowledge that the West *studies* all the world religions, whereas the East simply *practices* them."[1]

LANGUAGE AND SILENCE

Buddhism certainly does possess a highly developed and sophisticated intellectual tradition, and Buddhists themselves have discussed and debated interminably the interpretation of their own tradition. Buddhists, however, have also repeatedly questioned the importance of such debates. Mahayana Buddhists treasure the story of Vimalakirti, a wealthy householder who understood the Buddha's teaching with great depth and wisdom. One day the bodhisattva Manjushri, the incarnation of wisdom, went to visit Vimalakirti together with a large number of other bodhisattvas, people who are future buddhas. Each one explained his understanding of the central Buddhist teaching of nonduality.

When they finished, Manjushri asked Vimalakirti what he thought it meant for a bodhisattva to penetrate the doctrine of nonduality. Vimalakirti responded with a thundering silence, refusing to utter a single word. Manjushri praised him most highly, telling him: "Excellent! Excellent, noble sir! This is indeed the entrance into the nonduality of the bodhisattvas. Here there is no use for syllables, sounds, and ideas."[2]

In a similar vein, Japanese Buddhists tell the story that one day in a little country temple in Ohara, north of Kyoto, two monks were arguing endlessly over a point of Buddhist doctrine. Suddenly a statue of Amida Buddha in the temple began to glow with a supernatural light, putting an end to the wordy discussion and leading the participants into silence.

For Buddhists, the deepest expression of wisdom is silence, as exemplified by the silence of the Buddha.[3] Absolute truth or ultimate reality cannot be expressed in words.[4] To understand Buddhist perspectives on human life, however, we have to use words. Words are necessary even for understanding silence, for silence is only meaningful in relation to language. Silence always invites interpretation. Without the interplay of language and silence, we cannot distinguish the silence of the wise from the silence of fools. The Vimalakirti Sutra itself acknowledges this by rejecting the unenlightened silence of other disciples who do not know how to respond to questions. It is because Vimalakirti's words are so insightful that his silence is so powerful.

While using words to explore Buddhist and Christian perspectives, I do not want to forget my first lessons in Buddhist meditation at Wat Rempoeng or the thundering silence of Vimalakirti or the statue of Amida Buddha with its miraculous light. The point of all our words in dialogue is to lead us to the silence beyond words.

SKILLFUL MEANS

This principle is closely related to a fundamental premise of Buddhism. All the teachings of the Buddha and his followers are like a raft which takes us from a dangerous shore to the other shore which is safe; once the other shore is reached, the raft should not be carried on our head. The teachings can help us reach the other side of the river but should not be grasped at for their own sake.[5]

Mahayana Buddhists distinguish two levels of truth: ultimate truth and conventional truth.[6] Ultimate truth, the insight of enlightenment, can be adequately expressed only by the noble silence of the Buddha. No language or theory, no explanation can express the Buddha's experience of reality as it is. In addition to ultimate truth there is also conventional truth expressed in language. While conventional truth can never perfectly express the Buddha's enlightenment, it is nonetheless important because it can lead us to share for ourselves the Buddha's experience of wisdom. The words that express conventional truth can undermine our false views of reality, they can overthrow the illusions that dominate our normal existence, and thus they can lead us on the path to enlightenment. But all the teachings of Mahayana Buddhism, all its practices and devotions, are to be understood as the skillful means of the Buddha to guide his followers.[7] They are not the truth itself, but they are instruments to assist our awakening to the truth.

Thus Buddhists can say that the Buddha taught 80,000 doctrines and never said a single word. Even the title given to the Buddha expresses his silence. After his enlightenment, Siddhartha Gautama became known as Shakyamuni Buddha. *Buddha* means the enlightened or awakened one, and *Shakyamuni* means the sage of the Shakya clan. *Muni*, translated as "sage," originally meant "the one who keeps silent"—the enlightened one is the silent one. The ultimate insight of the Buddha is beyond words.

The Buddha, nonetheless, did spend about forty-five years preaching out of compassion for all living beings, to enable them to find liberation and final bliss. The Buddha's words were so many skillful means that expressed a wisdom and compassion that transcended words.

The view of Buddhist teaching as skillful means has been extremely influential on the way the tradition has developed. Like Christianity, Buddhism has flourished in a wide variety of forms in different cultures, and so there is no one Buddhist perspective on wisdom and compassion or on the meaning of the transformation of human existence. Buddhism has been an important unifying force in much of Asian culture, for it has spread its influence in a wide variety of forms through much of Southern, Central, and Eastern Asia.[8]

While Buddhism is little practiced today in India, the land of its birth, it, like Christianity, has enjoyed great success as a missionary religion in other lands. Theravada Buddhism, so called because it follows the "Way of the Elders," is a dominant force today in the life of Sri Lanka, Burma, Thailand, Laos, and Kampuchea. Theravada Buddhism is the only surviving school of Hinayana Buddhism, so called because it was viewed as the "Lesser Vehicle" by members of the Mahayana tradition. Mahayana Buddhism in turn takes its name from its claim to be the "Larger Vehicle" of liberation. It has played a major role in shaping the cultures of China, Tibet, Mongolia, Japan, Korea, and Vietnam. The spread of Buddhism to so many different cultures has led to a wide diversity.

The goal of Shakyamuni Buddha was to transform the lives of his followers by showing them the path to liberation. In their efforts to share the teaching of the Buddha, later generations of Buddhists have felt authorized to adopt a wide variety of approaches in different lands in order to meet the needs of their situation. An old Zen saying tells us, "If we expounded the Dharma the same way all the time, the weeds in front of the teaching hall would be ten feet deep."[9]

Mahayana Buddhists understand all the teachings and practices of their tradition as skillful means in the service of enlightenment. In undertaking a comparison of the two traditions, it is important to remember both the diversity within each tradition and the status of religious language in each religion. The Christian tradition has also long been aware of the inadequacy of human language to communicate the reality of God in any literal, univocal fashion. Where Mahayana Buddhists insist that all their stories and theories and practices of meditation are so many skillful means, the goal of all Christian preaching, prayer, and theology is to lead us into the mystery of God, a mystery which exceeds all names. Neither Buddhism nor Christianity is interested in simply describing realities external to us. Both are movements of transformation that seek to overcome suffering and to liberate us from the prisons in which we find ourselves.

DIALOGUE AMID DIFFERENCE

Dialogue between Christians and Buddhists is increasing, partly because of increased global awareness, partly because of the vitality of Christianity and Buddhism in much of Asia, as well as the growing communities of Buddhists in North America, and also the attractive power of Buddhism to many persons in North America and Europe. Dialogue is important for both traditions' self-understandings in the global community, but genuine understanding is difficult because of the very different assumptions that Buddhists and Christians bring to their religious practices.

Augustine set the tone for most of the Western Christian theological tradition in his dialogue between himself and Reason in the *Soliloquies*. He heard the voice of Reason ask him, "What, then, do you desire to know?"

Augustine answered, "I desire to know God and the soul."

Reason pressed, "And nothing more?"

Augustine responded, "Nothing whatever."[10]

Most of Western Christian thought has followed the lead of Augustine and focused its attention on God and the human soul. Theologians have discussed the relation between God and the human person at great length. This relationship runs throughout the whole structure of Christian theology, from creation to redemption, Christology, grace, and eschatology.

Buddhism, by contrast, denies the existence of an independent, permanent self and refuses to rely on a transcendent creating and redeeming God.[11] The Buddhist premises of no-God and no-self have been interpreted by Buddhists themselves in a wide variety of ways, but in all their forms they are a radical counterpoint and challenge to Christian presuppositions.

Both the similarities and the differences between these two paths of liberation demand attention throughout this discussion. One of the most important aspects of their relationship is difference between the faith in God of Jesus and his followers and Shakyamuni Buddha's silence on God. This issue poses one of the most fascinating and most perplexing questions in Buddhist-Christian dialogue: What difference does it make for a *religion* to affirm or not to affirm the reality of God?

The beginning of the Nicene Creed states one of the fundamental assumptions of Christian faith: belief in God, the creator of all things. Belief in creation serves as a fundamental principle for interpreting all Christian beliefs and perspectives: every finite reality is dependent for its very being on the incomprehensible ultimate reality which Christians name God. For Christians, however, the meaning of creation becomes fully apparent only in the revelation of God in Jesus Christ, the incarnation of the Word through whom all things were created. To appreciate the significance of creation, Christians turn to the mystery of God becoming human and the grace of God given in Jesus Christ.

Instead of creation, the Buddhist tradition speaks of dependent co-arising: every reality arises from all the other realities in the universe. Because this is, that is. This is one way of formulating the central insight of the Buddha. Neither creation nor dependent co-arising is simply a cosmological theory about the universe, but the two perspectives do give rise to very different ways of interpreting the problem of human existence and the path of transformation. Christianity uses what we might call a hermeneutics of creation, that is, an approach to interpreting all language about God and humans in light of the relation of Creator to creatures. Buddhism, by contrast, employs a hermeneutics of dependent co-arising, an approach to interpretation which sees all realities as interdependent, arising from one another, and flowing into one another. All the terms used by Christians are set in the context of belief in God as Creator, on whom all things are dependent for their very being and without whom nothing would be. All the language used by Buddhists is set in the context of dependent co-arising and the radical interdependence of all things that results from this vision. Both traditions are aware, however, that human language cannot express the full meaning of these perspectives. For both traditions, religious language must in some way be negated in order to fulfill its purpose and communicate the truth of ultimate reality.

How fundamental is the difference between these two perspectives? Directly conflicting answers can be given to this question. On the one hand, one can caution that because Christians believe in God and Buddhists do not, any similarities between Buddhist and Christian language are superficial. It can be claimed that Buddhist enlightenment is an awakening from suffering to knowledge of who we already are; Christian salvation is a supernatural gift from God, who is both beyond anything we can imagine and closer to us than we are to ourselves. From this vantage point, the differences between Buddhism and Christianity appear far more fundamental than any alleged similarities. This then poses the question of whether one or both of these traditions is simply wrong.

On the other hand, some scholars have claimed that the experience of ultimate reality itself is fundamentally the same in Buddhism and Christianity or in any great religion.[12] While the outward forms and expressions obviously differ, it is argued, the same divine reality is fully manifest in every genuine religious tradition. On the deepest level, some maintain, the experience of Reality itself as such is the same. Christians interpret this experience through their belief in God while Buddhists, not believing in God, inevitably use different language and different categories.

Neither extreme of emphasizing similarity or difference to the neglect of the other can do justice to the complexity of the relationship between Buddhism and Christianity. On the one hand, it is not clear that the experiences of Buddhism and Christianity are fundamentally identical, for the linguistic expressions of these experiences differ in important ways, and expressions and experience always influence each other. Nor, on the other hand, are the two traditions so different that all similarities can be dismissed as superficial. Creation and dependent co-arising are not objective theories about comprehensible realities external to humans. Both perspectives arise from the experience of existence as a gift and both serve to mark out a religious path to be followed. Both challenge us to see and to live in new ways. The Christian doctrine of creation is a call to abandon worship of creation and surrender to the Creator. The Buddhist doctrine of dependent co-arising is a call to stop clinging to passing illusions and open our eyes to impermanence.

Rather than argue for either fundamental unity or radical difference, this book will undertake the more modest and more complex strategy of identifying and discussing the similarities between the Christian and Buddhist traditions while also insisting on acknowledging their differences. The purpose of my discussion is twofold: (1) to offer Western Christians an introduction to major Mahayana Buddhist themes and traditions and (2) to identify similarities and differences in the dynamics of the Christian and Mahayana Buddhist traditions. I am writing, as a Catholic Christian, primarily for Western Christians who may not be familiar with many Buddhist perspectives, and so at each stage of the discussion I will first present an introduction to aspects of the Mahayana Buddhist tradition and then will turn to a comparison and contrast of the traditions. One of the first effects of interreligious dialogue is often a renewed appreciation of themes in one's own tradition.

The discussion will proceed in three sections. Part I will examine the foundations of the two traditions in the lives and teachings of Shakyamuni Buddha and Jesus Christ as remembered by their followers. Part II will explore four classic paths of following the Buddhist or Christian way: two Mahayana Buddhist traditions, Zen and Pure Land; and two early Christian interpreters who have had wide influence, Dionysius the Areopagite and Augustine of Hippo. Part III will turn to two major figures who practice and interpret their respective traditions in the contemporary world: the Vietnamese Buddhist monk and teacher Thich Nhat Hanh, and the Peruvian Catholic priest and theologian Gustavo Gutiérrez.

Within each section the chapters will alternate between a discussion of the Buddhist tradition and a comparison and contrast with the Christian tradition. Chapters 1, 3, 5, and 7 will explore aspects of the Mahayana Buddhist tradition, focusing on the life and teaching of the Buddha (Chapter 1), the structure of Mahayana Buddhist thought and the Ch'an and Zen traditions (Chapter 3), the development of the Pure Land Buddhist tradition (Chapter 5), and the life and teaching of Thich Nhat Hanh (Chapter 7). The alternating chapters will compare and contrast major aspects of the Christian tradition to Buddhist perspectives. These chapters will explore the memory of Jesus in the New Testament in relation to the Buddha (Chapter 2), the mystical theology of Dionysius the Areopagite in relation to Mahayana and especially Zen Buddhism (Chapter 4), the life and teaching of Augustine in relation to Mahayana perspectives (Chapter 6), and the liberation theology of Gustavo Gutiérrez in relation to the engaged Buddhism of Thich Nhat Hanh (Chapter 8).

SIMILARITY AND DIFFERENCE

We can only understand a truly different perspective on the basis of our own experience. From the point of view of Christianity, the love of God extends throughout all human experience, affecting all persons, whether they are aware of God or believe in God or not. Thus it is almost inevitable that a Christian interpret a Buddhist's experience of enlightenment as an experience of the incomprehensible and universal reality that Christians name God.

Christians, however, must be wary of forcing Buddhist experience into a preconceived Christian mold. Genuine dialogue requires us to respect another perspective on its own terms, and this often means acknowledging it as genuinely different from our own perspectives. This means envisaging possibilities that are really new to us and requires a strenuous work of the imagination.

In approaching the question of the meaning of God or the absence of God in religion, it is crucial to be conscious of the status of religious language. Christians need to remember and take to heart the repeated insistence of the Mahayana Buddhist tradition that words and categories and concepts cannot express the meaning of enlightenment or absolute truth. Mahayana Buddhists are not proclaiming objective theories that claim to express the truth univocally; they are offering skillful means that lead to enlightenment.

Buddhists, on the other hand, need also to be aware that Christian theology itself has a long tradition of negating the literal meaning of any image or concept that humans apply to God. No concept or idea or image can capture the reality of God, because God exceeds all that we can think or imagine. In the classical language of Thomas Aquinas, the essence of God exceeds our understanding. We cannot know what God is, but only what God is not, and thus we have no means for saying how God is, but only how God is not.[13] Language and images can serve as signposts pointing the path to God or as sacraments bearing the presence of God. God is not one more being alongside of other beings.

While contemporary Christians can affirm that the reality that Christians name God is truly and redemptively present in the Buddhist tradition, it is nonetheless extremely important to remember that the ways in which Buddhists experience this incomprehensible reality are indeed very different from Christian experiences of God.

PART I

The Buddha and the Christ

Introduction

Both Buddhism and Christianity have enjoyed widespread success as missionary religions, transforming entire cultures with their spirit and being themselves transformed in the process. Both have flourished over many centuries in a wide variety of regions and cultures and political and social systems. While Buddhism has taken a wide variety of forms in different countries and while Buddhists have disagreed on many points of interpretation, they are united in their veneration of Siddhartha Gautama, who became Shakyamuni Buddha. The account of his life is perhaps the most accessible way to enter into the meaning of Buddhist life. Christian history has also been marked by wide variety and by intense doctrinal disputes which have contested almost every possible issue concerning the significance of Jesus Christ. While Christians have often disagreed bitterly with each other over many central questions of interpreting their tradition, Christians agree in honoring the name and memory of Jesus Christ.

Examining the lives of these two remarkable figures in relation to each other is an important aspect of dialogue, for the narratives of each figure set a tone for all that follows. The lives of the two leaders play a number of differing roles in their later respective traditions. While both traditions acknowledge that it is impossible to state absolute truth literally, they both look to the lives of the Buddha and the Christ as concrete embodiments of the truth they taught. The narratives of the lives of Shakyamuni Buddha and Jesus Christ serve as unifying threads through the histories of their respective traditions, as normative models of thought and action for their followers, and also as concrete exemplifications of the ideals their teachings present. For Buddhists, Shakyamuni Buddha exemplifies the ideal of awakening to wisdom and practicing compassion, and he also later came to be interpreted as the manifestation of absolute reality itself. For Christians, Jesus Christ is the presence of God among us, the revelation of who God is and of the deepest meaning of human existence.

Part I will examine the accounts of the two leaders from whose lives these two traditions are inspired. The first chapter will explore one of the most influential accounts of the life of Shakyamuni Buddha, the Buddhacarita of Ashvaghosha, and will examine his central teachings and some later interpretations of his significance. The second chapter will then examine the life, death, and resurrection of Jesus Christ in relation to the life and teaching of Shakyamuni Buddha. In each case my focus will be on the way the tradition remembered its leader rather than on the quest for the historical Jesus or the historical Siddhartha Gautama. While the role that each figure plays for his tradition is in many ways very different, the effort to hear the accounts of their messages and lives together can illumine the relation between the two figures and their later followers.

Most Buddhist accounts of the life of Shakyamuni have focused primarily on his early life, his search for wisdom, his awakening, and his initial preaching. The canonical Gospels, by contrast, never describe a search for wisdom or an awakening from ignorance by Jesus. The focus, with a few important exceptions, is almost exclusively on his public life, preaching, death, and resurrection.

1

The Life and Teaching
of Shakyamuni Buddha

SHAKYAMUNI BUDDHA

Buddhism is unique among the religions of the world in that its founder, Shakyamuni Buddha, never claimed to be a prophet or emissary of God and rejected any conception of God as the absolute creator transcendent of the universe.[1] Siddhartha Gautama claimed simply to be awakened or enlightened and thus a Buddha, and sought to show others the path to enlightenment and liberation. Neither prophet nor incarnation of God, the Buddha was a pathfinder, a teacher who invited others to follow the way to liberation.

EARLY RECOLLECTIONS

The earliest written accounts of the life of Shakyamuni Buddha come from centuries after his earthly life had ended and are heavily influenced by later additions, including many legends and mythological interpretations.

Even the dates of his life are debated. There are three different chronologies currently accepted. Most scholars of Buddhism in Europe, America, and India would date his birth about the year 566 B.C.E. and his death about 486 B.C.E. Theravada Buddhists in Sri Lanka and Southeast Asia, however, maintain the Buddha's life dates were about sixty years earlier (placing his birth in 624 and his death in 544 B.C.E.). Other scholars, including many Japanese, believe his dates were somewhat later: 448 to 368 B.C.E.[2]

Despite the uncertainty on the dates of his life, there is, nonetheless, a genuine historical core to the life of the Buddha.[3] He was born to the Gautama family of the warrior caste and of the Shakya clan at the southern foot of the Himalaya Mountains in present-day Nepal. His father was the leader of the clan and a leading citizen of Kapilavastu. Though later Buddhist tradition presented his father as king, he may have been an elected head of an aristocratic oligarchy. Siddhartha married and had a son, and then, probably at about twenty-nine years of age, he left his family and palace in order to enter the ascetic life. After a decisive experience of enlightenment at about the age of thirty-five, he organized a community of followers and began to make known the path of liberation. He preached the path to liberation throughout northern India for about forty-five years, and died at the age of eighty. Many scholars believe that it is difficult to be certain of much more than this, because even the earliest accounts of his life and teaching are so heavily influenced by legendary and mythological interpretations.[4]

The earliest writings of Buddhism in the Pali language focus more on the teaching of the Buddha than on the events of his life.[5] These writings do, nonetheless, record the central events of his life, especially his decision to renounce his comfortable life in Kapilavastu, his enlightenment, his public teaching and preaching, and his passing into nirvana.

THE BUDDHACARITA

Whatever the original historical details may have been, the story of Shakyamuni Buddha has profoundly marked the consciousness of later generations of Buddhists.[6] One of the earliest and finest accounts of the life of the Buddha is a work called the Buddhacarita, "The Acts of the Buddha," by a first- or second-century C.E. Indian poet named Ashvaghosha, who wrote in Sanskrit.[7] Since he had an extensive knowledge of the Hindu tradition, Ashvaghosha was most likely born into the priestly caste as a Hindu Brahmin, but later converted to Buddhism. His works reflect the teachings of the Hinayana tradition, but he also expresses perspectives and themes that resonate deeply with the Mahayana tradition, and thus he has been described as both "a Hinayanist and a Mahayanist."[8] The Buddhacarita has enjoyed great popularity and influence among both Hinayana and Mahayana Buddhists, for the narrative presents or suggests in narrative form many of the central themes and doctrines of Buddhism.

CONCEPTION AND BIRTH

The story begins with the conception of the Buddha. His mother is named Maya, and she is married to a wise and just king named Suddhodana. The name of his mother already introduces a central theme of the Buddhacarita and of all Buddhism, for *Maya* in Sanskrit means illusion.[9] Traditionally, Indians considered women themselves to be a form of illusion, as temptations to male ascetics. Ashvaghosha assures us, however, that Maya was free from Maya—she was not bound by illusion (1.5; p. 2). The experience of an illusion that is not an illusion will be crucial later on for Maya's son. Moreover, the experience of awakening from illusion to enlightenment is at the very heart of the Buddhist tradition.

According to the Buddhacarita, both the conception and the birth of the future Buddha or bodhisattva are miraculous events. The future Buddha is not conceived through normal sexual relations. Rather, he chooses his mother, takes the form of a huge white elephant — a symbol of wisdom, power, purity, and goodness — approaches Maya in a dream, and enters her womb.

Some time later the queen yearns to go to the forest grove in Lumbini, about nineteen miles from the family's home in Kapilavastu. She leaves the palace and goes into a garden in Lumbini. While she is there, the future Buddha comes forth from her side without pain or illness. Suddhodana gives his newborn son the name Siddhartha, which in Sanskrit means "Goal Attained." The name was not uncommon, and could refer either to the child's excellent qualities or to the parents' attaining their goal of having a male child. Siddhartha's family name was Gautama, which literally means "superior cow." In India such a name was an indication of the family's high social status.

The birth of Siddhartha near a tree in a garden introduces a second major theme of the Buddhacarita: trees and forests. By giving birth in a garden, Maya is associated with the powers of nature and is often pictured reaching up to grasp a branch of the tree. The pose of a woman reaching up to grasp a flower or a tree was a traditional image in Indian art, often depicting a goddess or identifying the real mother of the child as the power of vegetation itself.[10] Maya — illusion — appears in the form of a goddess who is almost the power of nature itself, bringing the Buddha into the world.

Later on, trees and forests will play a major part in the life of Siddhartha. He will be tempted in a forest, he will seek wisdom by going into a forest, he will debate the meaning of responsibility under a tree in a forest, and it will be under a tree that Siddhartha will become enlightened. The forest will be a place of transformation. The forest in India was the opposite of the city: the place where ascetics withdrew to live a life of austerity, renouncing the ordinary patterns of social and family life. In India a sage was expected to withdraw to the forest at one stage of his development, after he had married and fathered a son. In some respects, the forest in India plays roles similar to the desert in the Bible — it is a place away from civilization, a place of temptation and trial, of asceticism, of transformation and new beginnings.

At the very beginning of his life, the newborn Siddhartha already knows his destiny. As soon as he is born he proclaims: "I am born for Enlightenment for the good of the world; this is my last birth in the world of phenomena" (1.15; p. 4). Even though at his birth he proclaims the reason he has come into the world, later in his life, he will not remember this. As a young man he will be quite ignorant in many respects. He will be surprised by the reality of human suffering, old age, and death, and he will have to search long and hard before he learns the lessons of wisdom and suffering and awakens to reality.

The confident proclamation of the newborn infant expresses the Mahayana perspective that the Buddha has been Buddha from the limitless past and "merely takes human form to demonstrate the experience of enlightenment to the world."[11] The eventual enlightenment of the infant is assured.

The birth is attended by miraculous signs. Two streams of water fall down from heaven to refresh the infant's body. The earth shakes "like a ship struck by the wind," and a shower of lotuses perfumed with sandalwood fell from heaven (1.21; p. 6).

Shortly after the birth of Siddhartha, Brahmins (members of the priestly caste) famous for their religious learning proclaim that the child "will certainly become either an enlightened seer or a Chakravartin monarch" (1.34; p. 8). A Chakravartin was a world-conquering emperor who "turned the wheel" of political and military power, defeating all his foes. They predict that if the child desires earthly power, he will conquer all rivals. If, on the other hand, he seeks salvation by going to the forest, he will overcome all creeds by his knowledge.

PROPHECY

Then a sage named Asita arrives on the wind and examines the child, finding special marks which set him apart: "the soles of his foot marked with a wheel, the fingers and toes joined by a web, the circle of hair growing between his eyebrows" (1.60; p. 13). These signs, Asita explains, foretell the destiny of the newborn child: "For he will give up the kingdom in his indifference to worldly pleasures, and, through bitter struggles grasping the final truth, he will shine forth as a sun of knowledge in the world to dispel the darkness of delusion" (1.69; p. 15).

The circle of hair on the infant's forehead represents the "eye of Dharma" which allows him to see what is otherwise invisible.[12] The wheel can be a sign of either a Chakravartin, a great king who "turns the wheel" of conquest, or of a Buddha, who "turns the wheel" of *dharma* (true teaching). The original meaning of the webbed hands and feet is not clear.[13]

Having explained the child's destiny, Asita expresses his own disappointment: since this child is born, it is Asita's time to depart (1.68; p. 15). Asita laments that he will not hear the preaching of this child and sees even dwelling in the highest heaven as a misfortune in comparison with the opportunity to hear the message of the future Buddha (1.77; p. 17).

KING SUDDHODANA AND THE DEPARTURE OF QUEEN MAYA

King Suddhodana, however, is ambivalent; while delighted to have such a son, he is worried by the prophecy and hopes desperately that his son will not be a world-renouncing ascetic (1.79). He tries to prevent the fulfillment of the prediction and forestall his son's renunciation of the palace. Even though he has been told the truth directly by a sage, he is nonetheless caught in the delusion of his own desire and does his utmost to thwart his son's vocation. He knows and yet does not know the meaning of his son's birth.

While Suddhodana worries about the future loss of his son, there is very soon a different loss in the family. Not long after giving birth, Maya sees the glory of her newborn son and cannot sustain the joy which it brings. Thus, Ashvaghosha tells us, "she went to heaven to dwell there" (2.18; p. 23). Her sister will serve as stepmother, raising the child as if he were her own.

The departure of Maya introduces a third theme that will be crucial to the life of Siddhartha and to the Buddhist tradition: separation. As soon as Siddhartha is born, he is separated from his mother, and his father already dreads the inevitable separation that will come. One of the central truths of the Buddha's teaching will involve the meaning of separation, the proper way to endure the inevitable pain of human loss and tragedy.

The departure of Maya to heaven has an important symbolic significance because of her name. The purpose of the Buddha's coming is to destroy Maya in the sense of illusion. As soon as the Buddha is born, Maya his mother departs. Where the Buddha is, Maya cannot be. The central dynamic of Buddhism is presented in symbolic, narrative form.

YOUTH OF SIDDHARTHA

Suddhodana, meanwhile, does his best to foster illusion in order to prevent his son from ever learning that life is filled with pain. He tries to satiate his son with sensual pleasures. The young Siddhartha grows up in a world of illusion, protected from the pain of separation. When his son grows older, the king arranges for the prince to marry a beautiful woman named Yasodhara, and he prepares a special dwelling for the couple in the recesses of the palace far from contact with any unpleasant scene. Suddhodana does everything possible to keep his son in an ivory tower, ignorant of the harsh realities of human suffering. The royal apartments are lavishly furnished, and abundant women delight Siddhartha with music and dancing and the arts of love.

Yasodhara bears a son, named Rahula, a name that means "obstacle."[14] The son can function either as an obstacle to asceticism, binding Siddhartha to the world, or as an opportunity for liberation. According to Indian custom, the birth of a son fulfills Siddhartha's obligation to society. Indian tradition held that as soon as a man sees the face of his son, he can renounce the world. He has fulfilled his duty to his wife and to his ancestors and he is free to become an ascetic. This causes Suddhodana to be diligent in religious practice, "hoping that, now that the prince [Siddhartha] has seen the face of his son, he would not go to the forest" (2.54; p. 31).

Suddhodana fears that the journey to the forest will free Prince Siddhartha from the bond of illusion and awaken him to his destiny.

FOUR SIGNS

Siddhartha does not leave immediately, however. He has yet to experience his first enlightenment in one of the most famous scenes in all Buddhist literature. One day he resolves to go to the forest — not the forest of the ascetics, however, but the enticing forests and groves beloved by women. His father orders a pleasure party to be prepared. Resolved to keep Siddhartha in ignorance, the king orders that his son not see any sign of suffering on the road.

People line the streets, and women in particular come out to see the handsome young prince. At first the journey is pleasant, but then the Indian gods decide to intervene and create an illusion in order to tell the truth. Because the king has arranged for reality to be a lie, the gods create the illusion of an old man walking along "in order to incite the king's son to leave his home" (3.26; p. 37). Siddhartha has been so sheltered that he has never seen anyone suffering from the effects of old age before, and he has to ask his charioteer the meaning of this sight.

Even though the king had ordered the charioteer to protect Siddhartha from any knowledge of suffering, the gods bewilder the mind of the charioteer to make him answer the question truthfully. The charioteer explains that this is the visage of old age, "the murderer of beauty, the ruin of vigour, the birthplace of sorrow, the grave of pleasure, the destroyer of memory, the enemy of the senses" (3.30; p. 37). Siddhartha wonders whether this may happen to him, and the charioteer assures him that it will. It is noteworthy that the future Buddha's first worry centers on himself; he worries about himself, about the inevitable loss of youth and vigor.

Siddhartha orders the charioteer to return home, where he ponders what he has seen. He decides to leave the palace a second time, and the king takes the same precautions. This time the gods create the illusion of a man afflicted with illness all over his body. Siddhartha sees and questions his charioteer a second time. On learning the cause, Siddhartha asks if illness strikes all people. Hearing that it does, he again retreats to the security of his palace.

He departs a third time, and again the king orders that no sign of suffering be visible. Again the gods intervene, this time creating the illusion of a dead man being carried by four men and followed by mourners, but the illusion is visible only to Siddhartha and the charioteer. Siddhartha again asks the meaning of the sight, and the charioteer's mind is overcome by the gods and he tells the prince the truth that this is the final end of all living beings.

Siddhartha orders the charioteer to turn back, but the charioteer takes the prince instead to the forest where groups of beautiful women await him with eager passion and do their best to seduce him. Siddhartha now knows, however, that the forest of sensual delights is not the forest that gives lasting contentment and peace. Even though surrounded by voluptuous women who literally throw themselves upon him, Siddhartha reflects on the reality of old age, disease, and death and refuses their advances. A counselor named Udayi advises him to honor women and not to spurn their advances, but Siddhartha responds with a reflection on the impermanence of such pleasures and the suffering they cause. His reflections anticipate the later Buddhist maxims that all things are full of sorrow, that all things are momentary, and that all things are void. This awareness will later become the first of the Four Noble Truths, but Siddhartha has not yet found the answer to his quest, and thus does not understand the full meaning of impermanence.

The prince continues to ponder the problem of suffering, and on a later day goes out again to a forest. He sits under a rose-apple tree and attains the path that leads to firmness of mind and the first stage of contemplation. As he sits in passionless meditation a man dressed as a beggar approaches. When the prince asks him who he is, the man explains that he has become a *shramana*, a homeless, wandering ascetic who seeks truth for the sake of liberation. As soon as he finishes speaking, however, he flies up to the sky, for in fact he was a heavenly inhabitant who had come in the form of an ascetic. His words, however, point out the initial steps on the path to liberation: ascetic renunciation. The fourth and final sign is once again an illusion that tells the truth.

At that, the future Buddha sets his mind on enlightenment. The experience of the four signs is the decisive turning point in the life of Shakyamuni Buddha. The first three signs express the problem of the human condition: old age, sickness, and death. The fourth sign points the way to the solution: voluntary renunciation is a clue to a way out of suffering. Later on the seeker of wisdom will discover that renunciation by itself is inadequate, but it is at least the beginning of the path to liberation.

ILLUSION, FOREST, SEPARATION, AND DHARMA

The three themes of illusion, the forest, and separation intertwine in the narrative. Paradoxes run through each of them. The real world that the young Siddhartha experiences is actually a well-crafted illusion designed by his father. The reign of illusion is a parable of the normal human condition. In contrast to the "real" world that is a lie, the illusions created by the gods awaken Siddhartha to true awareness of human existence. The systematic denial of pain is the first obstacle to be overcome. The harsh realities of separation must be faced and accepted before Siddhartha can be awakened. Separation freely chosen allows him to endure and overcome the pain of forced separation. Separation is both the cause of great suffering and the beginning of the path to freedom.

The forest plays a dual role in Siddhartha's journey. The forest is the place both of sensuous, alluring women and also of wandering ascetics; it is the place of illusory pleasures and also of the resolution to seek enlightenment. The forest is the place of seeking and debating what is the proper path for humans in this world. The forest is the place of separation from the world and of the overcoming of illusion.

As the narrative progresses, a fourth theme comes more and more to the fore and becomes the central concern: What is the proper *dharma*? *Dharma* (*dhamma* in Pali) is a word that is difficult to translate, for it has many significations. The Sanskrit root *dhr* means "bearing" or "supporting," and dharma can be translated as "duty, law, or teachings"; it is "the ground of the path of salvation."[15] Dharma refers to the social and moral order, to the duty of one's place in society and family, to the wisdom and cosmic order of the universe. At times it has been translated as "religion."[16] Dharma normally means one's ethical responsibilities as interpreted by the Indian tradition, but in the quest of Siddhartha, these are called into question.

Much of the Buddhacarita is a debate over what is the proper dharma for Siddhartha. Ashvaghosha tells us that at his birth dharma blazed forth (2.16; p. 23). Suddhodana himself was extremely virtuous in relation to his people and thus practiced dharma himself, but by surrounding his son with sensual pleasures Suddhodana was actually keeping young Siddhartha from dharma (2.55; p. 31). As a young man Siddhartha must face the question of what dharma calls him to be and do. Should he fulfill the expectations of his warrior caste and his father and wife and thereby fulfill the traditional interpretations of dharma? Or should he separate himself from the palace and his family in order to seek a more radical liberation which will be his true dharma?

Both Suddhodana and Yasodhara will reproach the prince for violating dharma by abandoning them. His eventual awakening will involve a new insight into dharma which places all relationships in a new light, and the Buddha will call his own path and teaching the dharma. Ashvaghosha will even say that the Buddha himself appears as "Dharma incarnate" (10.6; p. 142). Early Buddhist sutras record Shakyamuni as saying: "Whosoever sees me sees the Dharma and whosoever sees the Dharma sees me."[17] Since it is difficult to say precisely what dharma is, the narrative presents the true meaning of dharma through the struggles and questioning and eventual awakening of one individual.

DEPARTURE

On the day of his meeting with the divine ascetic, Prince Siddhartha decides to leave his father's home. He requests permission of his father, but his father urges him to delay his renunciation of the palace. Suddhodana warns that to practice the ascetic life too young is against dharma, the wisdom and order of the cosmos. The king insists that there is a fixed order in life, and that old age is the proper time to renounce the world and go to the forest. To seek dharma in the forest prematurely would be to go against dharma. Siddhartha, however, persists in his resolve: "And seeing that separation is the fixed rule of the world, is it not better to make the separation myself for the sake of dharma?" (5.38; pp. 68–69).

That night Siddhartha prepares to depart, and he looks upon the women of the palace, lying asleep with their limbs and clothes in unseemly disarray. Their disorderly postures reveal how illusory the physical charms of the palace courtesans really are. The sight strengthens his resolve to leave, and he rides his horse out of the palace grounds. The gods throw open the gates and bear up the hoofs of his horse as he rushes away in silence. Outside the city he looks back and resolves: "I shall not be entering the city named after Kapila, till I have seen the further shore of life and death" (5.84; p. 79).

He goes to the forest and gives his horse and jewelry to his groomsman, Khamdaka. He cuts off his hair as a sign of renouncing the world and tells his servant to inform King Suddhodana that he has entered the ascetic wood to destroy old age and death. He sends a message to his father, urging him not to grieve for his son, but rather for those who are slaves of passion (6.18; p. 83). Khamdaka is distressed and cannot bear the thought of returning alone to the city. Siddhartha explains to him the inevitability of separation:

> As birds collect on their roosting tree and then go their separate ways again, so inevitably the union of beings ends in their parting. And as clouds come together and depart asunder again, so I deem the meeting and severance of creatures that draw breath. And since this world is in a state of continuous separating, therefore the feeling that "this is mine" is improper with regard to a coming together that is transitory as a dream (6.46–48; p. 87).

From this point on in the narrative, the gods will no longer assist Siddhartha on his search.[18]

ASCETIC PRACTICE

In the forest Siddhartha meets a group of ascetics doing penance in the hope of a happy rebirth in heaven. The future Buddha, however, is not impressed. The best reward for penance, he reflects, is a period of time in heaven; but all worlds—even heaven, in Indian belief—are subject to change, and thus the penitent's labor brings little gain in the long run. Siddhartha seeks a more lasting peace than this. He seeks not a better place in the cycle of change, but liberation.

Moreover, he questions whether the expectation of a better future rebirth is really in accord with dharma. If the ascetics are simply seeking a pleasurable rebirth as a reward for their austerities, he reflects, "then dharma in this world bears as its fruit what is contrary to dharma" (7.26; p. 97). The austerities of the forest dwellers are still trapped in illusion: The austere ascetic, by seeking pleasure in the future, "does not perceive the evils of the cycle of existence and seeks by suffering nothing but suffering" (7.22; p. 96). Siddhartha's first disillusionment with the life of the palace is followed by a second disillusionment with the life of the forest-dwelling ascetics.

As he is leaving the wood, one of the ascetics advises him to seek out the master Arada to learn the path to truth. Siddhartha sets out. In the meantime, his wife and his father are distraught with grief. Yasodhara laments that her husband has failed in his responsibility to her by abandoning her. She recalls the example of kings of old who took their wives with them into the forest and laments that Siddhartha "has become miserly of dharma towards me" (8.63; p. 117). The king mourns bitterly and sends a counsellor and the family priest to find Siddhartha and entreat him to return.

DEBATE OVER DHARMA

The counsellor and the priest find the prince sitting by the side of the road under a tree and begin a debate over the meaning of dharma. The family priest, speaking in the name of the king, appeals to Siddhartha as a "lover of dharma" to "give up this purpose for the very sake of dharma" (9.15; p. 126), for the sake of duty to his wife, his child, his father, and his city. Siddhartha should first exercise earthly rule and then later in life return to the forests. The priest points out that liberation can be attained by householders: "The dharma of salvation has been attained by kings, even though they remained at home" (9.19; p. 126).

The Bodhisattva listens patiently but refuses to accept responsibility for the sorrow of his family. Separation is inevitable, what is important is how one experiences it: "the cause of affliction is neither the son nor the father; this distress is the outcome of ignorance" (9.34; p. 130). He also rejects the claim that kings have found liberation while remaining at home: "How can the dharma of salvation in which quietude predominates be reconciled with the dharma of kings in which severity of action predominates?" (9.48; p. 133). The rule of a king demands a ferocity which is incompatible with the dharma of salvation.

The counsellor then intervenes, acknowledging the worth of Siddhartha's resolve to practice dharma but questioning its timing. He notes the uncertainty of any life hereafter and urges the future Buddha to "enjoy the sovereignty that offers itself to you" (9.55; p. 134). The counsellor notes the uncertainty of all theories, and appeals to the future Buddha's sense of dharma and urges him to return. The Bodhisattva refuses to accept theories based on another's words; he seeks to learn the truth for himself. He rejects the authorities that the counsellor had cited, and renews his resolve not to return home until he has discovered the truth on his own.

SEARCH FOR A TEACHER

Siddhartha then sets off to study with different masters, crossing the river Ganges. He is intercepted by Shrenya (also called Bimbisara), the king of the Magadhas, who offers the future Buddha half of his kingdom if he will abandon his religious quest for the moment and enjoy the pleasure, the wealth, and the dharma of power. Old age will offer time enough for the prince to go to the forest. Siddhartha, however, reaffirms his resolve. "For the passions are ephemeral, robbers of the treasury of good, empty, like will-o'-the-wisps in the world. The mere expectation of them deludes men's minds, how much more then their actual possession?" (11.9; p. 150). He wants to end the insatiable tyranny of desires; even when we are successful in enjoying them, we are defeated, for we only become intoxicated when our desired pleasures are attained.

Siddhartha seeks out the hermitage of the sage Arada Kalama and asks him how one may be freed from old age, sickness, and death. Arada explains that passion is delusion and that through meditation one can still its power and reach a point where one is liberated from the body. The future Buddha is not satisfied with this teaching because it does not envision the end of egoism: "as for this imagined abandonment of the ego-principle, so long as the soul persists, there is no abandonment of that principle" (12.76; p. 179). Siddhartha seeks a more radical liberation through a more radical abandonment: "I deem complete success in reaching the goal to derive from the abandonment of everything" (12.82; p. 181).

Judging Arada's teaching to be incomplete, Siddhartha seeks out another sage, Udraka Ramaputra. Udraka teaches a higher state of the intellect that is beyond consciousness and unconsciousness. The future Buddha finds his teaching also unsatisfactory, however, for Udraka's teaching assumes the existence of the soul and leads to return to the world. In both cases Siddhartha quickly learns all that these masters have to teach him, but he still does not believe he has found the way to liberation.

THE ASCETIC LIFE

Afterwards he meets five mendicants and is inspired to begin the practice of difficult austerities and fasting. For six years of ascetic practice, he deprives his body of food and drink, wasting away so that only skin and bone remain. At length, he decides that this is not the way to perfect knowledge or to liberation. Instead, he remembers the time that he sat under the rose-apple tree and reflects that that was certainly the true way.

To follow this path, however, requires strength of body and mind, and thus food and drink for nourishment.

Abandoning the path of rigorous asceticism, he goes down to bathe in the Nairanjana River. Indians normally bathe frequently in a river or pond, but Indian ascetics often covered their bodies with dirt, resolving never to wash themselves clean. Thus Siddhartha's immersion in the waters of the river symbolizes his rejection of the path of extreme asceticism.[19] Coming up from the river, he takes refreshment from some milk offered him by a young woman named Nandabala (in other sutras often called Sujata), the daughter of the cowherd chief. Where earlier women had appeared in the story as temptations and obstacles to enlightenment, Nandabala appears as an indispensable aid to enlightenment, for she enables Siddhartha to attain the highest knowledge by restoring his physical health and strength.

TEMPTATION AND ENLIGHTENMENT

Fixing his mind on enlightenment, he sits under the Bodhi tree and resolves not to rise until he has obtained his goal. The dwellers in heaven rejoice at this; but Mara, the tempter, the enemy of liberation, is afraid that if Siddhartha succeeds, others will become enlightened as well, and Mara's own realm will become empty. "Mara" literally means "destruction" or "killing," and thus essentially means "death."[20]

Mara resolves to break Siddhartha's resolve, sending his sons (Caprice, Gaiety, and Wantonness) and his daughters (Discontent, Delight, and Thirst) to tempt the future Buddha. Mara himself repeats the call to dharma: a member of the warrior caste is supposed to accept the civic and military responsibilities of his position and not abandon the world before old age.

When this approach fails, Mara's children entice and threaten Siddhartha. Warriors with the faces of boars, fish, horses, camels, tigers, bears, lions, and elephants dance before him. Many are grotesque figures, with one eye or many mouths or three heads or half-mutilated faces. One has flames blazing forth from every hair. As the conflict begins to rage in the night, the sky loses its brightness, the earth shakes, and the wind rages. The assault is, however, in vain, for the future Buddha is as untroubled as a lion seated in the midst of oxen.

Mara then launches a full assault. His warriors lift up stones and trees, but are unable to throw them, and so they fall down together with their weapons. Others leap up into the sky to hurl rocks and trees and axes, but the objects remain in the sky and do not return to earth. Another hurls a mountain-sized blazing log, but the sage shatters it into fragments in midair. Still another launches a shower of live coals, only to see them turn into red lotus petals as they fall harmlessly beneath the Bodhi tree. Still others transform themselves into thunderclouds and hurl down stones upon the tree, but they become a shower of flowers.

As the battle continues, Ashvaghosha interprets the weapons of the enemy as metaphors of human emotions. One of Mara's archers sets an arrow in his bow. It glistens there, but it refuses to come forth "like the anger of a poor ill-tempered man, when it is fanned in his heart" (13.46; p. 197). Another warrior charges the future Buddha with a club, only to fall powerless to the ground, like people who, "not obtaining their desires, fall helplessly into calamitous sins" (13.48; p. 197). A woman brings a skull in her hand, but she herself cannot remain settled and wanders aimlessly, like "the intelligence of a man of inconstant mind wandering uncertainly among the various sacred traditions" (13.49; p. 197). Another tries to hurl a heavy rock but finds his efforts frustrated and himself baffled, "like one who desires to obtain by affliction of the body the dharma which is the ultimate good and which is only to be reached by knowledge and concentration of mind" (13.51; p. 198).

The metaphorical interpretations make it clear that the real battle is not with outward mythological monsters but with the emotions and passions and temptations Siddhartha finds within himself. Mara is often interpreted to symbolize the mental afflictions that cause suffering, especially the principal afflictions of greed, anger, and stupidity.[21] While Siddhartha continues to sit solidly on the ground, unperturbed by the tumult around him, Mara becomes more and more frustrated and angry.

Finally, a heavenly being advises Mara to cease his efforts, telling him:

For to-day is the appointed time for the ripening of those deeds which he has done in the past for the sake of illumination. Thus he is seated in this place exactly like the previous sages. For this is the navel of the earth's surface, entirely possessed of the highest power; for there is no other spot on earth which can bear the force of his concentrated thought (13.67–68; pp. 200–201).

Mara withdraws in defeat. With this, the regions of the sky grow clear, the moon shines forth, and showers of flowers fall down from the sky upon the earth.

In many accounts of the enlightenment, Shakyamuni has a conversation with Mara and finally puts an end to the temptations by putting his right hand on the earth and calling upon the goddess of the earth as a witness to his steadfast resistance to the temptations of Mara.

Nagao points out, however, that the departure of Mara, and of the mental afflictions that Mara symbolizes, is not yet the full meaning of enlightenment.[22] Victory over temptations and mental afflictions is important, but the light of wisdom, the ability to see clearly, is the heart of being a Buddha.

ENLIGHTENED MEDITATION

Having vanquished Mara, Shakyamuni Buddha spends the night in meditation. In the first watch of the night he remembers all his past lives, sees the truth that the cycle of existence is without substance. In the second watch of the night he is filled with growing compassion for all beings as he sees the countless ways they suffer without escape. He sees that evil deeds bring inevitable consequences of suffering. Even those who are born in heaven are still disturbed by sensual passion and thus fall from heaven. No state of existence is free from illusion and death.

> This stream of the cycle of existence has no support and is ever subject to death. Creatures, thus beset on all sides, find no resting-place. Thus with the divine eyesight he examined the five spheres of life and found nothing substantial in existence (14.47–48; p. 208).

In the third watch of the night he understands the real nature of the world in the cycle of causation. One factor leads to another and causes the cycle of birth and death and suffering to be repeated endlessly. Ignorance is what allows the cycle to continue. The Buddha "saw no self anywhere from the summit of existence downwards and came to tranquillity, like a fire whose fuel is burnt out, by the eightfold path of supreme insight, which starts forth and quickly reaches the desired point" (14.84; p. 213).

As the fourth watch begins and dawn approaches, Shakyamuni "reached the stage which knows no alteration . . . the state of omniscience" (14.86; p. 213). The earth swayed, lotuses and water lilies fell from the sky, and the world became tranquil.

VISIT OF THE GODS

He understands the Four Noble Truths and the Eightfold Path, which will form the core of his teaching. After the Buddha's night of enlightenment and meditation, the gods come and praise the Buddha and celebrate with him for four weeks. Moved with compassion for all suffering beings, he resolves to share his wisdom with the world (15.7). This promise, a model of the vows of the bodhisattva, expresses the oneness of the Buddha's wisdom and compassion. To be enlightened is to have compassion on all sentient beings.

Other narratives of the Buddha often portray him hesitating and doubting that anyone else could understand what he has learned. He fears that his spiritual breakthrough is too difficult and too subtle for others to comprehend and decides to give up the idea of communicating his wisdom. At this, the god Brahma intervenes:

> In spite of all the trouble you have been through to reach enlightenment and become the highest Buddha, to enter Nirvana without explaining to others what you have realized would be a tragic loss to them. I beseech you, please expound the Dharma. . . . There should certainly be people who can understand you.[23]

PREACHING OF THE BUDDHA

In either version, compassion is the motivating force in the preaching of the Buddha. He sees the suffering of the world and begins his public ministry of preaching and teaching. He journeys to the Deer Park in Varanasi (Benares) to find the five ascetics with whom he had fasted for six years. His former companions think that he has abandoned the ascetic life from loss of self-control and resolve not to greet him. As soon as they see him, however, his serene appearance draws them to him, and they take his mantle and begging bowl and offer him water to wash his feet.

He proclaims to them that he has become enlightened and preaches to them of the cause of suffering in the idea of the self and the path of liberation. During the first sermon the five ascetics attain enlightenment themselves.

LATER LIFE

The extant Sanskrit text of the Buddhacarita ends with the enlightenment of the Buddha. Most narratives of the life of the Buddha treat the remaining forty-five years of his life much more generally than his path to enlightenment and initial teaching. Shakyamuni Buddha did return to Kapilavastu some years later and was welcomed by his wife and father and son, and his son and half-brother joined the company of his monks. In the later sections of the Buddhacarita, Suddhodana comes out to meet his enlightened son; Shakyamuni performs some wondrous feats and preaches the Four Noble Truths to his father. At this, Suddhodana is reported to have acknowledged that his son had indeed followed dharma: "Rightly You toiled with great labour, and rightly, beloved as You were, You left Your dear relations and have had compassion on us" (19.31; p. 88). At the core of the Buddha's later ministry were his preachings concerning the meaning of his awakening and his central teachings.

THE FOUR NOBLE TRUTHS

Later generations of Buddhists have differed in their interpretations of just what Shakyamuni Buddha's experience of enlightenment was. The most widespread distillation of the experience is contained in the Four Noble Truths and the Eightfold Path.

Shakyamuni Buddha is remembered as expressing the significance of his enlightenment in the Four Noble Truths in the famous initial sermon to the five ascetics in the Deer Park in Varanasi, the "turning of the wheel of Dharma." These truths together constitute the core of the Buddha's teaching.[24] Together these truths form "an existential path wherein one's own awakening awakens others."[25]

FIRST NOBLE TRUTH

The first of the Four Noble Truths proclaims that life is suffering (*duk-kha*), that is, unsatisfactory, meaningless, impermanent, culminating in death and decay. This does not mean that there is no happiness or joy, but such moments are fleeting. Even the most ecstatic experience passes. The awareness of suffering is closely linked to temporality. The Dhammapada remembers the Buddha as comparing impermanence to a burning fire: "How can there be laughter, how can there be pleasure when the whole world is burning?"[26] The image of fire, which causes pain and is ever-changing, is a powerful symbol of the link between impermanence and suffering.[27]

The attempt to deny the reality of impermanence and suffering is itself an illusion that blocks the path to wisdom, and a harsh encounter with suffering is a necessary stimulus to seek enlightenment. It was only when the young Prince Siddhartha left the sheltered world of his father's palace and saw a sick man, an old man, a dead man, and a mendicant that he became dissatisfied with his life of comfort and security and began to seek wisdom. The first truth challenges us to be aware of the suffering in ourselves and in others. Buddhist practice allows us to see the suffering, and once we see, we are challenged to seek the cause and a cure.

SECOND NOBLE TRUTH

Shakyamuni learned that the cause of suffering is our craving for things, our clinging to desires, our being addicted to some aspect of life's pleasures. The Buddha's cry, "Everything is burning," refers both to the impermanence of all things and also to the flames of desire within us.[28] The cause of suffering is the fire of desire at the base of our consciousness. This is the Second Noble Truth. Craving or thirst for existence and pleasure imprisons us in a beginningless and endless cycle of suffering. Craving includes all types of clinging attachments, whether to pleasures, wealth, possessions, power, or to ideas, beliefs, and concepts. The source of all the world's suffering is the grasping desire to accumulate more and more, to be more and more.[29]

D. T. Suzuki explained craving as "a wish to become something other than what is," "to change oneself into something else"; and commented that this craving "is the very foundation of all our existence, according to Buddhism."[30] Craving expresses itself in infinite forms, or rather, it is these forms themselves. In this impermanent world we are born and die in every moment, and the craving to exist is the chain that keeps us bound to the unsatisfactory world. The thirst arises from the illusion of a separately existing self.

The Buddha also discovered that freedom from such addictions brings freedom from suffering. When we no longer cling to our desires, we are free to experience life as it is. This is the Third Noble Truth. When we see our suffering for what it is, we awaken to a new awareness of ourselves. To be aware of the cause of suffering is to see the way to end suffering. When we awake from a frightening, painful dream and see the experience as a dream, we are no longer frightened or in pain; when we awaken from the suffering of our illusory self, we no longer suffer from the delusions of our false consciousness. The Buddha is reported to have explained this state to a wealthy householder, Anathapindika:

> Yes, always at ease he lives, the Brahmin, attained
>   to nirvana,
> Who is not stained by lusts, cooled, without "basis,"
> Having rent all clingings, having averted heart's care,
> Tranquil he lives at ease, having won to peace of
>   mind.[31]

The cessation of suffering is the experience of absolute truth, but this truth can never be adequately expressed in words. The extinction of thirst is often called nirvana, the cessation of suffering. Nirvana is absolute reality and truth beyond all duality and relativity, but because it cannot be expressed directly, it is usually spoken of in negations. This can be misleading if taken to be the literal extinction of a self. As Rahula cautions:

> Because Nirvana is thus expressed in negative terms, there are many who have got a wrong notion that it is negative, and expresses self-annihilation. Nirvana is definitely no annihilation of self, because there is no self to annihilate. If at all, it is the annihilation of the illusion, of the false idea of self.[32]

Nirvana is liberation from the illusion of the self, absolute emancipation from grasping, thirsting, clinging, and thus from suffering. Nirvana cannot be communicated through an objective description; it escapes all the categories of thought; it must be experienced to be understood.[33]

In Buddhism, insistence on the awareness of suffering and the harsh negations of our ordinary beliefs are always in service of an ultimately positive goal. The first truth of suffering is always to be read in light of the third truth that there is a release from suffering. The second truth points out the cause of suffering; the third truth confidently expresses the possibility of peace and joy; and the fourth truth points out the path to freedom. The Four Noble Truths together really form a single Fourfold Truth, which leads to liberation. They have often been understood on the analogy of four stages of medical practice: (1) identification of a disease, (2) analysis of the cause of the disease, (3) prospect for removal of the cause, and (4) the specific method of cure.

FOURTH NOBLE TRUTH

The last of the Four Noble Truths indicates the way out of suffering: The path to freedom is a middle way between extremes, a path of neither extreme sensuality nor extreme asceticism. It is an eightfold path based upon a proper view of all things and proper conduct toward all. The path consists of right speech, right action, right livelihood, right effort, right mindfulness, right concentration, right understanding, and right thought.

THE EIGHTFOLD PATH

The eightfold path is traditionally divided into three moments, sometimes called the Three Learnings: (1) ethical conduct (*shila*), which includes right speech, right action, and right livelihood; (2) mental discipline, which includes right effort, right mindfulness, and right concentration; and (3) salvific insight (*prajna*), which includes right understanding and right thought.[34]

The first stage of the eightfold path establishes a firm ethical foundation for all Buddhist practice. Since nirvana is beyond all duality and relativity, Buddhists often make paradoxical challenges to go beyond the discrimination between good and evil, but these challenges always presuppose a basic ethical practice. "Do not do what is evil. Do what is good. Keep your mind pure. This is the teaching of Buddha" (Dhammapada 14.183; p. 62). The five precepts express the minimum ethical standards expected of any Buddhist: (1) not to kill or injure life, (2) not to take what is not one's own, (3) not to misuse the senses, especially not to engage in sexual misconduct, (4) not to speak falsely or slanderously, and (5) not to use intoxicants or drugs that harm one's consciousness.

MEDITATION

The practice of the precepts makes possible the next stage of mental discipline and concentration. The practice of meditation establishes concentration (*samadhi*), which is the cultivation of mindfulness, awareness of reality. The teaching of the Buddha repeatedly calls us to be watchful: "Those who are watchful never die: those who do not watch are already as dead" (Dhammapada 2.21; p. 38). Mindfulness allows us not to lose ourselves in dispersion or in our surroundings. The close attention of Buddhists to breathing allows us to be watchful and to see reality and overcome anxiety and fear. In teaching methods of meditation, the Buddha was transforming the older tradition of yoga.[35] Meditation is at the center of the eightfold path, making possible the transition from ethical practice to salvific insight.

As Thich Nhat Hanh explains, "Breathing is a means of awakening and maintaining full attention in order to look carefully, long and deeply, see the nature of all things, and arrive at liberation."[36] The Theravada tradition of Buddhism still regards the sutras on the *Full Awareness of Breathing* (*Anapanasati Sutta*) and on the *Four Establishments of Mindfulness* (*Satipatthana Sutta*) as the most important texts, which monks often learn by heart.[37] The practice of meditation in turn leads to salvific insight, wisdom, which is the ineffable experience of truth and freedom in nirvana.

Nirvana is the extinguishing of the flames of addiction, the blowing out of the fire of desire, the quenching of thirst. While it is the end of the illusory, grasping self, the Buddha specifically rejected the interpretation of nirvana as absolute annihilation. Nirvana is "a realm of absolute calmness and quietness on 'the other shore.' "[38] In Mahayana Buddhism, the ideal of the bodhisattva challenges one not to remain in the peaceful calm of nirvana but to return to the world of impermanence out of compassion for all sentient beings.

Buddhism has sometimes been interpreted by Western writers as a "pessimistic" religion because of its insistence on the suffering that pervades life and its use of powerful negations to destroy our ordinary awareness. It is true that Buddhists negate our belief in an independent self, in separate objects, and in God, and that Buddhists can be relentless in undermining any belief to which we cling.

Buddhism is not, however, a pessimistic nihilism, but a path to liberation. The Dhammapada remembers the Buddha as saying: "When desires go, joy comes: the follower of Buddha finds this truth" (14.187; p. 63). The Buddha is also reported to have said: "My teaching is like the sea. It is wide and deep but it has only one taste. The taste of the sea is salt. The taste of my teaching is freedom."[39]

NO-SELF

Buddhists do agree that awakening to reality involves the insight that our ordinary sense of our self is an illusion. Normally we believe in a permanent, substantial self that underlies all our experiences and that is the source of our thirsts and desires. This clinging, independent self does not exist. This is what Buddhists call the doctrine of no-self or non-ego (*anatta* or *anatman*).

According to D. T. Suzuki, the Buddha's enlightenment involves two moments: the realization that (1) "all things are transient as they are composites (*skandha* or *khanda*) and go on disintegrating all the time, that there is nothing permanent; and (2) there is therefore nothing worth clinging to in this world."[40]

All the beings of our world—including ourselves—are impermanent and therefore causes of sorrow when we cling to them. We do not ordinarily recognize this, however, and live in a world of delusion. The foundation of this delusion is the belief in a permanent, grasping self underlying all our experiences. Impermanence is not simply an objective theory about a world in process; it expresses the radical finitude and mortality of my own existence. The suffering caused by impermanence is not simply physical or emotional pain, it is the unsatisfactoriness of a life based on the distinction between self and objects.

Awakening to wisdom is seeing things as they are, as impermanent and as radically interdependent. Buddhist wisdom (*prajna*) is the ability to see reality as it is. Wisdom dispels the clouds of Maya, of illusion, demolishes our false beliefs, and introduces us to a new world of values based upon compassion (*karuna*). Wisdom and compassion are inseparable. To see things as they are is to have compassion on all sentient beings. It is to realize nonduality, to realize that we are not separate from the other beings of the universe.

As long as we cling to the belief in an independent, substantial self underlying our experiences, we remain trapped in the prison of our own desires and are condemned to live a life of frustration. The illusions and delusions of the clinging self have to be destroyed if we are truly to live. The experience of wisdom requires the realization that the clinging self does not exist. This frees us to see things as they really are, that is, as radically interdependent, and leads to compassion for all living beings.

Buddhist practice challenges each person to follow the eightfold path: "It is you who must make the effort. The Great of the past only show the way" (Dhammapada 20.276; p. 75). But the effort is not made alone, for the path involves a continual taking refuge in the Three Jewels: the Buddha, the Dharma (the teaching of the Buddha), and the Sangha (the Buddhist Community).

LATER INTERPRETATIONS OF THE BUDDHA

MERIT TRANSFERENCE AND THE SOURCE OF DHARMA

In time, the Buddhist tradition accorded Shakyamuni a more exalted significance and he acquired more and more of a salvific role in later generations, especially for Mahayana Buddhists.[41] Early Mahayana Buddhists came to believe in a process of merit transference, through which practitioners, especially a Buddha or a Bodhisattva, could apply merit to persons less advanced on the path.[42] The idea of merit transference was based upon the principle of interpenetration, which sees every being as containing and being contained by every other being.[43] The development of the idea of merit transference became one of the distinguishing marks of Mahayana Buddhism in distinction to Hinayana Buddhism, and it would be particularly important for later Pure Land Buddhism.

Later Buddhist interpretations of Shakyamuni understood him as the manifestation of the ultimate reality of the universe. As the teacher of dharma, Shakyamuni was related to the *dharma-dhatu*, the "source of dharma." As Nagao explains,

> *dharma-dhatu* represents the realm which is the source of every possible existence, or the source of all teachings about existence. It is beyond human language, inconceivable and completely equivalent to emptiness in its content.[44]

The later interpretations were rooted in the close association between Shakyamuni and the dharma he taught. As Shakyamuni Buddha was dying, his followers were overcome with emotion, and Shakyamuni is reported to have told his disciple Ananda: "After I am gone the dharma (teaching) and the vinaya (discipline) which I have expounded will be your teacher."[45] Even though Shakyamuni himself died, his teaching lived on as a refuge to his followers, and the dharma itself continued to instruct Buddhist practitioners. As noted earlier, the Buddhist tradition would remember Shakyamuni as saying: "Whosoever sees me sees the Dharma and whosoever sees the Dharma sees me."[46]

THREE BODIES OF THE BUDDHA

As the later Buddhist tradition came to see the historical Shakyamuni Buddha as a manifestation of absolute reality itself, it began to interpret his historical appearance in terms of the *dharma-dhatu* becoming manifest through a series of bodies of the Buddha:

> The *dharma-dhatu* can also particularize itself in such a way as to become the *dharma-kaya*, the dharma body of the Buddha. . . . If we compare the *dharma-kaya* with the *dharma-dhatu*, the former is somewhat more concrete in a human way. But, as even the *dharma-kaya* is neither visible nor inferable, more concrete forms of the Buddha-body are expressed as the body of enjoyment (*sambhoga-kaya*) and the body of emanation (*nirmana-kaya*).[47]

The later Mahayana tradition used the terms *dharmata* (dharma-nature) and *dharma-dhatu* (dharma-realm) and *tathata* (suchness) and *shunyata* (emptiness) to refer to reality itself, the essence of dharma, the absolute. Shakyamuni Buddha came to be seen more and more as a superhuman figure who manifested *dharmakaya*. To explain this, the tradition distinguished three bodies of the Buddha: (1) the dharma-body or essence-body (*dharmakaya*), which is the basis for the other two; (2) the reward-body or enjoyment-body (*sambhoga-kaya*); and (3) the transformation-body (*nirmana-kaya*).

The *dharmakaya* is the eternal aspect of the Buddha, the essence of the Buddha which is one with absolute reality. The *sambhoga-kaya* (reward-body or enjoyment-body) is the body in which a Buddha (whether Shakyamuni or another Buddha) enjoys the rewards of diligent practice and vows fulfilled and preaches to others in the process of enlightenment. Shakyamuni Buddha enjoyed the fruits of his enlightenment in the *sambhoga-kaya* after overcoming the temptations of Mara and before he began to preach the dharma. As we have seen, the Buddha decided not to enjoy his rewards in solitude, but returned to the world to preach the dharma to others in order to share his enjoyment. Thus the Buddha's own enjoyment of dharma becomes the basis for his sharing the dharma and its delights with others.[48]

The reward-body is the body of the Buddha both enjoying the reward of enlightenment and also preaching to bodhisattvas; this body is not a physical body but an appearance visible only to bodhisattvas. The body of the infant Siddhartha that Asita saw bearing the supernatural signs would have been the Enjoyment-body.[49]

The third body was usually called the *nirmana-kaya* (transformation-body). This is the concrete physical, historical body of a Buddha, such as the physical body of Shakyamuni born of Queen Maya. This is the body that ordinary unenlightened humans can see and hear and touch. The enjoyment-body serves as the link between the *dharmakaya* and the transformation-body, for it transcends the human body of the Buddha and serves as the concretization of the absolute essence-body or *dharmakaya*.[50] As the tradition developed, the three-body theory (*tri-kaya*) became more and more widely accepted in Mahayana Buddhism, with the *dharmakaya* remaining the basis for the other two bodies.

Thus Buddhists have interpreted Shakyamuni Buddha in various ways. Some Buddhists have stressed the role of Shakyamuni as a human teacher, a pathfinder who points out the way to liberation. Other Buddhists, especially in the Mahayana tradition, have interpreted Shakyamuni Buddha as a manifestation of the absolute reality of the cosmos, presenting him as an appearance of the cosmic dharmakaya, the body of the dharma or absolute reality of the universe itself. In time, more and more Buddhas came to be imagined, each governing a different realm of the universe and each being an expression of the cosmic *dharmata*.

The entire universe itself came to be viewed as a spiritual reality designed as an instrument of grace to lead beings to enlightenment:

> The transcendent Buddhas and their realms that fill the universe are concretized expressions of the eternal Buddha-principle (*dharma*), which as the basic reality of the universe is ever active to lead all beings to enlightenment. In other words, the universe is the domain of the Buddhas and is, thus, fashioned and sustained by their work to lead beings to enlightenment.[51]

The *Avatamsaka Sutra* (Flower Ornament Sutra) presents the Body of the Tathagata or the Buddha as extending throughout the cosmos, universal in its wisdom and compassion, bestowing benefits on all beings. The historical person, Shakyamuni Buddha, is one manifestation of this cosmic reality in the world of time. The sutra proclaims:

> The Buddha's immense body
> Reaches the extremities of the cosmos;
> Without leaving this seat
> It pervades all places.[52]

The sutra also tells us:

> Buddha, with various bodies,
> Travels throughout the worlds,
> Unhindered in the cosmos,
> Beyond the ken of anyone.
> The light of his wisdom always shines everywhere,
> Removing all the darkness of the world;
> It has no compare at all:
> How can it be comprehended?[53]

2

Jesus the Christ and Shakyamuni Buddha

This chapter will explore some themes in the canonical Gospels' accounts of the revelation of God in Jesus Christ in light of the teaching of the Buddhist tradition. The four themes of the Buddhacarita — illusion, the forest, separation, and dharma — find analogues in the gospel narratives. These themes will weave back and forth through the discussion of the births of the Buddha and the Messiah, the temptations they face, their analyses of the problem of human existence, their strategies for transforming consciousness, the challenge of the cross, and the cosmic significance of both figures. While there can obviously be no question of a full discussion of many issues of New Testament scholarship, many New Testament themes exhibit both important similarities and differences from fundamental Buddhist teachings. I will focus particularly on the Sermon on the Mount and the sayings of the Buddha collected in the Dhammapada as representative of the teachings of the respective leaders.

As in the case of Shakyamuni Buddha, the earliest accounts of the life of Jesus of Nazareth are shaped by the later memories of the community that followed him. The earliest Christian communities celebrated the presence of Jesus as the Risen Lord in their midst and composed the Gospels in light of this experience; they were not guided by the concerns of modern historical scholarship. As in the case of the life of the Buddha, the earliest narratives of the life of Jesus are heavily influenced by legend and myth. Thus scholars have often sharply disagreed over what can be reconstructed of the life and teaching of Jesus as a historical figure.[1]

Nonetheless, as in the case of the Buddha, there is a central core of the life of Jesus that many scholars accept. E. P. Sanders has summarized what he claims are "almost indisputable facts" concerning Jesus' career and its immediate aftermath:

1. Jesus was baptized by John the Baptist.
2. Jesus was a Galilean who preached and healed.

3. Jesus called disciples and spoke of there being twelve.

4. Jesus confined his activity to Israel.

5. Jesus engaged in a controversy about the Temple.

6. Jesus was crucified outside Jerusalem by the Roman authorities.

7. After his death Jesus' followers continued as an identifiable movement.

8. At least some Jews persecuted at least some parts of the new movement (Gal. 1:13, 22; Phi. 3:6), and it appears that his persecution endured at least to a time near the end of Paul's career (II Cor. 11:24; Gal. 5:11; 6:12; cf. Matt. 23.24; 10.17).[2]

As in the discussion of the life of the Buddha, my concern here is not with the historical Jesus as reconstructed by modern historical critical scholarship but with the portrait of Jesus as the Christ, Jesus as remembered by the early Christian community and presented by the Gospel writers.

JOURNEYS OF INITIATION

The lives of both Jesus and Shakyamuni can be read as parables which set a model for their disciples to follow. Where the early Christian community proclaimed Jesus as "the parable of God,"[3] Buddhists have read the life of the Buddha as a parable for the later Buddhist tradition.[4] In each case, following the example of the founder leads the follower into a journey of initiation. In the Gospel of Mark the journey of Jesus leads from the initiation of baptism in the Jordan River to the initiation of the resurrection revealed at the empty tomb. Followers of Jesus are explicitly challenged to "take up their cross." The journey of Shakyamuni leads from his initiation into the truth of suffering in his first sight of an aged man to his initiation into ultimate truth under the bodhi tree to his turning of the wheel of dharma in the Deer Park.

In the language of Mircea Eliade, the lives of both Jesus Christ and Shakyamuni Buddha have served as hierophanies to their followers, manifestations of the sacred that overcome the alienation and fragmentation of temporal existence and offer an orientation for human life.[5] These manifestations of the sacred overcome the terror of historical existence by providing models, paradigms for existence within time. The hierophany or manifestation that occurs through Jesus Christ or Shakyamuni Buddha is an event within time that overcomes the alienating and destructive powers of existence, an event that frees us from the terror of history, allows us to endure the passage of time with creativity, and initiates us into an experience of liberation transcending time and death.[6]

In each case, the initiation of the Buddha or the Christ sets a pattern for others to follow. Jesus Christ is the firstborn of the dead, a foretaste of the end-time; the Buddha is the pathfinder who preaches the dharma and shows others the way to freedom. The Buddha, however, points out a path that all others can follow, and so all others can, in principle, become a Buddha. The Christian tradition has placed a greater importance on the particular historical events of the life, death, and resurrection of Jesus Christ and has distinguished the unique sense in which Jesus is the Christ and the Son of God from the status of followers of Jesus, who are not and never become children of God in the same sense as Jesus. Where Shakyamuni Buddha bears a message that, at least in principle, could be learned by oneself or communicated by another, Jesus Christ is the unique incarnation of God in this world (Jn. 1:14). Jesus does, nonetheless, give his followers the power to be born again from God and become children of God in an analogous sense (Jn. 1:11–13).

The narrative of the Buddha is a journey from illusion, through the experiences in the forest, through the acceptance of separation, to ultimate insight into dharma, to initiating others into this wisdom by forming the community, the Sangha, to continue to make the dharma available in the world. The main drama of the narrative in most lives of the Buddha is the movement of Siddhartha's own consciousness from illusion to enlightenment. Only after he has been awakened and initiated into absolute wisdom itself by his own efforts do the sutras present him teaching the dharma to the Buddhist community.

Jesus, by contrast, is never presented in the Gospels as himself subject to illusion or to sin, and so there is no account of progression in his consciousness comparable to the awakening of Shakyamuni Buddha. In the canonical Gospels Jesus does face temptations in the desert, but there is no indication that Jesus himself suffers from sin and needs forgiveness. On the contrary, John the Baptist questions the appropriateness of Jesus accepting his baptism of repentance (Mt. 3:13-15). Where the driving quest of Siddhartha is to find out for himself the meaning of dharma and the answer to suffering and then, as the Buddha, to share this with others, Jesus' ministry is, from beginning to end, dominated by his relation to God. While Jesus' identity is unique, he does bring humans the gift of sharing in the divine life (Jn. 1:11-13; 1 Jn. 1:2–3; 3:1). This divine gift, as expressed in the basic principle of Athanasius, has dominated much of Christian thought: God became human so that humans could become divine.[7]

BIRTH OF THE MESSIAH AND THE BUDDHA

The narratives of the births of Siddhartha and Jesus anticipate the major themes of their entire life journeys. Where Ashvaghosha presents the birth of the Buddha as a miraculous event which reveals his identity and foretells his life mission, Matthew and Luke present the entire message of the Gospel in symbolic narrative form in their accounts of the conception, birth, and infancy of Jesus as the Son of God, the presence of God among God's people, "God with us" (Mt. 1:23).[8] They reflect on the questions of who he is, how he came to be, where he comes from, and, by anticipating the passion narrative, where he is going.[9] These brief accounts, recounted by authors in light of the later lives of the religious leaders, present miniature summaries of the core of the Buddhist and Christian paths and thus serve as meditations on the meaning of Jesus Christ and Shakyamuni Buddha.

There are obvious similarities between the births of the Buddha and the Messiah. In each case the conception is miraculous, apart from normal sexual relations. Each birth is attended by cosmic signs: a star in Matthew, an earthquake, winds, and flowers from heaven in the Buddhacarita. Hindu gods rejoice at the birth of the Buddha, and angels celebrate in the heavens at the birth of Jesus.[10] Brahmins honor the newborn Siddhartha, and Magi come to honor Jesus. In each case a seer predicts the future of the child: Simeon in Luke and Asita in the Buddhacarita.

In each case, too, there is an ominous foreshadowing of a threat to the destiny of the child. King Suddhodana, for all his joy at the birth of a marvelous son, is not at all pleased by the prophecy of Asita and resolves to thwart the prophecy by surrounding the young Prince Siddhartha with pleasures. King Herod is not pleased at the prospect of a new rival and seeks to eliminate the threat by having all the infant boys in the area of Bethlehem murdered. Jesus is a king in hiding who must flee the power of an earthly king. Siddhartha is the child of a king and has an ambiguous future: Will he become an emperor or a Buddha?

In both the Buddhacarita and the Gospels there is also a forgetfulness of the infancy narrative which appears curious to modern readers. Neither Shakyamuni Buddha nor Jesus appear to profit from knowledge of the revelations made shortly after their births. Prince Siddhartha will not remember the proclamation of wisdom he made shortly after his birth, and the later narratives of Matthew and Luke will not recall the wonders and prophecies at the birth of Jesus. When Jesus later preaches in Nazareth, the people there evidently will not know the angelic proclamations at his birth (Lk. 4:16–30) or the visit of the Magi or the escape from the slaughter of infants by Herod (Mt. 13:53-58).[11] There is no later mention of the flight into Egypt in the Gospel of Matthew.

There is also an analogy between the position of Ashvaghosha, who interprets the Buddha against the background of earlier Hindu tradition, and the Christian evangelists, who interpret the Christ against the background of the Hebrew Bible and contemporary Judaism. While Ashvaghosha constantly takes up themes of earlier Indian thought and transforms them by relating them to the Buddha, the evangelists present the Messiah in light of the history of Israel. In both cases the language of the earlier tradition is profoundly transformed by being applied to the new figure. The meaning of such fundamental terms as dharma and Messiah will be reshaped by their new applications.

While each birth requires careful preparation beforehand, the form of preparation for each birth is very different, and so the relation to the older tradition takes a distinctive form in each case. Matthew presents Jesus as the fulfillment of the prophetic words of the Hebrew Bible in order to portray his entire life as the fulfillment of God's plan.[12] Luke, in contrast to Matthew, models his account on the Hebrew Bible's story of the birth and childhood of Samuel (1 Sam. 1–3). With this model, Luke structures his infancy narrative around the comparison and contrast between John the Baptist and Jesus, with Jesus emerging as the decisive figure.[13]

The Buddhist tradition never relates the birth of Siddhartha to a divine plan of preparation involving a specific people or an earlier prophet; it does, however, recount the Jataka tales of the previous lives of the Buddha which prepare him for his birth as Siddhartha Gautama.[14] The preparation of the Buddha is one of boundless generosity over many lifetimes. As Edward Conze comments: "The state of a Buddha is one of the highest possible perfection. It seems self-evident to Buddhists that an enormous amount of preparation over many lives is needed to reach it."[15] In Mahayana Buddhism the previous lives become less important as the Buddha comes to be seen as a cosmic figure, manifesting the nature of dharmakaya, of reality itself. In this case it is reality itself manifesting itself to humans in the form of Shakyamuni Buddha.

The names of the two infants are clues to their identity. Jesus receives his name because he is to save his people from their sins (Mt. 1:21), and he is further called Emmanuel, "God with us." The meaning of the life of each child is found in his name: Jesus will save people from sin by being the very presence of God in this world. Siddhartha's name means "goal attained": he proclaims immediately after his birth that he will indeed attain the goal of release from suffering, and he promises to make the path to this goal accessible to others.

The threat to the very existence of Jesus comes from sin: sin is the power from which he is to save people, and sin finds a most ominous expression in the rage of Herod. By clinging to his own power and, in effect, putting himself in the place of God and thus rejecting the entry of God into this world, Herod symbolizes the furious struggle of sin against God's presence among humans: sin is the power that prevents us from receiving God-with-us. Thus Matthew presents the infancy of Jesus as already dominated by the dynamics of the passion narrative.[16] The threat to the future Buddha is not so violent, but nonetheless real. The danger in this case is not sin, rebellion against God, but rather illusion, the clinging to thirsts which do not ultimately satisfy and the refusal to accept the necessity of separation. The question posed by Suddhodana is: Is earthly rule worth grasping, or should it be abandoned for the sake of enlightenment? The question posed by Herod is: Can the violence of earthly powers prevent God from entering the world?

The prophecies of the two children's futures are also very different. Simeon foresees conflict and violence: The child will be a sign of contradiction, a presence that will divide Israel, leading to the fall and the rise of many (Lk. 2:34). The child will bring the secret thoughts and commitments of people to light, arousing opposition, and Simeon warns Mary that a sword will pierce her soul (Lk. 2:35). Simeon himself is grateful to have looked upon the child who is the glory of God among God's people, and he is content to depart.

Asita's prediction is less violent, but his leave-taking is also less serene. The seer predicts no violence but only great success for the future Buddha: "he will throw open for the escape of living beings the door whose bolt is the thirst of desire and whose leaves are delusion and the dark of ignorance" (Buddhacarita, 1.74; p. 16). Asita weeps not for the child but for himself, lamenting that he will not live to hear the future Buddha preach: "I am distressed for my own disappointment. For my time to depart has come, just when he is born who shall understand the means, so hard to find, of destroying birth" (1.68; p. 15).

The later traditions will also interpret the births of these two children as revelations of absolute reality itself, the Gospel of John portraying the birth of Jesus as the eternal divine Word becoming flesh, and the Buddhist tradition interpreting the birth of Siddhartha as dharma-dhatu appearing, through the mediations of the three bodies of the Buddha, in the world of space and time. Dharma-dhatu is not, to be sure, a creating God; and the Buddhist tradition never developed a notion of a trinitarian God becoming incarnate, and so it is impossible to identify the later Christian and Buddhist interpretations. In later Christian terms, Buddhist interpretations of Shakyamuni appear docetist, for the visible physical body is seen as "unreal and fictitious."[17] The two traditions do agree, nonetheless, in finding the key to reality itself in the coming of a child into the world.

TEMPTATIONS: THE FOREST AND THE DESERT

Both Jesus and Shakyamuni go through a process of personal testing and decision before beginning their public preaching. For both Jesus and Shakyamuni, the path of liberation involves overcoming illusions and the distorting desires that arise from such illusion, and they must both face these temptations in themselves before they proclaim the path of liberation to others.

In both cases the temptations involve the very identity of the religious leader. The questions of Siddhartha turn on the meaning of dharma; those of Jesus on the meaning of being the Son of God. In the Theravada tradition it is only after Siddhartha has resisted the temptations of Mara that he is proclaimed a Buddha. In Mahayana interpretations, the temptations serve rather as a testing and manifestation of the identity of the one who has been the Buddha from the limitless past.

There is no sign that Jesus, as presented in the Gospels, went through a search for his identity or for the true meaning of wisdom.[18] In the Synoptic Gospels, Jesus' temptations follow immediately on his accepting baptism from John and the sound of the voice from heaven which proclaims Jesus to be the Son of God.[19] The proclamation alludes to Psalm 2:7 ("You are my son, today have I fathered you."), a psalm of royal enthronement which acknowledged the king of Israel to be the son of God and warned other nations to obey him.[20]

The voice's expression of divine pleasure in Jesus also alludes to Isaiah 42:1, where God expresses God's pleasure in the suffering servant. The combination of the images of Jesus as the royal Davidic Messiah and as the suffering servant of God begins to focus the meaning of Jesus' role as Son of God. As John Meier notes, in Matthew, "Jesus' sonship and royal enthronement are intimately connected with servanthood, suffering, and vicarious sacrifice."[21] This sets a very different context for the temptations of Jesus from those of Siddhartha. Where the temptations of Siddhartha involve the proper response to suffering and separation and the meaning of dharma, the temptations of Jesus test his identity as the Son of God, an identity which will involve a voluntary acceptance of suffering for the sake of his mission.

The temptations are debates over what it means to be the Buddha or the Son of God. In the forest Siddhartha faces not only the temptation of alluring women but also the rather more subtle temptation of religious practice itself. Both the seductive women and the world-renouncing ascetics that Siddhartha encounters promise peace and joy, but both are actually forms of illusion which cannot deliver what they promise. Siddhartha resolves to renounce both paths because he sees that they are both forms of selfishness. During his search for the truth, Siddhartha ponders and debates the meaning of dharma: Is his proper place in the palace with his family or in the forest, seeking the truth? One of the very last temptations of Mara invites Shakyamuni to follow his own duty and renounce the path of liberation. Siddhartha, however, reflects on the necessity of separation and continues his quest.

At the center of the temptations of Jesus in the desert is the question of his role as Son of God and his proper relation to God the Father. In both Matthew and Luke, the devil's opening words are: "If you are the Son of God" (Mt. 4:3; Lk. 4:3). Both of these temptations are examples of a religious identity gone awry. The third temptation demands that Jesus give to the devil the worship due to God alone. The temptations of Jesus can be read as false ways in which to be the Son of God—the wonder worker who performs miracles to astonish people or the political ruler who worships power more than God. The temptations of Jesus recapitulate the temptations that Israel faced in the desert—temptations involving food, power, and the proper object of worship.[22] In each temptation something finite threatens to usurp the place of God.

In each response the scripture passage that Jesus cites refers to the proper relation to God—trusting in God, not putting God to the test, and serving God alone. In each case Jesus responds with a quote from Deuteronomy on the need for trusting and worshiping God. Even God's own Son is not to put God to the test. His responses anticipate the type of rule that the Son of God will exercise in conflict with civil and religious authorities later in his life. While the temptations of Shakyamuni do not explicitly involve God, the temptations of both Shakyamuni and Jesus are false paths of liberation, paths which masquerade as religious. The temptations of both Jesus and Shakyamuni are paths dominated by illusion and desire, paths that promise liberation but deliver new forms of servitude.

ILLUSION AND SIN

The types of temptations that Shakyamuni and Jesus overcome are closely related to the question of why human existence is awry. The understanding of the central problem of human existence is very different for the two religious leaders. In each case, the diagnosis of the problem only becomes clear from the vantage point of liberation. It is only after awakening to wisdom that a Buddhist can truly understand suffering and grasping; it is only after being healed by grace that a Christian can understand the ravages of sin.

The young Prince Siddhartha resolves to seek enlightenment only after he has become aware of the suffering that is inevitably linked to human limitations: sickness, old age, and death. Siddhartha comes to recognize the inevitability of separation in human existence and searches for a way to accept and thereby overcome the suffering it brings. The central problem of existence for the young Prince Siddhartha, as for the later Buddhist tradition, is the unnecessary suffering caused by ignorance and illusion. As presented in the Gospels, the central problem for Jesus is not human finitude—it is sin. Jesus' public ministry begins not with the discovery of the suffering of old age, illness, and death. Rather, Jesus encounters the fiery preaching of John the Baptist, who warns of the wrath of God that is to come as judgment upon a sinful world and calls for a baptism of repentance (Mk. 1:4; Mt. 3:4–12; Lk. 3:3–18).

In the Buddhist tradition there is no "sin" in the Christian sense of the word, only ignorance or wrong views which arise from illusion.[23] The difference between Buddhist ignorance and Christian sin is, to be sure, not absolute, but it is nonetheless important. For Christians, the reign of sin is founded upon illusion and deceit. According to the Book of Genesis, sin entered the world through a deception (3:4). For Buddhists, ignorance is not simply a lack of knowledge; it involves a fundamental warping of our relationships with all other beings and causes tremendous suffering. This pernicious warping of human existence is comparable to what Christians name sin, but the implications of the two terms are not the same.

In Christianity the central dynamic of sin is idolatry (e.g., Rom. 1:18–32). In the Book of Exodus, the Ten Commandments are founded upon the first: We are not to worship any finite reality. The first commandment, in turn, is rooted in Israel's experience of deliverance by God from slavery in Egypt. An historical encounter with God opens up the possibility of liberation which is expressed in the covenant, but it also imposes the responsibilities involved in accepting the covenant.

In Christian understandings of sin, we delude ourselves into making finite objects or concerns into our ultimate concern. We erect false gods and offer them worship. They deceive us and lead us to our destruction. In Buddhism the central dynamic of ignorance is the positing of an independently existing self that is a delusion. This false, clinging self makes itself the center of its universe, is addicted to its desires, and thus traps itself in an endless cycle of suffering. Buddhist awakening means seeing through this illusion, awakening from this dream. Christian sin is making some created reality absolute against the Creator; Buddhist ignorance is clinging to something that appears to be permanent against impermanence.

The Buddhist precepts, while they resemble the Ten Commandments in content, are not received as commandments from God. While the violation of the Buddhist precepts does cause suffering, it does not result in guilt in the sense of responsibility before God. Buddhist teaching on ethical conduct does not appeal to the authority of God but points out what actions and illusions cause suffering and what actions and realizations stop it.

The wisdom literature of the Hebrew Bible offers a closer analogy to the Buddhist precepts than the Ten Commandments. The sayings and warnings of Proverbs and Ben Sira are rooted in the experience of many generations, and point out what leads to lasting happiness and what does not. Not all the sayings are matters of sin and guilt; many simply point out what is wise and what is foolish, without making any moral judgment. The wise person acts in harmony with the wisdom God implanted in creation, and therefore the wise person flourishes; the fool goes against the wisdom and perishes in ignorance.[24] Where the Buddhist precepts would not presuppose any wisdom implanted by God in creation, they are based on a vision of what reality demands and a sense that suffering follows from certain actions.[25] The wisdom tradition, together with the covenantal and prophetic traditions, forms an important part of the background of the preaching of Jesus and of the Gospel of John.[26]

Both Jesus and Shakyamuni agree that our ordinary consciousness of ourselves is imprisoned in illusions. Jesus calls for repentance and Shakyamuni for awakening. Both teachers see illusions and distorted desires as integrally connected. From our self-deceptions come our addictions. The Buddha discovered that the false belief in a substantial ego-self causes great anxiety, conflict, and unnecessary suffering; the way to freedom is through liberating knowledge. Jesus expressed the proper relation to God in the proclamation of the reign of God.

DHARMA AND THE REIGN OF GOD

Both Jesus and Shakyamuni propose paths for transforming human consciousness in light of their understandings of what is wrong with human existence. As the First Noble Truth of the Buddha concerning suffering must be interpreted in light of the Third and Fourth Noble Truths (which point out the solution and the path to freedom), so the sharp condemnations of sin by John the Baptist and Jesus must be interpreted in light of the proclamation of the reign of God as the overcoming of sin.

Mark presents a summary statement of the teaching of Jesus in the very first chapter: "The time is fulfilled, and the kingdom of God is close at hand. Repent, and believe the gospel" (Mk. 1:15). There has been endless debate over what the kingdom or reign of God meant for Jesus, and whether it was a present or a future reality.[27] The reign of God combines elements of present experience with future expectation: It is the power of God breaking into human experience, forgiving sinners, healing wounds, and challenging all to live out of love.

The experience of Jesus is in stark contrast to the portrait of the Buddha. Where Shakyamuni seeks the path of awakening for himself and later proclaims it to others, Jesus is portrayed as gripped by the experience of God's reign breaking into this world, and he calls people to repent and accept the good news of God's reign.[28] For Jesus, the experience of the reign of God is central to his entire existence — to his preaching and healing, his actions, his challenge to established authorities, his dining with tax collectors and sinners. Moreover, everything in the life, teaching, death, and resurrection of Jesus must be interpreted in light of his relationship to God as Father, addressed as Abba. Like Shakyamuni Buddha, Jesus sees our normal existence as distorted and twisted by a false consciousness. Jesus, again like Shakyamuni, proclaims a path of liberation through a transforming experience of conversion to the truth.

Shakyamuni Buddha, as we have seen, receives the help of the traditional gods of India in the Buddhacarita, but Shakyamuni nowhere describes an experience comparable to Jesus' intimacy with God as Abba. Prince Siddhartha himself needed the assistance of the traditional gods of India in his first awakening to the reality of human suffering and the possibility of an escape in the four signs. The Indian gods do offer the gift of the initial insights to the young prince, but they do not offer him the final enlightenment. In Indian tradition these gods are themselves finite, though powerful, beings who dwell in the heavens; they are not the ultimate creating and redeeming reality that Christians name God. Indeed the Hindu gods have reason to envy Shakyamuni after his enlightenment: "Even the gods long to be like the Buddhas who are awake and watch" (Dhammapada 14.181; p. 62). ·

Shakyamuni's path leads him to awaken to the truth of his own identity, but he does not turn to a loving God to resolve the problem of human suffering. Where Jesus places his trust in the creating and redeeming God that he addresses as Abba, Shakyamuni Buddha discovers for himself the all-pervasive power of suffering in life and the path to freedom. The Dhammapada remembers him as saying: "I have conquered all; I know all, and my life is pure; I have left all, and I am free from craving. I myself found the way. Whom shall I call Teacher? Whom shall I teach?" (Dhammapada 24.353; p. 85). In accord with his own awakening, the Buddha advises others: "It is you who must make the effort. The Great of the past only show the way" (Dhammapada 20.276; p. 75).

The question of the existence or nonexistence of God does not arise in the preaching of Shakyamuni, and he appears to have rejected such questions as mere speculation. For Shakyamuni Buddha, the desire to speculate on God is itself an indication that one is still caught in illusion. Such speculations about the existence or nonexistence of God cannot liberate us, and they can increase our suffering.

The center of the preaching of Jesus is not speculation, but the experience of the reign of God, God's dominion breaking into human experience as both judgment upon and forgiveness of sins. This is the central reality of Jesus' life, dominating the parables he tells and the actions he performs. The reign of God is grace, the forgiving presence of a loving God, and also a critical judgment upon all who reject the invitation.

Jesus' proclamation of the reign of God comes as a sword that divides hearers into opposing groups, setting even members of a family against one another (Mt. 10:34–36; Lk. 2:34; 12:51–53). The Gospel of John portrays the results of this challenge in the division of humans into two opposing groups, the children of light, who accept the message of Jesus, and those who refuse to believe and choose to live in darkness (Jn. 3:16–19; 12:35–48). For John, the world appears as a battleground where the prince of this world opposes the entry of the bearer of salvation and must be driven from power (12:31; 14:30; 16:11). While the Buddha recognizes the destructive power of ignorance and illusion in the world and wields the sword of wisdom, the proclamation of the dharma challenges Buddhists to overcome all divisions and dualisms, including the division of the human race into opposing groups of light and darkness. Instead of a harsh condemnation of sinful rebellion against God, the Buddha issues an urgent summons to awaken from illusion.

The center of the teaching of Shakyamuni Buddha is found in the Four Noble Truths which diagnose the problem of human life and prescribe the proper cure. Shakyamuni Buddha did not claim to experience the presence of a transcendent and immanent, creating and redeeming God, but rather found the path to liberation and shared it with others. Shakyamuni Buddha himself did not claim to offer salvation as a gift but pointed out the way to attain insight and liberation. He was not a savior but a pathfinder.

THE DHAMMAPADA AND THE SERMON ON THE MOUNT

The Dhammapada, one of the earliest collections of the Buddha's sayings, expresses the heart of his wisdom. *Pada* means "path," and *Dhammapada* means the "path of dharma," the path of truth, of life, of perfection, of nirvana.[29] The work consists of a series of brief sayings, aphorisms, observations, comparisons, and exhortations.

The Sermon on the Mount in Matthew is a summary of the teaching of Jesus, an epitome edited by Matthew to present the core of the vision of Jesus.[30] The sayings of the Sermon on the Mount are heavily influenced by the earlier Hebrew and Jewish wisdom tradition and express a wisdom of life rooted in a theology of creation.[31] While the present form of the Sermon on the Mount is a product of the early church and the evangelist, many of these sayings probably contain a historical core of the preaching of Jesus himself.[32]

Seeing Clearly

In both the Dhammapada and the Sermon on the Mount, the exhortations are based upon a vision of reality and urge the hearer to live in accord with reality and in harmony with other people: "Many do not know that we are here in this world to live in harmony. Those who know this do not fight against each other" (Dhammapada 1.6; p. 35). The core of the Buddha's vision is the interdependence and impermanence of all realities. Jesus also stresses the importance of seeing clearly:

The lamp of the body is the eye. It follows that if your eye is clear, your whole body will be filled with light. But if your eye is diseased, your whole body will be darkness. If then, the light inside you is darkened, what darkness that will be! (Mt. 6:22–23).

For Jesus, seeing clearly is the key to wholeness and living in harmony with God and creation. A darkened consciousness perpetuates the reign of sin. The images of enlightenment or "seeing clearly" have been central to the quest of the Buddhist tradition, and Buddhists have long named the central problem of human existence ignorance. In both traditions the wise person sees reality as it is, lives in accord with this reality, and finds true life. Thus in the Sermon on the Mount in the Gospel of Matthew, Jesus stresses the importance of having the proper consciousness, and he chides his followers for living in dominion to distorted desires. Like Shakyamuni, Jesus also insists that seeing clearly involves liberation from desires.

Beatitudes and Consciousness

Jesus begins the Sermon on the Mount with the beatitudes, pronouncements that certain people are blessed, happy, joyful because of a certain state or attitude.[33] Beatitudes were found in the Hebrew and Jewish wisdom tradition (e.g., Sir. 25:8–9) and in the Greek world,[34] but Jesus uses the form in the distinctive context of his proclamation of the reign of God. The beatitudes are eschatological pronouncements, declarations that people are blessed because of the reign of God. In the preaching of Jesus, the wisdom sayings now promise eschatological salvation and open up a new way of being in the world. The reign of God comes as sheer gift from beyond our control, but followers of Jesus are to live in a new way because of this gift.

While in Matthew the beatitudes focus on attitudes, the beatitudes in Luke focus more on persons in a particular condition. It is likely that in this respect Luke is closer to the earliest tradition of the sayings of Jesus.[35] In the beatitudes concerning poverty, mourning, and hunger found in both Matthew and Luke, Luke's version in each case focuses on a condition referring to those who are economically poor, who hunger and weep.[36] In Luke the poor as poor are the special recipients of God's concern. As Herman Hendrickx comments, "They are called blessed, not because of their virtue, their internal disposition, their openness to the kingdom of God, but simply because they are poor and as such benefit from God's disposition towards them."[37] It is also to be hoped that as the reign of God becomes present on earth, they should also benefit from the concern of those with more economic resources than they.

Matthew changes the description of those proclaimed blessed and focuses the sayings on the attitude of those who follow Jesus. To be "poor in spirit" (Mt. 5:3) is to have the proper disposition in the reign of God. It is freedom from preoccupation with material goods: "Poverty in spirit is not necessarily opposed to possessions, but it is always opposed to attachment."[38] Poverty in spirit also implies a proper humility and freedom from self-importance.[39] The later beatitudes in Matthew spell out other aspects of the attitudes of those who have accepted the reign of God: to be merciful, pure in heart, peacemakers, even at the cost of persecution (Mt. 5:7–12).

Given the reticence of Shakyamuni Buddha on the question of God, there is nothing in his teaching to parallel the perspective of the Lukan beatitudes that God has a special concern for the poor simply because of their poverty. Nonetheless, the attitudes of renunciation, nonattachment, and freedom from material worries of the Matthean beatitudes do find analogues in Buddhist perspectives on wealth, especially in the ideal of virtuous householders such as Vimalakirti, who may be wealthy, but who do not cling to their possessions and share their wealth with the Buddhist monks who own nothing.

The beatitude to those who mourn promises divine comfort, the passive voice expressing divine action which is beginning in the preaching of Jesus and will find its culmination in the end-time. The beatitude to the meek, which is not in the Lukan beatitudes, anticipates the image of Jesus as the meek king entering Jerusalem on an ass and thus challenges the hearers to adopt the attitude of Jesus (cf. Mt. 11:29; 21:5). The meek are also those who surrender all to God, including their own dreams and desires. The promise of land may refer not to physical possession of territory but to participation in the reign of God, to finding a space in which to be free.[40]

The attitude of meekness is not, however, a subservient surrender to the status quo. Jesus' own meekness in entering Jerusalem (Mt. 21:5) was followed by his cleansing of the Temple (Mt. 21:12–17), and the beatitudes that follow link meekness to the pursuit of justice, to mercy, and to peacemaking. The meek, like Jesus, renounce the use of violence (Mt. 26:52–55), but they do not abandon the struggle for justice.

Where Luke promises happiness to those who literally hunger, Matthew shifts the focus to those who seek righteousness. The hunger and thirst for righteousness suggest that this righteousness comes only as a gift from God, but it demands active longing and effort in living out righteousness. Righteousness encompasses all that is in accord with the will of God, including both personal uprightness and proper social relations.

As the Sermon continues, Jesus escalates the demands of the Torah, warning his followers not to nurture anger, not to regard another's wife with covetous desire (Mt. 5:21–30). The reign of God that Jesus proclaims means liberation not only in external actions but also in internal attitudes.

Parallels between the teaching of Jesus and the sayings of the Buddha abound. Both urge their hearers to seek the true righteousness and lasting treasure (Dhammapada 9.116–18; p. 52; and 14.187; p. 63; Mt. 5:20; 6:19–21). Both warn against judging any evil deed to be of small account, even in the least matters. Jesus warns against infringing the least of the commandments and teaching others to do the same (Mt. 5:19). The Buddha warns: "Hold not a sin of little worth, thinking 'this is little to me'. The falling of drops of water will in time fill a water-jar. Even so the foolish man becomes full of evil, although he gather it little by little" (Dhammapada 9.121; p. 52).

Where Jesus tells us to take the beam out of our own eye before trying to remove the splinter from another's (Mt. 7:3–5), the Buddha cautions us: "Think not of the faults of others, of what they have done or not done. Think rather of your own sins, of the things you have done or not done" (Dhammapada 4.50; p. 42–43).

Both figures warn against allowing life to be dominated by lustful desires (Dhammapada 20.284; Mt. 5:27–28). Both warn that the path of wisdom is difficult and is followed by only a few (Mt. 7:13–14; Dhammapada 6.85; p. 47), but both promise rewards of joy to those who do live wisely (Mt. 5:3–12, 19; Dhammapada 7.92, 96–99; pp. 48–49).

Jesus warns against fasting or praying in public for all to see (Mt. 6:1–4, 16–18), and Shakyamuni warns against fasting without the proper consciousness (Dhammapada 5.70; p. 45) and criticizes those who desire recognition and a reputation, precedence among monks, and veneration among people (Dhammapada 5.73–74; p. 45). Where Jesus advises us not to nurture anger and to settle with one's opponent before going to court (Mt. 5:25–26), Shakyamuni advises: "Never speak harsh words, for once spoken they may return to you. Angry words are painful and there may be blows for blows" (Dhammapada 10.133; p. 54).

NON-DISCRIMINATING LOVE

Jesus proclaims a non-discriminating love modeled on the love of God for all creatures. This love resolutely refuses to reduce other persons to objects of desire or outlets for emotional frustration. Jesus also challenges his followers to transcend the division of people into friends or enemies and imitate the love of God by loving enemies:

> But I say this to you, love your enemies and pray for those who persecute you; so that you may be children of your Father in heaven, for he causes his sun to rise on the bad as well as the good, and sends down rain to fall on the upright and the wicked alike. . . . You must therefore set no bounds to your love, just as your heavenly Father sets none to his (Mt. 5:22, 27–28, 43–45, 48).

The perfection of righteousness manifests itself in the love of one's enemy. This is not merely a matter of an inner feeling toward an enemy; it involves creative action, nonviolent ("meek") peacemaking in the pursuit of justice that leads the situation of hostility to be reconciled. Jesus' examples of turning the other cheek, giving the extra garment, and going the extra mile are all examples of creative responses to oppression that prod the enemy to rethink the situation. Since the left hand was used only for unclean tasks in the culture of Jesus' day, one would strike someone only with the right hand. Thus one would strike an inferior with the back of one's hand and a peer with one's fist or open hand. To strike the right cheek (Mt. 5:40) was an insult, since it meant hitting someone with the back of one's hand. To turn the left cheek after being struck on the right cheek forces the opponent to strike the left cheek with the right fist or open hand, and this means treating one as an equal.[41] Even though the violence may continue, the dehumanizing degradation of being treated as inferior is ended.

Giving the extra garment would mean nakedness, which was taboo in Judaism, and those who saw the naked person were held responsible (Gen. 9:20–27). If a poor person were sued in court for his or her garment (the wealthy would have other resources to offer), the offer of the extra garment would place the plaintiff in the position of violating the Torah, since Exodus specifically forbade taking the cloak as a pledge for debts (Ex. 22:26–27; Dt. 24:12–13).

Similarly, going the extra mile would put the oppressor in a difficult position. Roman soldiers were authorized to force subject persons to carry their pack one mile and no further. Since the Romans did not want to be seen as unbearably oppressive, there were strict and severe penalties for forcing someone to go an extra mile. Jesus' advice to go the extra mile would place the Roman soldier in the uncomfortable position of violating Roman military law and risking serious punishment. Again, the strategy of creative nonviolent response places the oppressor in a difficult position and prods the opponent to view one in a new light.[42]

While not as detailed in example, the strategy of the advice of the Buddha is similar: "Overcome anger by peacefulness; overcome evil by good. Overcome the mean by generosity; and the man who lies by truth" (Dhammapada 17.223; p. 68). Where Jesus warns against anger (Mt. 5:22) and judgment (Mt. 7:1–2), the Dhammapada warns us not to cling to the memory of past injuries: " 'He insulted me, he hurt me, he defeated me, he robbed me.' Those who think such thoughts will not be free from hate. . . . For hate is not conquered by hate: hate is conquered by love. This is a law eternal" (Dhammapada 1.3, 5; p. 35).

Buddhists insist that awakening brings freedom from desire and discrimination, including the desire for revenge and the discrimination between friend and foe. This does not mean that Buddhists no longer have emotions or desires, but that the awakened person does not cling to desire and is not dominated by emotions and desires. Buddhists also speak of a non-discriminating compassion that is beyond good and evil, for the awakened Buddhist does not discriminate between friend and enemy but looks on all beings with compassion.

The Japanese Buddhist philosopher Keiji Nishitani accepts Jesus' command to love one's enemies as one's friends as what Buddhists know as "non-differentiating love beyond enmity and friendship."[43] Nishitani also accepts Jesus' mention of God sending sun and rain upon all equally as an example of this perfection; it manifests "the indifference of love. It is a non-differentiating love that transcends the distinctions men make between good and evil, justice and injustice."[44] Nishitani understands this indifference of love not as a reduction of things to an abstract common denominator. Rather, "the indifference of love embraces all things in their most concrete Form—for example, good men and evil men—and accepts the differences for what they are."[45]

POSSESSIONS AND FREEDOM

After stressing the importance of the eye as the lamp of the body (Mt. 6:22–23), Jesus goes on to explain that seeing clearly is related to the outcome of a conflict that rages within us: "No one can be the slave of two masters: he will either hate the first and love the second, or be attached to the first and despise the second. You cannot be the slave both of God and of money" (Mt. 6:24). For Jesus, to see clearly is not simply an intellectual matter. It is immediately related to our relationship to God, for it involves the central choice that each of us is always making: the basic decision to worship God or some finite reality—whether money or some other object of our concern.

Shakyamuni Buddha is remembered as issuing a similar warning to his followers about the pursuit of wealth. In the Dhammapada Shakyamuni cautions: "But one is the path of earthly wealth, and another is the path of Nirvana. Let the follower of the Buddha think of this and, without striving for reputation, let him ever strive after freedom" (Dhammapada 5.75; p. 45).

For both Shakyamuni and for Jesus, wealth, or indeed any object of desire, can be a snare trapping us in illusion, but the way they interpret the dynamics of illusion is different. For Shakyamuni, the central illusion is clinging to the false belief that our ego-self is real; for Jesus it is elevating a finite reality such as money to the position of being god in our lives. In the Sermon on the Mount, wealth is a danger when it becomes a god that rules over us or when it blinds us to the needs of others or causes us to dominate others.

In the Gospel of Luke Jesus tells the parable of the rich fool to illustrate the illusion that people bound by desire for material security can fall into. In the parable a rich farmer enjoys a great harvest and decides to build more barns, in effect hoarding his crop and manipulating the price of grain on the market. He tells himself: " 'My soul, you have plenty of good things laid by for many years to come; take things easy, eat, drink, have a good time.' " Jesus comments on his self-deception: "But God said to him, 'Fool! This very night the demand will be made for your soul; and this hoard of yours, whose will it be then?' " (Lk. 12:19–20).

In a similar warning in the Dhammapada, Shakyamuni describes a fool as expressing a deluded self-confidence. The fool says to himself: " 'These are my sons. This is my wealth.' " Shakyamuni comments: "In this way the fool troubles himself. He is not even the owner of himself: how much less of his sons and of his wealth!" (Dhammapada 5.62; p. 44).

For the Buddha, awakening from illusion means the realization that the clinging ego-self is not real. We do not own ourselves, much less the objects or the persons around us. Jesus also warns us that we are not our own masters. We are not the owners of ourselves. As Jesus repeatedly emphasizes, worshiping God, accepting the reign of God, means surrendering ourselves completely, accepting the loss of family, of possessions, even of life itself. Jesus expresses this surrender of self in his instruction on prayer in the Sermon on the Mount: "your kingdom come, your will be done" (Mt. 6:10). To accept the reign of God is to surrender our will to God's. To worship God means to follow on the path of Jesus and take up our cross.

The choice of money, or indeed of any finite object or concern, is, in effect, a form of idolatry—an illusion, for we turn to false gods in order to seek our true identity and lasting security, gifts which idols are powerless to impart. The power of these illusions is often deeply embedded in our consciousness, and so Jesus often uses harsh language and unexpected images to cut through the illusions that bind us to our false gods.

The Buddhist tradition ascends the path of wisdom by using negations to destroy the illusions of our ordinary consciousness. The beginning of wisdom for Christians involves an attack on the idols that delude us.

Because false gods normally rule over our world, the assault on their power must proceed by way of negation, and thus Jesus' proclamation of the reign of God is a battle cry that declares war on any other reality that usurps the place of God. "The reign of God is at hand" means that every false god must be destroyed.

PRAYER AND MEDITATION

The center of the Sermon on the Mount is the Lord's Prayer (Mt. 6:9–13), which inscribes all the admonitions within a life of prayer that ask the grace and the forgiveness of God. The prayer implicitly acknowledges that we cannot put Jesus' teaching into practice without divine support. The prayer begins by hallowing God's name and asking that God's reign and will may become effectively present on earth. Then it focuses on the needs of the praying community, asking for the bread that will sustain us, the forgiveness that will heal us, and freedom from trial and temptation. Our reconciliation with God manifests itself in reconciliation with those who have wronged us. The prayer seeks the divine sustenance which allows us to live out of God's love and to practice God's righteousness, and it seeks God's protection in time of trial, both the trial of the everyday and the great trial of the end-time (Mt. 25:31–46). Since the demands of Jesus are beyond our capability, we rely on the grace of God and pray for the reign of God to come. Christian prayer is a surrender of oneself to God.

Buddhist meditation can also be seen as a surrender, but there is no God to surrender oneself to, and no self to surrender. In meditating, we let go of our illusory self. While the Buddha insisted on the importance of concentration and proper mental discipline, Buddhist meditation is very different from the prayer of Jesus. The Buddha insisted that humans are their own masters (Dhammapada 12.160) and urged his followers to be a refuge to themselves,[46] and so there is no series of petitions to God. Buddhist meditation attends to the present moment, frees one from illusions, and allows one to see clearly. In the *Sutra on the Full Awareness of Breathing*, the Buddha instructs his followers to be aware of every breath, short or long, and of the peace and joy that awareness of one's breath brings to the body and mind. Awareness of one's breathing leads to awareness of one's body, of one's feelings, and to mental stability and understanding. Persistence in meditation leads to increased energy, joy, ease, concentration, and the letting go of all attachment and clinging.[47]

ANXIETY AND FREEDOM

However different their forms, both Buddhist meditation and the prayer of Jesus lead to the abandonment of the anxieties that normally dominate our lives. In the second half of the Sermon on the Mount, Jesus develops the theme of the reign of God by attacking the illusory sources of anxiety and worry in our lives. His followers are to look to the lilies of the field and the birds of the air and not worry about the morrow: "So do not worry about tomorrow: tomorrow will take care of itself. Each day has enough trouble of its own" (Mt. 6:34).

The worrying that Jesus warns against is not simply an inner feeling but a matter of practices and external attitudes. We often worry about matters that are less important (such as clothes) or beyond our control (such as the past and the future). Misplaced worries allow us to avoid the one thing we should worry about: our present relation to God, the one who cares for all creation and who gives us time itself.[48] The reign of God and its righteousness is the only experience that ultimately matters, but humans prefer to avoid this genuine concern by worrying about other matters.

For Jesus, as for Shakyamuni Buddha, most of our lives are lived in illusion, our vision distorted by mistaken priorities. To see life as it really is frees us from the illusions that dominate our lives and the misplaced anxiety that they cause. For both leaders, our worries distort our vision and lead us to misplace our energies. Such anxieties also warp our sense of time, so that we do not live in the present, but worry constantly about a future that does not exist. We live constantly in worry about realities that are not present and are thereby deprived of experiencing the only time in which we can live: the present. The *Sutra on Knowing the Better Way to Live Alone* presents the Buddha as saying: "Do not pursue the past. Do not lose yourself in the future. The past no longer is. The future has not yet come."[49]

Shakyamuni discovered the source of suffering in our cravings and addictions. Freedom from craving brings freedom from suffering. Jesus also warns against craving for things that affect our bodies and our material security. Jesus suggests that in such anxieties we are really misplacing our worry. Instead of worrying about God, about the reign of God and God's saving justice, we worry about less important matters, material concerns or future questions over which we have no power. Thus Jesus seeks to negate our ordinary sense of priorities.

There is a similar dynamic of negating our ordinary consciousness, of awakening from illusion, of living in the present, and of liberation from anxiety in the teachings of Jesus and Shakyamuni. For both figures, freedom from illusion brings freedom from craving, and freedom from craving means liberation from the dominion of conflicting and contradictory desires. This frees us to experience the world as it is—the birds of the sky, the flowers of the field, the present day.

CREATION AND DEPENDENT CO-ARISING

The explicit basis for their respective teachings is rather different, however. At the core of the Sermon on the Mount is a theology of creation.[50] Jesus' challenge and his advice are founded upon faith in a God who continually creates and provides for the world. The liberation from false worries that Jesus proclaims is possible because of the love of a gracious heavenly Father who providentially cares for the world. If God cares for birds and flowers through the processes of nature, Jesus suggests, how much more will God care for us!

Shakyamuni Buddha would agree with Jesus' assault upon the illusions and worries that dominate so much of ordinary life, but from a very different perspective. Buddhists reject an anthropocentric view of the universe, and thus in reply to Jesus' question: "Are you not worth much more than they?" the American Buddhist scholar Francis Cook answers: "No."[51] In Buddhist perspectives, it is wonderful to be born as a human, because humans have a special opportunity to awaken to the dharma, but humans are not worth more than the birds of the sky.

The difference between the Christian tradition, which looks to God as Creator, and the Buddhist nontheistic vision of dependent co-arising is especially important here. For Buddhists, dependent co-arising is the web of mutual interrelationships that binds all beings into a whole and makes them one. The Buddha's intuition of dependent co-arising is an intuition of pure contingency and of universal connection. All things are what they are, arising from the other things of the universe. Nothing arises from nothing, and so there is no question of a Creator calling things to be out of nothing. The Buddhist sage Nagasena reportedly explained to King Menander: "Precisely so, great king, there are not any things that exist which come out of things that did not exist. Only out of things that existed, great king, come things that exist."[52]

For the Buddha, there is no providential love of God supporting creation and clothing the flowers of the field and caring for the birds of the air. Moreover, there is no system of values that decides one reality is worth more than another. The birds of the air are precious, and so are humans, but we are not worth more than they.

The Jesuit theologian Raimundo Panikkar comments on the meaning of dependent co-arising: "The Buddha's great intuition consists in 'seeing' contingency in itself, divorced from any fundament. ... The Buddha did not see the 'beyond.' He saw the totality and interdependency of the 'right here.'"[53] The Buddha and his followers do not look to a providential God as the basis of their freedom from anxiety, but rather to the direct experience of reality as such.

SEPARATION AND DEATH

The third theme of the Buddhacarita, separation, also finds analogies in the Gospels. As we saw in the Buddhacarita, young Prince Siddhartha made his initial decision to seek enlightenment only after he became aware of the inevitable pain of separation in human life. To overcome the suffering of inevitable separation, he chose a voluntary separation.

Jesus repeatedly demands separation in one form or another from his followers. Jesus calls his followers away from their fishing nets and their families, and he later warns them: "No one who prefers father or mother to me is worthy of me. No one who prefers son or daughter to me is worthy of me" (Mt. 10:37).

The physical separation from one's home and family is only the beginning of the deeper and more difficult separation or loss which marks the entire path of discipleship. Jesus insists that we must lose even our very lives: "Anyone who does not take his cross and follow in my footsteps is not worthy of me. Anyone who finds his life will lose it; anyone who loses his life for my sake will find it" (Mt. 10:38–39).

When a rich young man comes to Jesus and asks how he may obtain eternal life, Jesus first reminds him of the usual commandments of morality and love of neighbor (Mt. 19:16–20). The young man notes that he has kept these, and then Jesus tells him to sell his possessions, give the money to the poor, and follow him (Mt. 19:21). At least for this young man, the path to the reign of God leads through voluntary separation from all attachments.

Shakyamuni is recorded as saying: "Good men, at all times, surrender in truth all attachments. The holy spend not idle words on things of desire. When pleasure or pain comes to them, the wise feel above pleasure and pain" (Dhammapada 6.83; p. 46). For Jesus, as for Shakyamuni, separation voluntarily chosen can set one free. For Jesus, separation is always for the sake of the reign of God, and brings true freedom. For Shakyamuni, separation brings release from illusion and desire and offers freedom.

FINAL SEPARATION

The theme of separation dominates not only Jesus' challenge to his followers but the end of Jesus' own life as well. Jesus undergoes separation from his friends and followers, even from life. But the most frightening and paradoxical separation of all is his apparent separation from the God he had addressed as Abba. In the Gospels of Mark and Matthew, Jesus prays to God in the garden of Gethsemane without receiving an answer. The prayer in the Garden echoes the Lord's Prayer from the Sermon on the Mount, in which Jesus had taught his followers to pray, "Your will be done." In Matthew's version of his prayer in the garden, Jesus prays: " 'My Father,' he said, 'if it is possible, let this cup pass me by. Nevertheless, let it be as you, not I would have it'" (Mt. 26:39).

At the most difficult moment of his own life, Jesus prays the prayer he had taught his disciples. In both the Gospels of Mark and of Matthew, Jesus offers this prayer without receiving any reply from God. After Jesus' lifelong dialogue with God, God's response in his agony is silence.

Jesus dies abandoned by his disciples, betrayed by one and denied by another. In the Gospels of Mark and Matthew Jesus cries out from the cross, "My God, my God, why have you forsaken me?" (Mk. 15:34; Mt.

27:46). This is the beginning of Psalm 22, a psalm that begins in despair and abandonment but ends in trust in the power of God's love. Both aspects of the psalm intertwine in the passion account. The anguished lament is itself a cry to God, and thus an expression of trust even beyond the limits of human endurance. As some commentators note, by reciting the opening line of the psalm, Jesus is implicitly looking forward to the more hopeful conclusion of the psalm; nonetheless, the cry itself expresses the painful separation of Jesus from any outward sign of God's love and protection.[54]

Shakyamuni also voluntarily chooses separation, and through this choice finds enlightenment, but the dynamics of Shakyamuni's separation are very different from the Gospel accounts of Jesus. Shakyamuni freely leaves his father's palace, renounces desire and attachment, and finds enlightenment. For Shakyamuni, wisdom comes through realizing the inevitability of separation, accepting this inevitability, and becoming free by seeing and accepting reality as it is. For Jesus, the experience of the reign of God breaking into this world calls him and his followers to separation from home and family and to radical self-sacrifice, even to the point of his life. The most powerful and frightening separation of Jesus in the Gospels of Mark and Matthew is the separation from the God he had named Abba. God remains silent at the end of his life, and Jesus cries out in despair.

The climax of the Buddha's life is the night of his temptations by Mara and his enlightenment. As recounted by the Buddhacarita, Shakyamuni had generated so much power and resolve from his earlier practice that the struggle's outcome was never in doubt. Amid the assaults of Mara's forces, Shakyamuni is not troubled or frightened (Buddhacarita 13.54–55; p. 198), and a heavenly being explains to Mara that this is the result of his previous perseverance,

> in view of the meritorious deeds accumulated by him through many ages he cannot abandon his resolution. For such is his vow, his energy, his psychic power, his compassion for creation, that he will not rise up till he has attained the truth, just as the thousand-rayed sun does not rise without dispelling the darkness (Buddhacarita 13.58–59; p. 199).

The question of the role of God that we encountered earlier recurs in the decisive moments of the two leaders' lives. For Jesus, every decision and action must be related to the reign of God, and the most difficult moment of his life ends with a despairing lament that nonetheless expresses trust in God. For Shakyamuni, the determined search for wisdom leads to awakening to impermanence, for, as the heavenly being explains to Mara, "nothing is impossible of achievement to the man of perseverance. Everything that is undertaken by the proper method is thereby necessarily carried out with success" (Buddhacarita 13.60; p. 199). Shakyamuni does not rely on the Hindu gods; with his enlightenment he is superior to them in wisdom.

The physical postures of the decisive moments in the lives of Jesus and Shakyamuni are powerful symbols of the differences between their respective paths to wisdom. Jesus dies an agonizing, violent, and bloody death, the result of a direct conflict with the powers of his time. Shakyamuni Buddha finds enlightenment seated under the bodhi tree. Hanging on the tree of the cross is a position of absolute powerlessness and extreme pain. Being seated under a tree is a position of extreme stability and rest, a posture of peace and repose amid the onslaught of Mara's temptations.

THE CHALLENGE OF THE CROSS

Christians are so accustomed to the image of Jesus Christ hanging helplessly on the cross that it is sometimes hard for us to appreciate how shocking, even scandalous, this image can be to Buddhists. In a very revealing passage, D. T. Suzuki expresses his own inability to accept the cross of Christ:

> The crucified Christ is a terrible sight and I cannot help associating it with the sadistic impulse of a physically affected brain. Christians would say that crucifixion means crucifying the self or the flesh, since without subduing the self we cannot attain moral perfection. This is where Buddhism differs from Christianity. Buddhism declares that there is from the very beginning no self to crucify. To think that there is the self is the start of all errors and evils. Ignorance is at the root of all things that go wrong. As there is no self, no crucifixion is needed, no sadism is to be practiced, no shocking sight is to be displayed by the road-side.[55]

For Shakyamuni Buddha, suffering is caused by the illusions of our ego-self, and liberation is found in awakening to our true identity. There is, of course, a struggle in the process of awakening, but, as Suzuki reminds us, the struggles of Shakyamuni's life never took so violent a form of suffering as the cross of Jesus. Suzuki stresses that "In the East, there is no ego. The ego is non-existent and, therefore, there is no ego to be crucified."[56] Buddhist awakening is rather more like awakening from a bad dream.[57]

Suzuki acknowledges the importance of the Christian idea of oneness with Christ, but he asks: "Could not the idea of oneness be realised in some other way, that is, more peacefully, more rationally, more humanly, more humanely, less militantly, and less violently?"[58]

Christians may well question whether Suzuki's interpretation of the cross as involving a sadistic impulse really applies directly to God or to Christ. It was, after all, the Romans who devised this form of execution to deter radical political agitation within the empire. And yet, Suzuki could reply that the Gospels and much of the Christian tradition have interpreted this violent death as the fulfillment of the will of God.

A full exploration of the reasons for Jesus' death on the cross would take us beyond the limits of this discussion. It would inevitably require us to examine the social and political dimension of Jesus' proclamation, as well as to undertake a historical investigation of the conflict between Jesus and the Jewish and Roman authorities of his time.

Jesus died in a public execution. Crucifixion was the form of death that the Roman Empire used for political agitators who were dangerous to the peace of the empire. While Jesus' proclamation of the reign of God was not a direct political program to overthrow the Roman Empire, it would have been impossible to proclaim the reign of God in first-century Palestine without political overtones being evident.[59] Jesus directly challenged any finite reality that usurped the devotion due to God alone. In doing so, he inevitably set the stage for conflict with an emperor who proclaimed himself divine. Jesus also challenged the Jewish authorities in Jerusalem. His purification of the Temple was a direct provocation directed at the Jewish religious authorities; it seems most probable that he made a public prediction of the destruction of the Temple in light of the coming reign of God and performed a prophetic action symbolizing this threat.[60] While Jesus rejected violence as a strategy, he persevered in his quest for the righteousness of the reign of God and thus inevitably provoked the confrontation that led to his death.

Suzuki's challenge, nonetheless, provides matter for reflection for Christians. How do we understand the violence of Jesus' death? What does the Christian tradition mean in calling Jesus' death the fulfillment of the will of God? Was the cross simply an arbitrary ending to the life of Jesus? As presented in the Gospels, the path of Jesus leads inexorably to Jerusalem and to the cross. Because Jesus proclaims the justice of the reign of God, because he challenges authorities even in Jerusalem itself, he is put to death. While the cross is not "chosen" by Jesus in any masochistic sense, he accepts it as a consequence of his entire mission. In Matthew the cross is both a personal acceptance of suffering and death by Jesus and also a public witness to his obedience to God and his unflinching challenge to the authorities.[61]

Many contemporary theologians, such as Karl Rahner, interpret Jesus' death not as a price to be paid for redemption or as an event somehow changing God's will toward humankind, but rather as a manifestation of the universal salvific will of God, which is always active in all human experience.[62] Leonardo Boff explicitly rejects any interpretation of the cross as a "masochistic symbol":

Christian hope looks not to the cross, but to the crucified, for he is now the one who lives, the one who was raised up. He is the living and exalted one because God has shown that to be crucified because of identification with the oppressed and the poor of this world has an ultimate sense so bound up with life that it cannot be swallowed up in death.[63]

The cross expresses the love of God manifested in Jesus, a love which identifies with the oppressed, the suffering, and the outcast, a love which comes into conflict with the established powers of his day but offers forgiveness even to the agents of violence. The power of God's love transforms the cross, a brutal instrument of execution, into a sign of God's forgiveness and healing.

Edward Schillebeeckx poses the question of the meaning of Jesus' death in rather different terms than those of Suzuki:

> That Jesus identified with all oppressed and outcast people is quite obvious from the analysis of his message, preaching, beatitudes and whole way of life. Can we suppose that it was actually God himself who set him through his trial and execution among the oppressed and outcast, thus to make his solidarity with the oppressed a *de facto* identification? Or is such a view not rather a blasphemy, in that it ascribes to God what the course of human wrong and injustice did to Jesus?[64]

The cross is ambiguous: It expresses the solidarity of Jesus and of God with the oppressed, but also expresses the absurd violence and cruelty of human history.

For Christians, the cross creates a crisis in our understanding of God and of ourselves, for it raises the question of the power of God in history and the presence of God's love in suffering. For the original followers of Jesus, the cross was indeed a crisis in their own decision to follow Jesus. Their hopes seem to have collapsed in utter failure.

Suzuki's question reminds us that the cross is not easily accommodated to rational, explanatory models. If we fit the cross into our explanations too neatly, we may have lost a sense of its shocking, revelatory power. When Paul proclaimed that true wisdom was found in Christ crucified, he knew that this was folly for the Greeks and scandal for the Jews (1 Cor. 1:21–23). In some ways the cross functions like a Zen koan, which refuses to be explained in ordinary logic, which brings our normal process of thinking about God and ourselves to a halt and forces us to a different level of awareness. In the Acts of the Apostles, Peter is presented as preaching to the people of Jerusalem: "The author of life you put to death" (Acts 3:15; NAB). The very notion of putting to death the author of life seems absurd. Yet the drama of the crucifixion is that the author of life enters into death, and death itself is transformed.

RESURRECTION

For Christians, the cross is not, of course, the end of the story of Jesus, but finds its full meaning only in relation to the resurrection. After their despair at the crucifixion of Jesus, the earliest Christians experienced the Risen Lord accepting and forgiving them and sending them forth to proclaim the Gospel. Through the experience of the Risen Lord, the first Christians became convinced that Jesus' trust in God as Abba and his proclamation of the reign of God had not been mistaken after all. In his death and resurrection the reign of God did indeed come, not in an outward physical triumph, but in the victory of a forgiving, transforming love.[65]

The early Church proclaimed the death and resurrection of Jesus as God's definitive act of salvation for all humankind. This experience established the basic structure of Christian faith: salvation and liberation, the forgiveness of sins and union with God, come to us from God through Jesus Christ. Death and resurrection is the basic pattern of sacred history and of the life of the Church.[66] As Jesus has suffered and died, so his disciples must be prepared to suffer and die for the sake of the Gospel. Matthew presents history as a battleground, with the ultimate reconciliation coming only at the end of time.

To live as a disciple of Christ means trusting in the power of God to bring life even out of the most violent death. The power of God may not always be evident in the working out of history, but Jesus and the Christian tradition hold out the hope of ultimate vindication. The teaching of the Buddha does not call for faith or hope in the Christian sense of the terms, but rather for seeing reality through one's own knowledge.[67] The Buddha can point out the way, but each person must understand and follow it.

COSMIC BUDDHA AND COSMIC CHRIST

In time, the Buddhist tradition came to attribute a cosmic role to the body of the Buddha, interpreting the historical Shakyamuni Buddha as the manifestation in our world of the dharma realm (dharma-dhatu), absolute reality itself, which particularizes itself as dharmakaya. Dharma-dhatu and dharmakaya are never personalized in the way the images of the Bible portray God, and neither dharma-dhatu nor dharmakaya is Creator of the universe. Nonetheless, dharma-dhatu is the source of all things, even though not other than all things, and it is the reality which the appearance of Shakyamuni makes known and effectively present. The dynamic of interpreting a historical figure as the manifestation of the power of the cosmos bears comparison with both the prologue of John's Gospel and the early Christian hymn at the beginning of the letter to the Colossians, which describes Christ:

> He is the image of the unseen God,
> the first-born of all creation,
> for in him were created all things
> in heaven and on earth:
> everything visible

and everything invisible,
thrones, ruling forces,
sovereignties, powers —
all things were created through him and for him.
He exists before all things
and in him all things hold together,
and he is the Head of the Body,
that is, the Church (Col. 1:15–18).

The hymn uses the language that described cosmic wisdom in the Hebrew Bible to interpret the event of Jesus Christ.[68] The power through whom all things came into being and in whom all things hold together is manifest in Jesus Christ. The hymn goes on to relate the cosmic process of reconciliation that Christ has accomplished, "making peace through his death on the cross" (Col. 1:20). Everything in heaven and on earth has been reconciled through the death and resurrection of Jesus, and Christians are initiated into this cosmic reconciliation in baptism (Col. 3:1–4). Thus Jesus Christ, like Shakyamuni, very soon came to be interpreted as the manifestation of the cosmic principle of order and reconciliation. In effect, the hymn affirms that we only understand the meaning of creation in light of the experience of Christ and the reconciliation he effects.

In the hymn in Colossians, the cross presents the power of God's reconciling, transforming love, a love which pervades the entire cosmos, drawing things into the fullness of Christ. The violent negation of the cross becomes the power of universal healing. In an analogous development, the Gospel of John presents Jesus as the incarnation of the Logos, the birth in time of the Word through whom all things were made (Jn. 1:1–14). The path of Jesus in John's Gospel leads inexorably toward the cross, but the cross itself becomes paradoxically the manifestation of God's glory, the moment of the exaltation of Jesus. Jesus is lifted up from the earth and draws all humans to himself (Jn. 12:32).

As Suzuki had noted, the body of the Buddha does not undergo as violent an ordeal as crucifixion, but it is also a cosmic power of reconciliation and healing, made manifest in Shakyamuni. The *Avatamsaka Sutra* tells us:

The Buddha's body emanates great light
With physical forms boundless and totally pure,
Filling all lands like clouds,
Everywhere extolling the Buddha's virtues.

All illumined by the light rejoice,
Beings in distress are all relieved:
This is the work of the Buddha's power.[69]

The first letter of John asserts that God, the source of all reality and the ultimate power in the universe, is love (1 Jn. 4:8, 16), and thus the Word made flesh is the concrete revelation of absolute love. Suzuki explains that the essential characteristics of the cosmic dharmakaya are *prajna* (wisdom) and *karuna*, the Sanskrit word usually translated as compassion, but which Suzuki himself on occasion translated as "love."[70] Thus, despite his insistence on the difference between the violence of the cross and the gentleness of the Buddha's awakening, Suzuki's interpretation of dharmakaya agrees with a long Christian tradition that finds love at the very heart of reality. Dharmakaya is not usually personalized or thought of as exercising direct agency in the world. But Suzuki himself quotes the *Suvarna Prabha Sutra*, a Mahayana text which affirms that Dharmakaya or Suchness

> is not possessed of any particular consciousness, but by virtue of the Spontaneous Will [inherent in the nature of Suchness, or what is the same thing, in the Dharmakaya], the Body of Transformation or of Bliss [as a shadow of the Dharmakaya] reveals itself in response to the spiritual needs of sentient beings.[71]

Suzuki himself comments on the text:

> According to this, it is evident that whenever our spiritual needs become sufficiently intense there is a response from the Dharmakaya, and that this response is not always uniform as the recipient minds show different degrees of development, intellectually and spiritually.[72]

Suzuki goes on to affirm that dharmakaya assumes a wide variety of forms in human history in response to different cultures and ages, and he interprets Christ as one of these, "a manifestation of the Dharmakaya in a human form. He is a Buddha and as such not essentially different from Shakyamuni."[73]

Karl Rahner affirms that the salvific will of God is universal and encounters all humans in their concrete situation, including their religious traditions. While affirming that the revelation of God in Jesus Christ is definitive and unsurpassable, Rahner goes on to affirm that other religions make present the supernatural grace of God. For every person, Rahner asserts: "That which God has intended as salvation for him reached him, in accordance with God's will and by [God's] permission (no longer adequately separable in practice), in the *concrete* religion of his actual realm of existence and historical condition."[74]

For both the Christian and Buddhist traditions, the absolute, which is beyond all human images and concepts and comprehension, graciously responds to the human dilemma by making itself salvifically present in the world. Both traditions assert that this gracious presence reaches all humans, and both find their own definitive understanding of this presence in the form of a bearer of the good news of liberation, even though the concrete way that Jesus and Shakyamuni bring their salvific message is quite different. For both traditions, the process of reconciliation focuses on one concrete bearer of good news, but involves not only humans, but the entire cosmos.

The similarities in the descriptions of the cosmic dimensions of the Buddha and the Christ do not, however, dissolve the real differences between the two traditions. The Christian understanding of creation through the cosmic Christ cannot be simply equated with all things arising from the cosmic dharmakaya. The Christian notion of the creation of a universe distinct from God, yet interpenetrated by God, sets the stage for the drama of the incarnation, for God becoming human to redeem humankind. Since dharmakaya is not creator, there is not the same relation of distinction and union of divine and human that the early Church struggled to affirm in Jesus Christ. Thus Buddhist descriptions of the Buddha as the manifestation of dharmakaya often sound docetist to Christian ears: it seems that the Buddha merely appears to be human. While the creation of the universe through Christ is not the same as the dependent co-arising of all realities, the two traditions do nonetheless offer a vision of a dynamic transformation of human life, a transformation which extends to the entire cosmos.

PART II

Classical Paths
of Transformation

Introduction

One sign of the depth of a religious tradition is its ability to give meaning to human life in radically different contexts, in different cultures and different ages. The messages of the Christ and of the Buddha come to us across centuries of interpreters, who have explored different aspects of the original event. The meaning of Jesus Christ or of Shakyamuni Buddha is fully displayed only in relation to the concrete ways in which their followers have sought to live out the Christian and the Buddhist paths. The experiences of the Christian Church or the Buddhist sangha explore implications and aspects of the original event which may not have been apparent in the founding scriptures. As John Henry Newman insisted, to explore the ramifications and implications of a truly revelatory event requires significant time, even centuries. In their efforts to follow their respective paths, both Buddhism and Christianity have enjoyed both successes and failures in their long histories.

During the same centuries that early Christians were pondering the meaning of Jesus Christ in relation to Hellenistic culture and neo-Platonic thought, Mahayana Buddhists in China were translating sutras from Sanskrit into Chinese and were rethinking the meaning of Buddhist experience in light of Chinese culture and the traditions of Confucian and Taoist thought. These two experiences of inculturation have been among the most influential in the history of their respective traditions and, indeed, of the entire human community, for they have decisively shaped the later developments of European and of East Asian culture respectively.

While Mahayana Buddhist thought had its origins in India, it enjoyed a widespread flourishing in China and, through China, in Korea, Japan, and Vietnam. Christianity, for its part, quickly moved beyond its Palestinian birthplace into all areas of the Hellenistic world and later spread eastward through parts of Central Asia. There was no universal agreement among either early Christians or early Mahayana Buddhists in China on how the new interpretations of their traditions should proceed. Part II will examine two of the most influential developments in each of these processes of inculturation: two Mahayana Buddhist traditions, Zen and Pure Land, and two early Christian fathers, Dionysius the Areopagite and Augustine. The Zen and Pure Land traditions have been among the most vigorous and creative in the history of Buddhism, continuing to claim numerous followers today.

No figure since the fifth century has influenced Western Christian theology as profoundly as Augustine. Medieval and Reformation-era theologians sought to interpret his perspectives and claim his authority. Roman Catholic and Protestant theology has been indelibly marked by the personal and intellectual struggles of Augustine and his expressions of his resolution of these struggles. The mysterious writer known as Dionysius the Areopagite has had a profound influence on both Eastern and Western Christianity. He was quoted by medieval Latin theologians more than any other Greek father. Thomas Aquinas quoted him among the patristic writers second only to Augustine. The entire Eastern theological tradition, both Orthodox and Catholic, has been inspired by this anonymous genius.

Each of these strands—Zen and Pure Land, Dionysian and Augustinian—has given a particular character to its interpretation to the meaning of its tradition, and each has had a powerful role in shaping the way its respective tradition has developed into the contemporary world.

3

Ascending and Descending

The Structure of Mahayana Buddhist Experience and the Zen Tradition

This chapter will begin by focusing on the experience of wisdom and compassion in the dynamic twofold movement that is characteristic of Mahayana thought in general, and then it will examine the way this twofold movement is expressed in the later Ch'an and Zen traditions in China and Japan.

Much of Mahayana Buddhist practice and teaching seems deliberately baffling and often appears nonsensical. Zen masters make seemingly outrageous statements such as: "A bridge flows, whereas water does not flow."[1] Zen is also noted for asking impossible questions and demanding an immediate answer:

It is like a man up a tree who hangs from a branch by his mouth; his hands cannot grasp a bough, his feet cannot touch the tree. Another man comes under the tree and asks him the meaning of Bodhidharma's coming from the West. If he does not answer, he does not meet the questioner's need. If he answers, he will lose his life. At such a time, how should he answer?[2]

The Mahayana tradition often delights in disorienting its students and in subverting any objective or merely conceptual understanding of itself. Examples of paradoxical, seemingly nonsensical statements abound in the earliest Mahayana scriptures, the Prajnaparamita sutras. *Prajnaparamita* in Sanskrit means "perfect" or "transcendent wisdom"—literally "the wisdom of crossing over." A sutra is a preaching of the Buddha that has been recorded either in oral memory or in written documents. The Prajnaparamita sutras, the sutras of transcendent wisdom, were written in Sanskrit in India beginning about 100 B.C.E.[3] They are the foundation of later Mahayana Buddhist thought and set basic patterns of thought that have decisively influenced later Buddhists in East Asia.

The goal of Buddhist practice is enlightenment. In one of the Prajnaparamita sutras Manjushri, the bodhisattva of wisdom, explains the experience of enlightenment in rather puzzling language:

> Enlightenment is not discerned by anyone, nor is it fully known, nor seen, nor heard, nor remembered. It is neither produced nor stopped, neither described nor expounded. Insofar as there is, Sariputra, any enlightenment, that enlightenment is neither existence nor non-existence. For there is nothing that can be fully known by enlightenment, nor does enlightenment fully know enlightenment.[4]

The Prajnaparamita scriptures also tell us there is no duality between enlightenment and ignorance and thus all beings enjoy original enlightenment. When the Buddha gained enlightenment, he realized that all beings were already enlightened.

The Prajnaparamita scriptures cherish the ideal of the bodhisattva, a person who could become a Buddha but assists other beings in their search for enlightenment. In the *Ashtasahasrika Sutra* (*The Perfection of Wisdom in 8,000 Lines*), the Buddha himself uses baffling language to explain the role of the bodhisattva:

> Here a Bodhisattva, a great being, thinks thus: "Countless beings I should lead to Nirvana, and yet there are none who lead to Nirvana, there are none who should be led to it." However many beings he may lead to Nirvana, yet there is not any being that has been led to Nirvana, nor that has led others to it.[5]

According to the Prajnaparamita scriptures, we are to seek enlightenment, and yet there is no one to seek enlightenment and no enlightenment to seek. We are to become a bodhisattva, and yet there is no bodhisattva to become. "No wisdom can we get hold of, no highest perfection, no Bodhisattva, no thought of enlightenment either."[6] If we understand the paradoxical logic of these sayings, we will have a key to the meaning of much of later Mahayana Buddhist thought.

Much of the challenge of entering into Buddhist practice, thought, and logic is to find a path through the constant negations. Any theory or explanation that we can devise will be negated in Buddhist logic, but that does not mean that it is not true or useful if properly understood and applied.

ASCENT AND DESCENT

While there have been many paradoxical and often directly conflicting forms of Buddhist teaching and practice, there is a dynamic two-directional movement of ascent and descent that runs throughout the Mahayana tradition. The Japanese Buddhist scholar Gadjin Nagao suggests that this two-directional movement offers a clue to interpreting the startling contradictions of much Buddhist language. Indeed, Nagao claims that this twofold activity "constitutes the characteristic feature of the Mahayana."[7]

ASCENT

The upward movement is the ascent from this world to the wisdom of the world yonder, to the experience of enlightenment. This path requires a series of negations of our ordinary way of thinking and acting in order to lead us to a new way of being. The downward movement is the return from the experience of enlightenment to a renewed affirmation of human existence in the world. The downward path of the return proceeds in the opposite manner from the ascent, through a series of renewed affirmations. The two directions correspond to the two fundamental Buddhist virtues: The upward path is the path of wisdom; the downward path is the path of compassion.

The ascent to a higher insight requires a negation of our present awareness. Our normal awareness of ourselves is distorted by illusion and imprisoned in a world of unnecessary suffering. Our true identity is covered over by clouds of ignorance. By clinging to belief in an illusory self, we cause great suffering both to ourselves and others. This false belief must be destroyed if our lives are to be transformed. Thus to find wisdom, the Buddhist must negate the beliefs of everyday life.

Buddhists use a wide variety of strategies to destroy the false beliefs that imprison us. Sitting and walking meditation bring our ordinary consciousness to a halt. The negations and contradictions of the Prajnaparamita scriptures subvert our ordinary sense of logic. The paradoxical sayings and questions called *koans* by the Zen tradition overturn our ordinary processes of thinking. Buddhists in the Pure Land tradition attack our false self-confidence by insisting that we are powerless to save ourselves. The concrete strategies differ, but the dynamic of negating our ordinary self dominates them all. In whatever form it takes, the path of ascent is a deliberate assault upon our ordinary sense of ourselves. As Nagao comments, "Ascent is always nihilistic in character—through self-negating practice, a practitioner finally reaches the summit of negation, which may be called shunyata, 'negatedness,' or 'zero-ness.' "[8]

SHUNYATA

Even though the journey upward proceeds through the dynamic of negation, the goal is positive. The path of ascending leads to wisdom, to insight into *shunyata*, a Sanskrit word which is often translated as "emptiness," though the verb form "emptying" may be more appropriate.[9] The adjective form, *shunya*, empty, probably came from the root *shvi*, which means "to swell."[10] Something that is swollen on the outside is hollow inside, and thus empty. Mathematicians in India used the word shunya for the mathematical zero.

The term shunyata, emptiness, is one of the most important and fundamental terms in all of Mahayana Buddhism. It names the summit reached by the path of ascent, and it is the key to all of Mahayana Buddhist experience. Yet it is difficult, indeed impossible, to state conceptually precisely what shunyata is. Beyond all concepts and beyond all distinction between subject and object, shunyata is perfectly expressed only by the Noble Silence of the Buddha. It is grasped through a nondiscriminating, intuitive knowledge that is beyond the categories of our thought.

In one sense, shunyata is indeed a negation, the climax of the negations of the path upward. To say that all things are empty means that things do not possess their own existence. The objects of our experience are empty of reality—they have no inherent substance and thus are illusions. I myself am empty, I am no-self, for I have no independent, substantial being that perdures from one moment to the next.

The negating power of the term shunyata is not intended as an objective theory about external reality but as an object for meditation to transform ourselves.[11] To say all things are empty is a skillful means to destroy our deluded selves and to assist us in abandoning desire and attachment to an illusory world.

The negation expressed by shunyata is not mere nothingness, however, for the negation of being leads into a positive affirmation of ultimate reality. Shunyata is beyond affirmation and negation, beyond existence and nonexistence.[12]

Insight into emptiness is the climax and fulfillment of the journey upward and also the beginning of the journey downward. The dual character of shunyata as both negative and positive marks the transition from wisdom to compassion, from the negations of the ascent to the affirmations of the descent. Buddhists warn against "getting stuck" in enlightenment. The desire to remain on the peak of the mountain, enjoying the experience of enlightenment, is itself a temptation and an illusion. Even enlightenment can be a snare if it becomes an object to be grasped.

DESCENT

The enlightened one must employ the non-discriminating knowledge attained on the summit for the good of all beings. The intuition of the nonduality of all reality must flow into the bodhisattva's compassionate activity in the world. On the descending path the bodhisattva again discriminates among beings and affirms the reality of everyday life, but the newly affirmed world both is and is not the same as the original world of illusion. The upward path negated the existence of ourselves and the particular beings of our world. The downward path affirms the particularity and individuality of ourselves and the beings we encounter in a dynamic unity beyond oneness or duality.

The experience of shunyata is a dynamic movement that includes both negation and affirmation. The experience moves through the negation of our ordinary world to an affirmation of absolute reality. Thus the word *shunyata* is sometimes translated into English as "absolute" rather than "emptiness." The initial negation of the reality of the world leads to a renewed affirmation, in effect a negation of the negation.

The two-directional activity of ascent and descent takes the logical form of a dynamic movement of negation and negation of negation. This dialectical logic dominates Mahayana Buddhist thought and practice. Nagao describes this as a "zigzagging logic . . . a paradoxical and dialectical logical process which evidences a dynamism continually moving from being to non-being and again to being, in which the former two are transcended."[13]

The twofold activity of going upward and coming down can help us to interpret many of the paradoxical and seemingly illogical and contradictory assertions of Mahayana Buddhism. It is important to bear in mind that the two movements naturally proceed in opposite directions, and thus they directly contradict each other at times. Both negations and affirmations can be true if understood properly and used as skillful means in the service of liberation.

The goal of the twofold movement is to overcome all dualities. The final duality to be overcome is that between the two directions themselves. Thus one final negation is necessary to complete the process of awakening. Even the difference between the ascent and the descent must be overcome. The two different directions are one and the same activity. The ascent is the descent and the descent is the ascent.

To explain this paradoxical identity-in-difference, Nagao turns to the twofold meaning of the English word *realization*. In English to realize can mean "to understand" something, as in "I realize what you are saying." To realize can also mean to make something real, actualize or bring something into existence, as in "I hope to realize my dream some day." The first meaning of *realize* corresponds to the upward path of wisdom, as we become aware of the truth of shunyata and we realize the truth of the dharma, the Buddha's teaching. The second meaning of realize corresponds to the downward movement in which truth actualizes itself in the compassionate activity of the bodhisattva. On the path upward, we are illumined by the teaching of the Buddha, and we realize the truth of his message. On the path downward, the teaching of the Buddha becomes real and actualizes itself in our own activity. We realize the compassion of the Buddha, making it a real and effective force in the world.[14]

In shunyata, Buddhists realize the truth of the Buddha's teaching, and this truth becomes actual in their lives. As Nagao comments:

[S]hunyata is not a mere nihilism which engulfs all entities in its universal darkness, abolishing all differences and particularities. On the contrary, shunyata is the fountainhead from which the Buddha's compassionate activity flows out.[15]

While shunyata is not normally expressed in personal language and is not to be identified with the creating and redeeming God of Christianity, it is noteworthy that Nagao can speak of it as the fountainhead of the Buddha's activity. In shunyata, Buddhists realize the nonduality of all beings, but in the next moment they return to the world of discrimination and differentiation.

ASCENT AND DESCENT IN THE LIFE OF THE BUDDHA

Mahayana Buddhists find the classic model for this twofold movement in the example of Shakyamuni Buddha. As we saw in the first chapter, the life of Siddhartha Gautama begins in a world of carefully constructed illusion. His initial awareness of the world is distorted by a deliberate deception planned by his father to conceal the reality of suffering. The basic movement of the first thirty-five years of his life is the ascent from the illusion of his sheltered life in the palace to the peak of enlightenment under the bodhi tree. This journey proceeds through a series of disillusioning experiences that repeatedly negate the prince's developing self-understanding. Through one negative experience after another, young Prince Siddhartha becomes disillusioned about human life, about the palace and its fleeting pleasures, and eventually even disillusioned even about the ascetics in the forest.

In his enlightenment, Siddhartha completes the process of negating the illusions of his early life and, in the language of the later Mahayana tradition, he realizes the truth of emptiness. After he is enlightened and has become the Buddha, he undergoes yet another temptation. Some versions of the Buddhacarita of Ashvaghosha tell us that Mara, the tempter, returns one last time and addresses an invitation to the newly enlightened Buddha: "O holy one, be pleased to enter Nirvana, thy desires are accomplished."[16] The last temptation of the Buddha is to accept the goal of nirvana, which he had earlier sought so ardently.

Shakyamuni Buddha, however, refuses to enter nirvana or to cling to enlightenment. Enlightenment itself is not an experience to be grasped at. Instead, he decides to descend from the lofty peak of his new awareness and return to the world to share his wisdom with others. He tells Mara: "I will first establish in perfect wisdom worlds as numerous as the sand, and then I will enter Nirvana."[17]

After the moment of his awakening, Shakyamuni spent another forty-five years on earth as a missionary, proclaiming the dharma, the truth of suffering and liberation. This is the movement of descent, of returning to the world with a new consciousness. According to the Mahayana tradition, the Buddha continues to guide his followers forever, even after his entering into nirvana at the end of his earthly life. The example of Shakyamuni set the basic pattern for Mahayana Buddhist life: first one must ascend to enlightenment, and then one descends with a message for all the world.

One of the most common titles of the Buddha expresses this dual movement: He is called *Tathagata*, which can mean either "thus gone" (*tatha-gata*) or "thus come" (*tatha-agata*).[18] The Buddha is "thus gone" because he has passed over to the attainment of wisdom. The Buddha is "thus come" because he has returned with compassion for all sentient beings.

THE BODHISATTVA

The Buddha's return from enlightenment to the world to aid all sentient beings forms the core of the Mahayana ideal of the bodhisattva. The term *bodhisattva* means a future Buddha, and the term was originally applied to Shakyamuni Buddha before his enlightenment. In Mahayana Buddhism a bodhisattva is a person who has attained wisdom and is able to enter into nirvana but freely decides to postpone the joy of nirvana until the moment when she or he can enter together with every other sentient being. There are certain figures, called "great bodhisattvas," who have already made this decision on behalf of all beings. All Mahayana Buddhists are encouraged to make the vows of the bodhisattva, vowing to save all sentient beings, to extinguish all passions, to master all truths, and to attain the Buddha-way.

The two central Buddhist virtues, wisdom and compassion, correspond to the twofold movement of the Buddha and constitute the heart of the bodhisattva ideal. The upward path of wisdom must lead to the downward path of compassion. These two virtues together are indispensable to the experience of enlightenment. If either is lacking, no claim of enlightenment can be genuine. Buddhists compare them to the two wheels of a cart or the two wings of a bird.[19]

This fundamental twofold activity of ascent and descent has taken many different forms in Mahayana Buddhist life. Among the most important of these are the Ch'an and Zen traditions of China and Japan.

CH'AN AND ZEN BUDDHISM

The tradition of Ch'an and Zen Buddhism has attracted much attention in recent Western thought, especially through the pioneering influence of D. T. Suzuki's essays on Zen Buddhism.[20] The word *Zen* is the Japanese pronunciation of the Chinese word *Ch'an,* which is itself an abbreviation of *ch'anna*. Thus the Chinese tradition of Ch'an Buddhism became known as Zen when it entered Japan, and has been generally known under this name in the West.

Ch'anna in turn is the Chinese transliteration of a Sanskrit word, *dhyana* (its Pali cognate is *jhana*), which means "meditation." As its name suggests, Zen is a Mahayana Buddhist school which stresses the importance of meditation. Nonetheless, as Carl Bielefeldt has pointed out, many Ch'an and Zen masters insist that "the religion has nothing to do with *dhyana*."[21] The dynamic of negations undermines any simple definition of what Zen awakening is.

ORIGINS

Zen traces its origin to Shakyamuni Buddha himself. The Zen tradition tells us that one day when Shakyamuni was preaching on the Vulture Peak, he held up a golden lotus blossom to the assembly. Only one disciple, Kashyapa, understood the significance of the gesture, and he smiled as a sign of his enlightenment. At that, Shakyamuni Buddha "turned to the assembly and said, 'I possess the True Dharma Eye, the Marvelous Mind of Nirvana. I entrust it to Mahakashyapa.' "[22]

This direct mind-to-mind transmission from teacher to disciple became the model for later Zen study. Zen claims to possess an unbroken line of direct mind-to-mind transmission from Shakyamuni to Kashyapa through a long series of Indian patriarchs to Bodhidharma and his successors in China, Korea, and Japan down to the present day.

According to Zen tradition, Bodhidharma brought this form of Buddhism from India to China in the late fifth or early sixth century C.E. Bodhidharma, who probably died in 532 at an advanced age, was the twenty-eighth patriarch of Indian Zen and the first patriarch of Zen Buddhism in China. For later generations, he came to symbolize the very heart of Zen. When later Zen masters asked their students what was the meaning of Bodhidharma's coming from India to China, they were asking about the very heart of Zen. A four-line stanza that has been traditionally attributed to Bodhidharma expresses the spirit of Zen:

> A special transmission outside the scriptures,
> Not founded upon words and letters;
> By pointing directly to [one's] mind
> It lets one see into [one's own true] nature and [thus]
>   attain Buddhahood.[23]

PRACTICE AND SEEING

Since Zen passes on its wisdom through direct mind-to-mind transmission, its teaching is "outside the scriptures, not founded upon words and letters." The heart of Zen is *satori*, the experience of enlightenment, and this cannot be attained by conceptual analysis or be completely expressed in words. Nor can the experience be identified with a trancelike state of meditation. Ch'an masters such as Shen-hui rejected any such identification as "dharma-bondage," a subtle form of self-deception.[24]

The words and actions of Ch'an and Zen masters proceed from enlightened consciousness transmitted through direct contact with an earlier master. No set pattern can capture the freedom that comes from this enlightenment. The act of awakening to enlightened consciousness is to become a Buddha, and so the tradition identifies the words and actions of the masters as the conduct of a Buddha.

Zen agrees with earlier Mahayana Buddhists that ultimate truth is perfectly expressed only by silence. One legend, which may have been modeled on the discussion in the Vimalakirti Sutra, tells of a conversation between Bodhidharma and four of his disciples at the end of his life. Bodhidharma asked each disciple to say what he had attained. The first three students explained their insights in words, and Bodhidharma praised them according to the depth of their attainment. Finally, it was time for Hui-k'o to reply. Hui-k'o bowed respectfully and stood silent. Bodhidharma awarded him the highest praise, saying: "You have attained my marrow."[25] Hui-k'o became the second patriarch of Zen in China.

Zen teachers warn that reading books or studying the scriptures alone will never awaken one to reality. Direct seeing is necessary. Clinging to words, even the true words of the Buddha in the scriptures, can be a form of illusion. While distrusting reliance upon words, Zen teachers insist, nonetheless, that their intent is the same as that of the Buddhist scriptures; and Zen masters have themselves produced a very rich literature expressing their experience.

The last two lines of the stanza quoted above express the goal of Zen: "pointing directly to [one's] mind/It lets one see into [one's own true] nature and [thus] attain Buddhahood." All the varied practices and paradoxical sayings and stories of Zen monks serve to attain this goal. The Japanese Zen master Zenkei Shibayama comments on these verses: "Zen teaches us to go beyond the dualistic discriminations of our ordinary consciousness, and to be directly and actually one with the True Nature."[26] Zen Buddhists describe our true nature as the Buddha-nature (*buddhata* in Sanskrit; *bussho* in Japanese), that is, as the nature that allows us to attain enlightenment and thereby become a Buddha.[27]

Seeing into one's own nature means casting off the illusions of our ordinary awareness and seeing reality as it is. This seeing is the immediate self-realization of our true nature. No words can express it. The thirteenth-century master Mumon said, "It is like a dumb person who had a dream. He has had it. That's all."[28] This experience is not the grasping of a new conception but a dynamic process of transcending both affirmation and negation.

MOUNTAINS AND WATERS

One of the most famous descriptions of this process comes from the Chinese Ch'an master Ch'ing-yüan Wei-hsin (Japanese: Seigen Ishin) of

the T'ang dynasty. The movement of the process follows the general Mahayana pattern of the twofold dynamic of ascent and descent. Wei-hsin
recounted his development:

> Thirty years ago, before I began the study of Zen, I said, "Mountains
> are mountains, waters are waters."
>
> After I got an insight into the truth of Zen through the instruction
> of a good master, I said, "Mountains are not mountains, waters are
> not waters."
>
> But now, having attained the abode of final rest [i.e., Awakening],
> I say, "Mountains are really mountains, waters are really waters."[29]

The twofold movement of ascent and descent provides the key to understanding this description of the process of awakening. The initial state of
seeing mountains as mountains and waters as waters represents our normal
understanding of the world. This state is dominated by ignorance. As Masao
Abe explains, this is the stage of differentiation, and it is dominated by the
belief in the ego-self, which distinguishes between itself and all other realities.[30] This ego-self, which is our everyday consciousness, makes everything
into an object which it then desires to possess or dominate.

In this state of ignorance the discrimination between different beings is
not just an intellectual mistake, it is a fundamental, existential distortion
of our true nature. The ego-self traps itself in illusion. Although it believes
itself and its world to be real, it is not our true self. It is in fact estranged
from the true self and is forever caught in a destructive cycle of grasping
and clinging. Thus it is driven by anxiety and desire, forever restless and
divided against itself. This is the initial state of thinking that "mountains
are mountains and waters are waters."

The beginning stages of Zen training launch an assault upon this ego-
self. The false ego has to be destroyed for us to be free. The various
disciplines of Zen alike aim at this goal. The destruction of the ego-self is
not simply a new intellectual insight, though it does involve a new way of
seeing the world. It is an existential realization that the ego-self is fundamentally a delusion.

The ego-self searches anxiously for the true self, but the true self continually escapes its grasp. The ninth-century Ch'an master Lin-chi (Japanese: Rinzai) described this process of the true self that is always present
but that recedes further and further from the clinging ego-self: "If you seek
him, he retreats farther and farther away; if you don't seek him, then he's
right there before your eyes, his wondrous voice resounding in your ears."[31]
The more desperately the ego-self strives to find and possess the true self,
the more hopeless the search becomes.

After the firm discipline of Zen practice, the ego-self collapses, and we
realize that the true self is unattained and unattainable. Our grasping ego-
self cannot find and dominate it. Masao Abe describes this process:

[T]he existential realization of the unattainability of the true Self culminates in a deadlock, the breaking through of which results in the collapse of the ego-self, wherein we come to the realization of no-self or no-ego-self. And when the ego-self disappears, then the "objective" world disappears as well.[32]

The clinging, grasping self must die. When this happens, the Zen practitioner realizes that "Mountains are not mountains and waters are not waters." The ego-self's initial differentiation of mountains and waters is overcome. The discriminating consciousness that creates a world of illusion is destroyed and replaced by the realization of no-self.

The collapse of the ego-self brings liberation from anxiety and peace of mind. The destructive cycle of desire, addiction, and suffering is broken through. The liberation is not yet complete, however, for there still remains a differentiation between the earlier stage of the ignorance of the ego-self and the newly attained realization of no-self. The new awareness of nonduality seems to be different from the earlier discriminating consciousness. As long as this differentiation persists, there is a danger of clinging to the experience of no-self.

We can objectify even the realization of no-self as a possession to grasp at, and then we begin another cycle of anxiety and attachment. We risk entering a state of spiritual pride in which we distinguish ourselves from the unenlightened and take a perverse satisfaction in our awakening. When emptiness is objectified and grasped at, it ceases to be true emptiness.

In the realization of no-self there is also a danger of falling into a nihilistic despair. If neither my ego-self nor the world of its desires is real, it seems that there is no positive basis for activity in the world, and we can fall into a paralyzing indifference. If nothing exists, nothing seems to matter, and creative action comes to a halt.

Because of these dangers, Zen insists on negating even the differentiation between the two stages of ego-self and no-self. We will not be truly free until even the differentiation between the ignorance of the ego-self and the realization of no-self is overcome.

Just as the initial illusion of the ego-self had to be negated, so also must the insight of no-self must be negated. This second negation is in fact an affirmation, and thus Wei-hsin could express his final realization by saying that "Mountains are really mountains and waters are really waters." In the second negation we transcend the nonduality of no-self and we can once again affirm particularity and individuality in the world, though in a different sense than before.

This is the movement of the descent, the return to the world with a different awareness, the nongrasping awareness of the bodhisattva who acts from compassion. The world is affirmed as real, but now there is an awareness of the mutual interpenetration and interdependence of all beings. All beings are one, and all beings are themselves.

In the final stage, Abe explains, "all forms of anxiety and all forms of attachment, open and hidden, explicit and implicit, are completely overcome."[33] This is the awakening to the true self and the full realization of emptiness in both wisdom and compassion. This awakening overcomes the difference between the first two movements and includes both the negations of the ascent and the renewed affirmations of the descent in a dynamic unity.

After Wei-hsin had explained the three stages of his awareness, he posed a question: "Do you think these three understandings are the same or different?"[34] Abe answers his question: "They are different and yet not different; they are the same and yet different at once."[35] By including both of the earlier stages in a dynamic whole, the third stage both affirms them and overcomes them.

Abe notes that for Zen there is not necessarily a temporal sequence between the second and third stages. The third stage can be realized simultaneously with the second stage, though Wei-hsin's account tells us that for him the two realizations came some time apart. In the end, even the image of "stages" must be negated in Zen. The final realization takes place in an absolute present which is beyond time. The separation of the three stages is itself an illusion if it is taken absolutely. While the stages are distinct, they are one.

The only adequate expression of this final realization is the Noble Silence of the Buddha. Zen tells us, "The instant you speak about it, you miss the mark." Master Mumon warns us:

> Words do not convey actualities;
> Letters do not embody the spirit of the mind.
> He who attaches himself to words is lost;
> He who abides with letters will remain in ignorance.[36]

The experience of Zen is unspeakable, beyond affirmation and negation, and yet including both; but the effects of Zen are manifest in the words and deeds and silence of the masters.

LIN-CHI CH'AN AND RINZAI ZEN

The Ch'an and Zen traditions have used different strategies to awaken their followers from the illusions of the ego-self. The two most common methods are sitting meditation (*zazen*) and koan practice. In China the Lin-chi tradition (named for master Lin-chi, d. 866, pronounced Rinzai in Japanese) focused more on koan practice, and the Ts'ao-tung tradition focused more on sitting meditation and silent illumination. Both of these early Chinese Ch'an traditions, however, used both sitting meditation and koans to transform students' awareness.

In Japan their later developments came to focus exclusively on one method or the other. The Japanese Soto Zen tradition, which developed out of the Ts'ao-tung Ch'an tradition, would eventually come to focus exclusively on "just-sitting." The Japanese Rinzai Zen tradition, which developed from the Lin-chi Ch'an tradition, became noted for using koans to cast off the discriminating mind.[37]

Chinese Ch'an masters apparently began the use of koans around the ninth century.[38] The word *koan* is the Japanese pronunciation of the Chinese word *kung-an*, which means "public notice" or "public announcement." A koan invites the hearer to take to heart what has been announced, but the announcement is a baffling, perplexing paradox which cannot be resolved by the normal intellect. The goal of a koan is to frustrate our ordinary process of thinking and force us to a new level of consciousness.

As the twentieth-century Zen master Zenkei Shibayama explains, koans have to be interpreted in light of the experience of awakening from which they arise and to which they challenge the hearer:

> Koans are sayings and doings that have come out of the old Zen Masters' deep Zen experiences. Behind their superficial expressions through words and actions there is the Truth of Zen, which really transcends such expressions. The primary significance of koan can be truly appreciated only when students personally plunge into the Truth of Zen behind such sayings and doings. Those who have not yet attained Zen experience can open their spiritual eye with the koan, and those who have broken through the barrier should refine and deepen their spiritual insight with it.[39]

To the unawakened consciousness, the koans seem meaningless or contradictory. To those who know how to see, they express the perfect clarity of enlightened consciousness. They confront the hearer with the fundamental challenge of human life. Suzuki notes that for Zen masters, "the universe itself is a great living, threatening koan challenging your solution, and that when the key to this great koan is successfully discovered all other koans are minor ones and solve themselves."[40]

Koans are not intellectual puzzles to be solved through reasoning, but challenges that perfectly express enlightened consciousness and demand an immediate response. In the collection of koans called the *Mumonkan*, Zen master Goso Hoen poses a koan: "If you meet a man of Tao [that is, someone who has attained the essence of Zen] on the way, greet him neither with words nor with silence. Now tell me, how will you greet him?"[41]

Master Goso deliberately drives his disciples into absolute contradiction. He places them in an unresolvable situation and demands a response. The koan pushes them to move beyond the limits of words or silence to act with absolute freedom. Zen master Mumon took up Goso's challenge and added two lines to the koan: "I'll give him with my fist the hardest blow I can—Get it at once, get it immediately!"[42]

As long as the student is trapped in an objectifying, discriminating consciousness, anxiety will block a free response. Lingering with abstract, intellectual reasonings only prolongs the anxiety. Koans seek to cut through the chain of reasoning, negate the discriminating self, and initiate the practitioner into a transformed awareness. As Shibayama comments:

[T]he True Self is one's original True Nature, in which not a thought of discrimination is working. It is the True Self awakened to the Buddha Nature. It is the True Self that is one with reality. . . . Ultimately speaking, however, the True Self can never be experienced in the realm of intellect or knowledge. There is no method for you to attain it other than to thoroughly cast away your intellect and reasoning, and personally plunge into the experiential fact which "you may describe, but in vain; you may picture, but to no avail." That is why Master Mumon cries out, "Stop all your groping and maneuvering."[43]

Koans destroy the thinking processes of the discriminating self and lead into a new consciousness. Suzuki describes this new consciousness as "a sense of the Beyond. . . . Even the 'Beyond' is saying a little too much."[44] He explains what happens:

The individual shell in which my personality is so solidly encased explodes at the moment of satori. Not, necessarily, that I get unified with a being greater than myself or absorbed in it, but that my individuality, which I found rigidly held together and definitely kept separate from other individual existences, becomes loosened somehow from its tightening grip and melts away into something indescribable.[45]

For Suzuki, the experience of satori which the koan practice makes possible is an overcoming or a breaking down of the barriers and restrictions of individuality. Suzuki generally restricts his discussion to abrupt experiences of satori and presents these as the heart of Zen, though he is aware of the alternative tradition which presented a gradual development of the experience.

Dumoulin also stresses that koans are not doctrines or theoretical instructions, but aids to enlightenment. Their function is to bring the mind to enlightenment through "a kind of spoof on the human intellect."[46] The student concentrates for long periods of time amid growing anxiety centering on the koan until the breakthrough occurs. Dumoulin notes that koans not only break down the old categories but also express the central unitive Mahayana vision of reality as nondual: "The purpose of practice is to clear away every trace of duality. All the koan are meant to serve this same purpose. Thus the metaphysical and religious role of the koan in Zen Buddhism is every bit as important as its psychological structure."[47]

Hee-Jin Kim, however, fears that Suzuki and Shibayama present too one-sidedly an "instrumentalist" view of koans, which separates the psychological process of frustrating usual thoughts from the realization of reality that occurs. This view of koans as "instruments," Kim charges, neglects the realization of reality that occurs in the koan. Kim seeks to "perfect" the instrumentalist view by complementing it with an awareness that reality expresses itself and actualizes itself in the koan:

> While the instrumentalist view maintains that the finger points to the moon, the realizationist view holds that the finger not only points to the moon but *is* the moon. To put it differently, the finger, according to the realizationist view, is not the moon, but the moon is invariably the finger, because it completes itself as the finger.[48]

Kim argues that Dogen, the founder of Soto Zen in Japan, developed such a realizationist view of language in koans.

TS'AO-TUNG CH'AN AND SOTO ZEN

The other major branch of Ch'an Buddhism is Ts'ao-tung, which became known as Soto Zen in Japan.[49] As it developed in Japan, Soto Zen became known especially for its practice of an approach to silent illumination through "just sitting." While in later Japanese tradition Rinzai became identified with the practice of koans and Soto with the practice of sitting, for the earlier traditions in China and also for the thirteenth-century Soto Zen master Dogen, this division was not yet firmly drawn, and masters from both traditions used both koans and sitting.

The Ts'ao-tung Ch'an and Soto Zen traditions trace their lineage from Hui-neng (638–713), the Sixth Patriarch of Ch'an in China, and base their practice on the perspectives of the mutual interpenetration of the absolute and the relative, as expressed in the Flower Ornament Sutra and Hua Yen Buddhism. According to the Chinese school of Hua Yen Buddhism, the absolute interpenetrates all particular realities and expresses itself in them, and is itself nothing other than this continuous realization of itself. The universal and the particular are integrated in all the universe, but we do not realize this ourselves because of the obstructions of our ordinary consciousness.

HUNG-CHIH

The Chinese Ts'ao-tung master Hung-chih Cheng-chüeh (1091-1157) developed an approach to nondual objectless meditation, advising his disciples not to focus on any object at all in their meditation. He taught that continued practice of "just-sitting" would overcome the subject-object dichotomies that rule our everyday perceptions and actions and would bring to radiant luminosity the unspoiled Buddha-nature within us. Hung-chih called our original nature "the bright empty field." This ultimate truth has always been within us as the true reality of ourselves, but it is obstructed by the distinctions of our discriminating consciousness:

> The field of boundless emptiness is what exists from the very beginning. You must purify, cure, grind down, or brush away all the tendencies you have fabricated into apparent habits. Then you can reside in the clear circle of brightness.[50]

While Hung-chih did use koans to overcome discriminating consciousness, his primary teaching for his followers was simply to empty their minds and allow the empty field to manifest itself.[51] For this, no words or discussions are necessary: "The practice of true reality is simply to sit serenely in silent introspection. When you have fathomed this you cannot be turned around by external causes and conditions."[52] He further explained:

> Vast and spacious, like sky and water merging during autumn, like snow and moon having the same color, this field is without boundary, beyond direction, magnificently one entity without edge or seam. Further, when you turn within and drop off everything completely, realization occurs. Right at the time of entirely dropping off, deliberation and discussion are one thousand or ten thousand miles away. Still no principle is discernible, so what could there be to point to or explain?[53]

For Hung-chih, just-sitting is not an avoidance of reality, but the true facing of reality and freely responding to it. Just-sitting allows us to attend to everything that is and not be attached, assuming the attitude of Shakyamuni in "leaving home," accepting separation for the sake of enlightenment: "Facing everything, let go and attain stability. Stay with that just as that. Stay with this just as this. . . . This is how truly to leave home, how home-leaving must be embodied."[54]

DOGEN

Hung-chih was very influential on the great Japanese master Dogen (1200–1253), acclaimed as the founder of Soto Zen in Japan. Even though Dogen himself refused to speak of a Zen or a Soto sect,[55] he was involved in struggles over the proper form of Buddhism, and insisted that his practice and interpretation of Buddhism was that of the Buddha himself.[56] Like Hung-chih, Dogen also stressed the practice of sitting meditation called *zazen* (seated meditation) and *shikantaza* (just-sitting) as the proper approach.

Dogen told his students: "[I]f you cast aside completely the thoughts and concepts of the mind and concentrate on *zazen* alone, you attain to an intimacy with the Way. The attainment of the Way is truly accomplished with the body. For this reason I urge you to concentrate on *zazen*."[57]

While Dogen placed an extraordinary importance on the practice of just-sitting and regarded this as itself enlightenment, Dogen himself did not restrict his own activity to sitting meditation. He reflected profoundly upon his experience with a great speculative mind and became one of the greatest philosophical religious thinkers that Japan has produced. Dogen came to see that language can function not only as a block to realization, but also as an expression of realization: "The monastics of future generations will be able to come to understand a non-discriminative Zen based on words and letters, if they devote efforts to spiritual practice by seeing the universe through words and letters, and words and letters through the universe."[58]

Thus he proposed a twofold approach, through studying Buddhist teaching and sitting:

> There are two ways to penetrate body and mind: studying with a master to hear the teaching, and devotedly sitting zazen. Listening to the teaching opens up your conscious mind, while sitting zazen is concerned with practice-enlightenment. Therefore, if you neglect either of these when entering the buddha way, you cannot hit the mark.[59]

Much of the power of his teaching comes from the relation between his insistence on just-sitting and his extraordinary use of language to open up the experience of true reality.

LIFE OF DOGEN

According to the traditional account of his life, Dogen's parents died when he was quite young, his father when he was two and his mother when he was seven. Shortly before her death, his mother urged him to seek the truth by becoming a Buddhist monk. The young boy was overwhelmed with grief as he saw the incense rising at his mother's funeral, and he experienced all too painfully the meaning of impermanence and separation.[60]

For the next five years Dogen was raised by an uncle of the Fujiwara family who wanted to prepare the boy to be his heir as an aristocratic lord. At twelve years of age, however, Dogen refused to go through the initiation ceremony for a young aristocrat and went to visit another uncle who was a Buddhist monk. Dogen undertook the discipline of Buddhist meditation and study of the sutras on Mount Hiei near Kyoto, and was ordained a Buddhist monk in 1213 at thirteen years of age. But he was plagued with a question that no one there could answer for him:

> As I study both the exoteric and the esoteric schools of Buddhism, they maintain that human beings are endowed with the Dharma-

nature by birth. If this is the case, why did the Buddhas of all ages — undoubtedly in possession of enlightenment — find it necessary to seek enlightenment and engage in spiritual practice?[61]

Dogen was posing the question of why, if all humans have the Dharma-nature or the Buddha-nature from the very beginning, the practice of Buddhist meditation and the study of the sutras should be necessary at all? This is the question of the relation between original enlightenment, which all sentient beings always already have, and acquired enlightenment, which is very rare and achieved only through disciplined practice. At this stage Dogen accepted the teaching of original enlightenment, but this seemed to empty the discipline of Buddhist practice of all meaning. As Abe comments: "In any case, while Dogen was studying Tendai Buddhism on Mt. Hiei, he unconsciously idealized 'awakening' and doubted the necessity of practice."[62] Abe suggests that the young Dogen understood the Dharma-nature as an unmediated reality that one could experience directly and thus without practice. If one already has it, why practice so diligently to achieve it? Then the Dharma-nature appears as the ground of awakening, and practice does not seem to play much of a role.

While Dogen does not seem to have approached the question from the other side, Abe points out that one could equally well ask why, if practice is indispensable, should one believe that sentient beings possess the Dharma-nature from the beginning.[63] If we must strive for awakening, then the Dharma-nature must not have been there from the beginning.

No one on Mount Hiei could answer the question to young Dogen's satisfaction, and so in 1223 he journeyed to China in search of a better master.[64] On his journey he met an old cook who changed his understanding profoundly. When Dogen's ship was anchored on the Chinese coast, an old Chinese monk journeyed eighty-five miles from his monastery to get a Japanese mushroom for the soup he was preparing. Dogen invited him to stay overnight, but the cook insisted on hurrying back to his monastery. Dogen insisted, pointing out that other monks could serve as cook. The old man replied that at his age he saw his duty as cook as "the practice of the Way for the rest of my life. How can I leave my practice to other persons?"[65] Dogen was puzzled and thought that an elderly monk should be practicing zazen or studying koans rather than serving as cook. At this, the old monk laughed out loud at Dogen and chided him: "You, a good man from a foreign country, perhaps do not understand what the practice of the Way is, nor what words and letters are."[66] While Dogen felt surprised and ashamed, the old monk hurried away into the evening.

Finally, in 1225, Dogen encountered a teacher, T'ien-t'ung Ju-ching (Japanese: Nyojo, 1163–1228), under whose direction he resolved his doubt. Ju-ching practiced zazen every day for hours and urged "zazen-only" to his students. In contrast to many monks of his generation, Ju-ching cared little for imperial favor, worldly distinction, or financial gain. He disliked the sectarian rivalries of his Zen counterparts and had a passionate devotion to the practice of zazen for its own sake. His ideal was a simple life of poverty, far from society.

Under Ju-ching's guidance, Dogen practiced zazen night and day. Early one morning in 1225 the monk next to Dogen fell asleep during meditation, and Ju-ching shouted at him: "In zazen it is imperative to cast off body and mind. How could you indulge in sleeping?"[67] At this moment Dogen found the answer to his question and the basis for his later teaching: the casting off of body and mind. Zazen meant the casting off of body and mind. This casting off of body and mind is enlightenment, the realization of our true nature, the overcoming of all concepts and discriminating ideas. To cast off body and mind is to realize the Buddha-nature in the present, to be enlightened by all the things of the universe, to overcome all duality between self and other. Casting off body and mind does not seek any external goals or objects, and thus is a mode of acting with absolute freedom. This experience sees and affirms the concrete individual, finite reality of the present moment in a nondualistic and interpenetrating union of self and world.[68]

Recent scholars have questioned whether Dogen's breakthrough under Ju-ching was as complete and definitive as the later Soto tradition remembered it and have argued for a more nuanced historical reconstruction of the development of his thought.[69] In his mature writings the older Dogen looked back to his experience of awakening under Ju-ching and found that this awakening clarified the dynamic unity and relationship between Buddhist practice and the attainment of enlightenment. This new insight answered the question which had driven him to leave Mt. Hiei.

THE BUDDHA-NATURE

The core of Dogen's mature thought involves insight into the relation of practice and attainment and the Buddha-nature. Practice and attainment are not two distinct experiences but rather, as Abe comments, "indispensable and inseparable components of a dynamic relationship."[70] On the one hand, the Buddha-nature is the ground of Buddhist practice and of awakening. On the other hand, Buddhist practice is the indispensable condition of casting off mind and body and awakening to the Buddha-nature or Dharma-nature. As Dogen explains: "This Dharma is amply present in every person, but unless one practices, it is not manifested; unless there is realization it is not attained."[71] The two are not the same, and they are not different. They must not be confused, lest one neglect the importance of either original enlightenment or practice; on the other hand they must not be distinguished as two separate realities or experiences over against each other.

Abe points out that the Buddha-nature is not a substantial ground but "a self-nihilating ground, or a nonsubstantial and nonobjectifiable ground."[72] The Buddha-nature, which is beyond space and time, is itself impermanence. To express this insight, Dogen altered the traditional interpretation of a famous line from the Mahaparinirvana Sutra, which stated that all sentient beings have the Buddha-nature. Dogen claimed that one should properly state that all beings *are* the Buddha-nature.[73] The Buddha-nature is not simply a potentiality to be realized; it is the very reality of the present moment and is realized by all beings, not only sentient (i.e., living) beings. The Buddha-nature is not other than all the things in the universe. Thus Dogen claims:

> Therefore, these mountains, rivers, and the earth — all constitute the sea of Buddha-nature. ... It has absolutely nothing to do with the inside or the outside, or the center of the universe. Thus to see mountains and rivers is tantamount to experiencing Buddha-nature.[74]

The Buddha-nature, however, is not realized immediately, but only through the mediation of practice. In zazen the Buddha-nature manifests itself, realizes itself in the practitioner and in the entire universe; but the Buddha-nature is not manifest apart from practice. The practice of zazen remains necessary as the condition of the Buddha-nature's realization. There is both (1) an irreversible relationship between the Buddha-nature and practice because the Buddha-nature is the ground of practice, and also (2) a reversible identity of the Buddha-nature and practice because the Buddha-nature is not a substantial ground but a self-emptying dynamic process which is not other than practice.[75] Practice is involved in the dimensions of time and space, but the Buddha-nature is beyond time and space. Thus in the realization of the Buddha-nature through practice we are at the point of nonduality of time and space and that which transcends time and space.

Abe points out the implications of this realization for human activity and for the relation of humans to the rest of the universe. Normally we act for a goal in the future. This goal-centered approach to life runs the danger of devaluing the present moment, which becomes merely a means to an end. This gives rise to the anxious restlessness of much of human life. We are always seeking an ever-receding future and never really abide in the present. Dogen's realization means that means and ends, without being confused, are one. The means as means not only contribute to the final goal but are the realization of ourselves and of the Buddha-nature in the present. Thus each moment is not only a means but also an end in itself, a realization of the nonduality of time and the transtemporal.[76]

This perspective has wide-ranging implications for the experience of time and for action in history. Abe points out that Dogen's perspective is a radical critique of any human-centered approach to ethics.[77] Awakening to the Buddha-nature cannot be a realization of the human personality over against nature; and nature can never be used simply as a means for human ends.

The casting off of body and mind is the liberation from all attachments, a liberation which frees us to engage in action in history without the entanglements of our deluded ego-self. Compassionate action is the realization of wisdom in the world, the manifestation of the Buddha-nature.

4

Dionysius the Areopagite and Mahayana Perspectives

Around the beginning of the sixth century after Christ, an anonymous writer described the climax of the Christian mystical journey in the image of Moses ascending Mt. Sinai and entering the cloud that symbolizes the divine presence: "Here, being neither oneself nor someone else, one is supremely united by a completely unknowing inactivity of all knowledge, and knows beyond the mind by knowing nothing."[1]

The anonymous Christian mystical author described the religious journey in terms of ascent and descent, of silence and negation, of the complete halt of the mind's activities, and of the overcoming of all duality between self and other to express the path of the Christian experience of God. The author assumed that ordinary human consciousness needs to be transformed and purified by passing through a process of negation so that it may be illumined and brought to perfect union with ultimate reality and truth beyond all duality.

While these themes bear similarities to themes of Mahayana Buddhism, they find their meaning in the very different context of Christian spirituality and practice, which is based on belief in a triune God who creates and redeems humankind. Even though the context and meaning of these themes in Christian thought differ significantly from the Mahayana use of negations, silence, and ascent and descent, both the similarities and the differences between the two traditions may be instructive.

For the history of the later Christian tradition, both Eastern and Western, the use of these themes by our unknown author was of lasting importance. The author is nameless because he wrote under the pseudonym of Dionysius (Letter 7.3 [1081C; p. 269]), and was identified with Dionysius the Areopagite, the disciple of Paul mentioned in Acts 17:34. The author was probably a monk living in the Eastern side of the Mediterranean world, possibly in Syria; but he presented his writings as those of a disciple of Hierotheus, who was a disciple of Paul the Apostle. The author also claimed to have been present at the dormition of the Virgin.

While the fictional authorship was accepted as authentic for centuries, modern scholars have established the date of the texts about 500 C.E. The texts cite the work of the non-Christian neo-Platonic philosopher Proclus, who died in 485; and they themselves are first cited in 532 or 533.[2]

The writings of Dionysius are significant for comparison with Buddhism because of their distinctive use of the themes of descending affirmations and ascending negations, the insistence on negating all language about God and then negating even the negation, and for their vision of final union with God as the overcoming of all duality, a state in which individuality is neither clung to nor annihilated. Much of the language of Dionysius could be used by Mahayana Buddhists, but the meaning in each case would be shaped by a very different context. The Dionysian writings are also noteworthy because it was largely through their influence that these themes entered much of the later Christian tradition, including the entire Greek tradition and much of the Latin theology of the High Middle Ages.

Because the fictional authorship was accepted as genuine, the writings of Dionysius were accorded an extremely high level of authority in later medieval thought, ranking just below the scriptures themselves. The Greek theologians Maximus the Confessor and Gregory Palamas and the Latins John the Scot, Thomas Aquinas, Bonaventure, and Meister Eckhart all took up the themes, images, and strategies of Dionysius in constructing their own theologies.

This chapter will begin by exploring the basic assumptions of Dionysius, especially the ascent-descent motif in his thought in relation to this motif in Mahayana Buddhism. Then it will compare the methods and strategies Dionysius proposed for transforming human consciousness with those of Mahayana, and especially Zen, Buddhism.

ASCENT AND DESCENT

PROCESSION AND RETURN

Dionysius views the universe as proceeding from and returning to its divine source. The universe itself is a vast movement flowing forth from God and turning back to its source, and the goal of all human and angelic existence is to return to God by becoming like God. Non-Christian neo-Platonic philosophers had offered a similar vision of all realities emanating from and returning to a first principle named the One or the Good, but Dionysius transformed this vision by grounding it in the Christian God who creates and sustains all finite realities. For Dionysius, finite realities are not a necessary overflow from the neo-Platonic One; they come into being by the free action of the Trinity (EH 1.3 [373D; p. 198], DN 10.1 [937A; p. 120]), and so God is the omnipotent source and goal of all that is (DN 10.1 [936D–937A; p. 119]).

This vision of all finite realities as proceeding from (*exitus*) and returning to (*reditus*) their origin lays the foundation for Dionysius's understanding of human life, his efforts to speak of God, and his vision of the mystical path. This fundamental assumption of Dionysius is important for any comparison of his language with Buddhist themes, for it establishes the framework of his thought and offers a major counterpoint to the Mahayana assumption of dependent co-arising. No matter how similar particular Dionysian themes or statements may be to Mahayana Buddhist perspectives, the context for Dionysius is always the creative presence and directing power of God.

To understand what this means, however, is difficult, indeed impossible in any literal sense. Dionysius warns us that since creation is an act of God and God is incomprehensible, we cannot understand fully what creation is or how God guides it. God's motives and methods are known to God alone (EH 1.3 [373C–D; p. 198]). The impossibility of directly stating ultimate truth in either Mahayana or Dionysian thought is an important interpretive principle for comparing their perspectives. On the one hand, Dionysius's belief in a creating and redeeming God is really different from Mahayana perspectives on dependent co-arising; on the other hand, similar themes are used by both, and both affirm that we only understand the meaning of their statements by undergoing a process of transformation of our consciousness, a process incomprehensible to those who have not experienced it. Neither the Dionysian process of procession and return nor Mahayana dependent co-arising can be grasped as objective descriptions of realities "out there."

Dionysius describes the relation of God and the world in paradoxical language which stresses both the immanence of God in all things and the radical transcendence of God beyond all things. On the one hand, God is wholly other than any finite reality, beyond anything that we can imagine or conceive, but God is also the source and goal of all that is, and is intimately related to the world. God is eternally the same, beyond all creation, but the scriptures affirm that God is also moving into all things. Dionysius interprets the biblical language to mean

> that God brings everything into being, that he sustains them, that he exercises all manner of providence over them, that he is present to all of them, that he embraces all of them in a way which no mind can grasp, and that from him, providing for everything, arise countless processions and activities (DN 9.9 [916C; p. 118]).

Dionysius's language at times seems almost to collapse the world into God: God "is the being immanent in and underlying the things which are, however they are. For God is not some kind of being. ... Rather, he is the essence of being for the things which have being" (DN 5.4 [817D; p. 98]). It is clear that for Dionysius, God is not simply another being alongside the world. Nonetheless, to prevent the simple identification of the world and God, Dionysius also strongly asserts the transcendence of God beyond all finite realities and employs negations to evoke some sense of divine otherness.

For Dionysius, God orders and guides the process of procession and return by using intermediaries arranged in two hierarchies, a celestial hierarchy composed of the angels, and an ecclesiastical hierarchy composed of the members of the Christian community.[3] We become like God by accepting our place in the hierarchies God has established.[4] If any finite reality accepts and fulfills its role in the hierarchy, it does the will of God and participates in an uplifting process of purification, illumination, and perfection leading to final union with God, *theosis*, in which all duality is overcome.[5]

While the central movement of Dionysius's thought takes the form of descent and ascent, it is important to note that because of the divine initiative in creating and redeeming, the movement typically moves in the opposite direction from the usual Mahayana ascent-descent motif. The ascent to God from deluded human self-consciousness always presupposes a prior procession from God in creation and the power of God's grace working through the sacred hierarchies. The contrast is an important indication of characteristic patterns, but it is not absolute: for both traditions, the sequence of ascent and descent could be reversed. Dionysius could easily view religious leaders, such as Moses ascending Mt. Sinai, as beginning from sin and ignorance and ascending to encounter God and then returning to share their wisdom with their people. Mahayana perspectives often emphasize the graciousness of dharmakaya in illuminating humans and leading them up the slope of wisdom, and thus begin the movement with a descent of wisdom which makes possible the human ascent to enlightenment. For both traditions, the ordinary consciousness of humans must be negated, and the power of absolute reality graciously makes this negation possible.

AFFIRMATIONS AND NEGATIONS

For Dionysius, the process of procession and return makes possible language about God and also provides the structure for interpreting such language. Affirmations are possible because of God's gift of being to creatures in creation and God's additional gift of inspired language in the scriptures. Even though God is present in all things, Dionysius denies that we could awaken to ultimate truth on our own and warns us that we would never be able to recognize God on the basis of our own rational powers:

> Indeed the inscrutable One is out of the reach of every rational process. Nor can any words come up to the inexpressible Good, this One.
> ... Mind beyond mind, word beyond speech, it is gathered up by no

discourse, by no intuition, by no name. . . . Cause of all existence, and therefore itself transcending existence, it alone could give an authoritative account of what it really is (DN 1.1 [588B; pp. 49–50]).

Language itself follows and interprets the movement of procession and return: all true language about God comes from God and leads us back to God. Where Dogen told his students to see the universe through words and letters and words and letters through the universe, Dionysius interprets the universe through the words and letters of the Bible and interprets the Bible through the experience of God's grace permeating the universe. For both Dogen and Dionysius, their respective scriptures illumine the universe, but we need an illumined consciousness to grasp what the scriptures proclaim. For Dionysius, as for Dogen and the entire Zen tradition, simply reading the scriptures is not enlightenment; we must learn how to read them through a process of interpretation involving both affirmations and negations. In this process reality itself becomes manifest, and we are transformed.

Dionysius uses "descending affirmations" to articulate the movement of descent from God. Descending affirmations assume the similarity of created realities to God and also the revelation of God in the scriptures. Because all things come from God and because the words of the scriptures make known God's presence in the world, we can make affirmations concerning God.

Dionysius calls theology that makes affirmations about God cataphatic or affirming theology. This positive form of language expresses the procession of all things from God: since all things come from God, they reflect their Source. God is "the Life of the living, the being of beings, it is the Source and the Cause of all life and of all being, for out of its goodness it commands all things to be and it keeps them going" (DN 1.3 [589C; p. 51]). The divine Source shares its goodness, beauty, and truth with all creation, and thus we can affirm that God is goodness, beauty, life, wisdom, power, peace, and truth. Moreover, the concrete images and symbols of the Bible and the Church's liturgical life can manifest God.

Like the skillful means of Mahayana Buddhism, Dionysian affirmations, properly understood, are true, but they can be misleading if we assume we know what they mean in any literal manner. For Dionysius, as for the Mahayana, no affirmation, not even the true affirmations of the scriptures, can express ultimate truth.

Even though Dionysius asserts that God is the being and essence of creation, God remains radically other than any created reality; thus every image, symbol, and concept of God must also be negated. Negating theology, called apophatic theology, corresponds to the return of all things to God and reminds us how different God is from creation.[6] The Good itself, the reality of God, is beyond the categories of our affirmations and denials.

Negations are of crucial importance for Dionysius because he ponders the meaning of Christian experience in light of the incomprehensibility and ineffability of God. He wrestles again and again with a central problem of Christian discourse: How can we talk about God when we know that we cannot really say anything about God? None of our categories applies to the divine reality. God neither is nor is not, because God is beyond being and nonbeing. Any image or concept that we have of God has to be negated, for our understanding of the image or concept is inevitably finite and inadequate. Every affirmation concerning God must be balanced by a corresponding negation. In developing this relation, Dionysius works out a logic of affirming and negating, a logic that propels language beyond itself into silence.

LOGIC OF AFFIRMING AND NEGATING

Where the movement of ascent and descent determines the "zigzagging logic" of all Mahayana language and action, the interplay of affirmation and negation dominates all three levels of knowledge of God in Dionysius's theology, and so Dionysius develops his own form of "zigzagging logic." This logic expresses a level of union which is beyond knowing and ignorance and which can only be described in a paradoxical logic dominated by negations. As Bernard McGinn describes this Dionysian logic:

1. God is x (true, metaphorically).
2. God is not-x (true, anagogically).
3. God is neither x nor not-x (true, unitively).[7]

This dynamic of affirming and negating and then negating the alternative of affirmation and negation bears some similarity to the logic of Mahayana Buddhism. Conze notes that the basic principle of Mahayana Buddhist logic and ontology is that "the truth 'lies in the middle' between 'it is' and 'it is not.' "[8] The classic expression of this Buddhist logic is the fourfold negation called the tetralamma. This pattern

considers four alternatives: (1) x exists, (2) x does not exist, (3) x neither exists nor does not exist, and (4) x both exists and does not exist. Having reviewed these possibilities, the Buddhists then tend to reject all four as merely so many kinds of attachment.[9]

Conze notes that this pattern is a constant amid the great variety of Mahayana traditions: "At all times and everywhere one-sided affirmation and negation have been rejected as erroneous, in favour of some 'non-dual' reality which is free from both being and non-being."[10]

The interpretation of the four-cornered negation follows the general pattern of Mahayana thought, negating any intellectual affirmation or negation to which one could cling in order to bring about awakening. For the

Mahayana tradition, awakening is beyond affirmation and negation and yet includes both; for Dionysius, true language about God is also beyond affirmation and negation and yet includes both.

In each case the logic is not simply an intellectual exercise but is the linguistic transcription of an experience of transformation which leads to a new way of seeing oneself and the universe. The movement of language follows the movement of the religious journey, which in turn follows the movement of the universe itself.

The entire theology of Dionysius is the articulation of a mystical journey, the expression of a religious practice. *Theologia* is a spiritual discipline that leads to union with God. Only those who have experienced this mystical path can have any real idea what the words that describe it mean. Dionysius plays on the Greek words *mathein* (learning) and *pathein* (experiencing, undergoing, suffering); learning and experiencing the divine things go together. His alleged teacher Hierotheus is his model: "not only learning but also experiencing the divine things" (DN 2.9; p. 65).[11] Dionysius assumes that those who have not experienced the divine things cannot understand the logic of Christian language or the meaning of Christian symbols and would laugh at Christians and pity them for being misguided if they witnessed the sacred rites (EH 7.3.1; p. 252). For Dionysius, as for the Mahayana in general and Zen in particular, everything turns on initiating learners into an experience that cannot be literally described and cannot be understood by those outside. The logic of both Dionysius and Mahayana presupposes a religious practice which allows one to see reality in a new way. Apart from practice, the logic will inevitably appear illogical.

The Dionysian vision leads to seeing God in all things and all things in God; the Mahayana journey leads to seeing all things in each and each in all things. The Dionysian logic expresses the movement of the mind through a process of purification to illumination and finally to a state of perfection in union with God. For Dionysius, the sinfulness of normal human consciousness must first be negated as a prelude to the ascent. Then images and concepts of God must be affirmed and negated in turn. The Mahayana logic expresses the negation of an illusory discriminating consciousness, denying the usual distinctions and categories of human thought and leading to the experience of shunyata or dharmakaya, reality itself. Only then can one return to affirm the world in a new sense. Both the Dionysian and the Mahayana journeys are borne by absolute reality itself: the grace of God permeating the universe makes possible the Dionysian path, and the graciousness of dharmakaya makes possible the skillful means of the bodhisattvas.

IMAGES AND CONCEPTS

For Dionysius, the dynamic logic of affirmation and negation is played out on the distinct levels of images and concepts. Symbolic theology interprets the concrete images of the Bible and the Christian liturgy, and conceptual or intellectual theology interprets conceptual language concerning God.

According to Dionysius, we need concrete symbols because the mind cannot be directed to the spiritual contemplation of spiritual realities unless we begin our journey with material things of sense. Beauty is an image of hidden spiritual things, and thus concrete symbols can manifest God. The experience of material realities can be uplifting, and this is critical for the soul's return to God.

We affirm material images of God from the Bible because, coming from God, they reflect their creator (and thus "God is x"), but we deny them because God is radically beyond them ("God is not-x"). Where Zen masters make seemingly outrageous statements, which, properly interpreted, express reality itself, Dionysius affirms that even seemingly bizarre images of God can be disclosive. For example, the Psalms present God "as drinking, as inebriated, as sleeping, as someone hung-over" (Letter 9.1 [1105B; p. 282]; e.g., Pss. 44:24; 78:65), hardly fitting images for the divine. Properly interpreted, however, they can be disclosive of the divine reality. Dionysius suggests that the sleep of God represents God's transcendence of all finite reality, and God's wakefulness represents the divine providential care for us (Letter 9.6 [1113B; p. 288]). God's drunkenness is a symbol of God as the "superfullness" of all good things, as surpassing all that is (Letter 9.5 [1112C; p. 287]). The use of concrete symbols for God has firm precedent: Dionysius notes that "Jesus himself speaks of God by means of parables, and passes on to us the mystery of his divine activity by using the symbolism of a table" (Letter 9.1 [1108A; p. 283]).

Where the Mahayana insists on both affirming and negating language about reality, Dionysius combines a positive and a negative use of symbols. The affirmative side of symbolic theology interprets God's revelation of Godself in scripture and the material things used in the liturgy to manifest God. To those properly instructed and initiated, these concrete images, no matter how bizarre they seem, communicate the unseen reality of God. The negating side of symbolic theology invites us to rise from our symbols and concepts and continue our ascent into God, an anagogical ascent that reaches its climax in a knowing beyond knowing in a silence beyond words.

On the level of sense, negations about God are true and affirmations are inconsistent, for we must negate any material image of God more than we affirm it. Thus dissimilar symbols are more appropriate to God than similar symbols. Because of their power to shock us, discordant figures lift up the mind more than the harmonious, noble images which may deceive us into thinking they are adequate to God. Dissimilar symbols impress upon us that God is not like anything we can imagine, and they help us strip away all images and eventually even all intellectual concepts. Thus God is more fittingly revealed in dissimilar symbols than in similar symbols.

Zen koans bring the ordinary activities of the mind to a halt and express a new vision of reality; Dionysius's dissimilar symbols also bring the ordinary process of the mind to a halt and express the truth of ultimate reality in symbolic form. For both Zen and Dionysius, what is critical is the way the koans or the dissimilar symbols function. If grasped at, they block awareness; if affirmed and negated, they can be disclosive.

Dionysius affirms that after we leave behind the images and symbols of the senses, we must also use and leave behind the concepts and operations of our intellect. Conceptual theology uses the intellect and reason for discursive or intellectual language about God. On this level we must follow the same dynamic movement of thought as in symbolic theology. Again, moving in the opposite direction from the usual Mahayana pattern, Dionysius begins by affirming concepts of God before proceeding to negate them. This allows him to place a greater importance on using the intellect before negating it than Zen Buddhism has usually done.

Zen masters such as Dogen did insist that "not-thinking" was to be negated in a state of "non-thinking" that included both thinking and not-thinking. Dionysius's state of unknowing beyond affirming and negating includes a similar union and transcendence of thinking and not-thinking.

For Dionysius, on the level of intellectual theology we affirm that God is Being, goodness, wisdom, but our concept of Being, goodness, wisdom is not God. The positive moment is affirming or cataphatic theology, which affirms statements about God (God is x). We can affirm predicates of God because we gain some conception of the Creator from the creatures. Nonetheless, God is unlike any created reality and unlike even the intellectual rational concepts we devise. Thus once again, affirmations about God are inconsistent and negations are true (God is not x). We must strip away all concepts from God in apophatic theology and move up to the level of unknowing, which is a union with God beyond all concepts and human affirmations and beyond all duality of subject and object.

The goal of Dionysius's theological reflection is to move us through and beyond the levels of symbols and concepts until we reach the level of mystical theology. Even though God is beyond both affirmation and negation, we reach God through this twofold movement of thought. Apart from the movement of the creature into God, there is no true theology, and the driving force of the ascent is the power of negation.

Mystical Theology: Union and Nonduality

Finally, Dionysius tells us, we arise by unknowing to union with what transcends all being and knowledge. Dionysius sees the third level of theology, mystical theology, as covered with dark clouds—this is the level of unknowing, the level of union with God as God is in Godself. In the end, the journey leads to mystical, hidden theology beyond images and concepts. On this level, God is neither x nor not-x, because neither affirmations nor negations can express the union beyond all knowing and understanding.

Again the language of Dionysius often resembles Mahayana statements about shunyata or dharmakaya or suchness: absolute reality, as such, cannot be described but can be experienced, and the experience yields paradoxical affirmations and negations which transcend themselves and move into silence.

For Dionysius, we cannot talk adequately about the hidden mystery, but we can reverence it in silence. This silence is the goal of "mystical theology," a new term apparently created by Dionysius. The term *mystica* had been used by Herodotus for something hidden, secret. Etymologically, a mystery is something you shut your mouth on (from *muein* in Greek). The term was then associated with the people initiated into mysteries which were kept secret from those outside.

For Dionysius, mystical theology is the goal of all believers, the culmination of the trajectory of the first two levels of symbolic and intellectual theology. While the treatise on *Mystical Theology* is very brief, it is the key to much of Dionysius's thought, for it tries to say what can be said of a reality we cannot talk about. To communicate some sense of this experience, he turns to the concrete biblical image of Moses plunging into the "truly mysterious darkness of unknowing" (MT 1.3 [1001A; p. 137]) and describes a state beyond all dualities or distinctions. Here we leave behind both the affirmations and the denials of images and concepts: "the cause of all is considerably prior to this, beyond privations, beyond every denial, beyond every assertion" (MT 1.2 [1000B; p. 136]).

The proper expression of the final stage of union is silence. The final stages of the ascent negate not only the affirmations made in images and concepts but also the negations themselves. Negative language is also inadequate to capture the divine reality, but it leads us into a wise silence beyond all language and rational processes. Dionysius describes the climax of the process of ascent:

> The fact is that the more we take flight upward, the more our words are confined to the ideas we are capable of forming; so that now as we plunge into that darkness which is beyond intellect, we shall find ourselves not simply running short of words but actually speechless and unknowing (MT 3 [1033B–C; p. 139]).

For both Dionysius and the Mahayana tradition, silence is the proper response to the experience of ultimate reality; but in both cases, silence only finds its meaning in relation to the words and actions of religious practice. For both, ultimate truth can only be expressed by a wise and reverent silence, but language, properly used, can lead us into the wordless experience of ultimate truth, and thus the language and practice of the preparation inevitably shape the formless silence that follows.

Again like the Mahayana tradition, Dionysius assumes that only a consciousness that has been negated, transformed, and purified of its illusions can understand the interpenetration of speech and silence before ultimate reality. Where Zen masters know that their language and actions appear nonsensical to the unenlightened, Dionysius asserts that to those outside the Christian community, Christian language and symbols must appear foolish. Thus, in a certain sense, the languages of Dionysius and the Mahayana are incommensurable. In each case, only silence properly communicates the experience, but silence is possible only in relation to words and actions. One can only understand what the words mean by having the experience of transformation. To those outside, the language and actions and silence will not be disclosive and may appear ridiculous.

While the Areopagite's vision is similar to the Mahayana Buddhist insistence that ultimate truth is perfectly expressed only by silence, important differences remain. Dionysius's experience of enlightenment is not simply seeing our own nature, as in the Mahayana, but having our nature changed and uplifted by the Incarnation of God in history. Moreover, the basis for language about ultimate reality remains different for Dionysius than for the Buddhist tradition. The Mahayana tradition never developed a theology of divine revelation, though it did interpret the life and teaching of Shakyamuni Buddha as the manifestation of absolute reality (dharmakaya) in our world for the sake of enlightening humans to the truth.

For Dionysius the entire movement is willed and guided by God. As Bernard McGinn comments on Dionysius's thought: "Divinization is a gift, not a birthright."[12] For the Mahayana tradition the question of a creating and redeeming God does not arise, and contemporary Mahayana Buddhists often insist that they are neither theist nor atheist in the usual Western sense of the terms. Mahayana awakening is not a gift of God, and much of the Zen tradition has stressed the importance of self-power, but the self itself is negated in the process of enlightenment, and the guidance of the skillful means of the bodhisattva can be crucial.

Much of the difficulty in comparing the two traditions lies in the insistence of each tradition that language cannot capture the experience. No description can express the Mahayana experience of shunyata. For Dionysius, it is impossible to state exactly who or what God is. God is clearly not some external reality separate from the world; God is the essence of the world, but God is also radically beyond the world. Dionysius explains the implications of God's relation to reality for language: God

> is all things since he is the Cause of all things. The sources and the goals of all things are in him and are anticipated in him. But he is also superior to them all because he precedes them and is above them. Therefore every attribute may be predicated of him and yet he is not any one thing. He has every shape and structure, and yet is formless and beautyless (DN 5.8 [824B; p. 101]).

The Mahayana tradition would not describe shunyata as Source and Cause of all things in the sense of creation. Shunyata is not other than impermanence. Ultimate reality is not other than this passing moment. While it is impossible to identify the Buddhist experience of shunyata with the Christian belief in God, it is noteworthy that in both traditions language is radically inadequate to state ultimate truth. Shunyata is clearly not a creating God, but it is impossible to state directly in either tradition what is meant by ultimate reality. Dionysius writes to a monk Gaius that God "solidly transcends mind and being. He is completely unknown and non-existent. He exists beyond being and he is known beyond the mind" (Letter 1 [1065A; p. 263]).

Both shunyata and God escape the web of human concepts, but both traditions acknowledge that the skillful use of language can lead humans to true awareness of shunyata or God. Where the Mahayana tradition uses both affirmations and negations as skillful means for discourse conveying conventional truth, Dionysius tells us that we must predicate both affirmations and denials of God, but in the end even our negations fall short of the divine reality, and we must negate even our denials. In both the Mahayana tradition and in Dionysian theology, it is impossible to separate the meanings of affirmations and negations from each other. Both types of statements find their proper meaning in relation to the other and to the illumined silence into which they lead.

Where the Zen tradition remembered the silence of Vimalakirti and of Hui-k'o as expressing the meaning of nonduality, Dionysius tells us that the proper reverence for God is expressed in silence: "With a wise silence we do honor to the inexpressible" (DN 1.3 [589B; p. 50]).

STRATEGIES OF TRANSFORMATION

In both traditions religious practice prepares and shapes the experience of absolute reality and enlightened silence. All the words and actions of Zen masters are expressions of an enlightened consciousness and strategies to bring others to this state. Where Zen has traditionally turned to koans and sitting practice under the guidance of a Zen master, the religious practice of Dionysius is based on the symbols and sacraments of the Christian liturgy under the leadership of a bishop.

For both Zen and Dionysius, our ordinary consciousness is so profoundly distorted that we cannot see reality itself which is right before us. Thus both insist on an initial moment of negation. For Dionysius the movement of the entire cosmos and of our redemption is a descending procession from God followed by an ascent, but our own starting point in sin and mortality requires an ascent that proceeds by way of negation. We must first be purified of ignorance and sin before we can begin to understand the symbols and concepts that lead us toward God. We need an initial moment of purification before we can advance to illumination and union.

Both traditions know that their outward forms of practice will mean nothing to those who do not understand their meaning from within. Zen masters mock those who simply imitate Zen sayings or actions without understanding and call them practitioners of "fox-Zen."[13] Dionysius assumes that those outside the Christian community cannot understand the meaning of the images, symbols, and concepts used of God. Anyone who has not undergone an inner process of purification will not understand the sacred rites and will defile them. To the uninitiated, the language of the Bible appears absurd (Letter 9.1 [1104B; p. 281]), and the discussion of the names of God provokes mockery and laughter (DN 1.8 [597C; p. 58]). Thus he repeatedly urges Christians to guard sacred matters from the disrespect of the uninitiated.

An Enlightened Guide: Hierarch and Bodhisattva

For both Zen and Dionysius, interpreting the language and actions of the tradition demands initiation into a higher level of consciousness. Since the ordinary consciousness of humans is distorted, it must be negated or purified, and this requires an enlightened guide, someone who has made the ascent through negations and shares the wisdom gained. Both Zen and Dionysius assume that we need a master who is enlightened to challenge our illusions and initiate us into enlightened consciousness.[14] The bodhisattva is the enlightened person who freely shares the wisdom of awakening; the divine hierarch of Dionysius models himself on God and "remains ever ready to give light to whomever approaches" (EH 2.3.3 [400B; p. 205]). Where the Zen tradition valued the direct transmission from mind to mind through generation after generation of Zen masters, Dionysius turns to the ecclesiastical hierarchy, and especially to its leaders, the hierarchs or bishops. The ignorant and sinners must be enlightened by those who have themselves undergone the process of initiation and purification.

The Mahayana tradition challenges all followers to take the vows of the bodhisattva. Dionysius, by contrast, sees the task of enlightening others as the special calling of the ecclesiastical hierarchy and sets the process of enlightenment in a Christian liturgical context. Even monks, the highest of the lower orders, who have been "purified of all stain" and "possess full holiness" (EH 6.1.3 [532C–D; p. 244]), are not called to illumine the lower orders but only to follow the higher levels of the hierarchy (EH 6.3.1 [533C; p. 246]).

Zen masters fulfill the role of the bodhisattva by using koans and sitting practice to negate the illusions of their students and initiate them into a new consciousness. Dionysius's hierarchy is composed of different orders with different liturgical roles. The process of initiation proceeds not by sitting meditation or by pondering koans but by a series of liturgical initiations. The deacons are to purify those outside of full communion with the Christian community. This includes catechumens preparing for baptism, as well as the possessed and the penitents awaiting reconciliation with the Church. The priests are called to illumine the faithful lay community. Hierarchs or bishops are called to perfect all the lower orders, but they have special care of the monastic community (EH 6.1 [529D–533A; pp. 243–45]).

Where the bodhisattvas use skillful means to reach different audiences, Dionysius's hierarchs have a special role in communicating the divine love to lower levels in ways they can understand. The first leaders of the ecclesiastical hierarchy employed material images to speak of the transcendent:

> They passed on something united in a variegation and plurality. Of necessity they made human what was divine. They put material on what was immaterial. . . . [O]ur own hierarchy is itself symbolical and adapted to what we are (EH 1.5 [376D, 377A; p. 199]).

Dionysius interprets the movement of the hierarch in celebrating the Eucharist as a journey toward the many who are assembled and toward the One, who is God. The hierarch shares his own illumination freely, using "a multitude of sacred enigmas" (EH 3.3.3 [429B; p. 213]) so that the community gathered together can journey with him toward God.

TRANSFORMATION OF DESIRES

In both traditions enlightenment involves a transformation of human desires. For the Buddhist tradition, the Second Noble Truth names "desire" or clinging or grasping as the source of our illusions and our suffering. For Dionysius, the tragedy of human existence is that human nature "turned to the life of the most varied desires and came at the end to the catastrophe of death"; humans have turned away from the peace of life in union with God and have been plunged "into the utter mess of passion" (EH 3.3.11 [440C; p. 220]).

The response of the Buddhist tradition to the illusions of desire is the twofold path of ascent and descent, a restructuring of consciousness that leads to a transformed mode of being in the world. In this transformation, desires are not clung to or grasped at. Desires and emotions still arise, but they are not the tyrannical masters of the self.

In Dionysius there is also a transformation of the meaning of desire. Even though turning to desires is the cause of sin, the restlessness of desire also reveals that we have a relationship to God as the Good: "Each being looks to it as a source, as the agent of cohesion, and as an objective. All things are returned to it as their own goal. All things desire it" (DN 4.4 [700A; p. 75]).

We experience a positive relationship to God through our desires and longings, which are not simply evil. Indeed, Dionysius tells us, the longing for the good makes angelic beings what they are (DN 4.1 [696A; p. 72]). There is a cosmic yearning (*eros*) which is good, which leads us into the divine self-giving love (*agape*). This eros is an awareness of one's own lack and a yearning for the Good and the Beautiful. Thus the title of the Good (Greek: *to agathon*) has a certain priority, because it expresses the attracting power of God for all reality.

Because the yearning for the good is also a yearning for beauty, Dionysius can also state: "Beauty unites all things and is the source of all things. It is the great creating cause which bestirs the world and holds all things in existence by the longing inside them to have beauty" (DN 4.7 [704A; p. 77]). Beauty, as another name for God, is the source and goal of all reality: "it is the longing for beauty which actually brings them into being" (DN 4.7 [704A; p. 77]).[15] Thus we praise God, the object of our desire, as Beauty and as the Good, but always also as the Nameless One (DN 1.6 [596A; p. 54]).

Later on he will say that God also has an eros, a divine yearning (DN 4.15 [713A; p. 83]), and this will be the key to our redemption. The eternal, impassible God is "beguiled by goodness, by love, and by yearning and is enticed away from his transcendent dwelling place and comes to abide within all things" (DN 4.13 [712B; p. 82]). Having brought into being a world other than God, God is so in love with the world that God yearns for the world and enters it to redeem humankind.

To predicate eros or yearning of God is one of the most daring moves of Dionysius, but he modestly attributes this to his teacher Hierotheus, who wrote "Hymns of Yearning," literally, *erotikon hymnon*, "erotic hymns," and allegedly applied the term eros both to God and to creatures (DN 4.15 [713A; p. 83]).

Eros traditionally had been identified with a need, a lack, and thus had been denied of God. For Proclus, Eros was one of the gods, but not the highest. Dionysius transforms the notion of eros into an overflow of divine goodness, a goodness that yearns even though it needs nothing. He adapts the Greek notion of eros to the Christian experience that God is love. God's creating love is ecstatic, that is, it draws God out of Godself and leads God to center God's being on the object of the divine love (DN 4. 13 [712A–B; p. 82]). As Andrew Louth comments: "Love is ecstatic because it is unitive; the lover is united to the beloved, who is, for him, a manifestation of beauty."[16]

The attribution of desire to God reveals a profound difference between the Dionysian and the Mahayana paths. While dharmakaya is compassion, the source of the bodhisattva's skillful means, the Mahayana tradition does not personalize the absolute and attribute desire or yearning to it. While dharmakaya manifests itself in Shakyamuni Buddha, the notion that ultimate reality "is enticed away from his transcendent dwelling place and comes to abide within all things" is foreign to Zen or Mahayana thought.

The desire of God leads directly to the climax of God's goodness to humans in the Incarnation of God in Christ:

It took upon itself in a most authentic way all the characteristics of our nature, except sin. It became one with us in our lowliness, losing nothing of its own real condition, suffering no change or loss. It allowed us, as those of equal birth, to enter into communion with it and to acquire a share of its own true beauty (EH 3.3.11 [441A–B; pp. 220-221]).

Dharmakaya is not other than the universe, and so there is no process of dharmakaya "becoming" one with us while retaining its own transcendent condition. In Shakyamuni Buddha, in the koans and sitting practice of the Zen masters, dharmakaya manifests itself as it is, the Buddha-nature is realized in practice. Dharmakaya, however, does not "become" anything, for it is always there. As Hung-chih remarked: "The field of boundless emptiness is what exists from the very beginning."[17] For Dionysius, we are not already divine, and God has not always been human; rather, the principle of Athanasius dominates: God became human so humans could become divine.

SYMBOLS, SACRAMENTS, AND KOANS

Both Zen and Dionysius use concrete strategies to transform desires and lead followers to enlightenment. Where the Zen tradition used the practice of sitting or koans to bring ordinary consciousness to a halt and radically restructure our awareness, Dionysius turns to symbols:

We use whatever appropriate symbols we can for the things of God. With these analogies we are raised upward toward the truth of the mind's vision, a truth which is simple and one. We leave behind us all our own notions of the divine. We call a halt to the activities of our minds. . . . It surpasses everything and is wholly beyond our capacity to know it (DN 1.4 [592C–D; p. 53]).

The dual movement of affirmation and negation brings our minds to a halt. In this halt we experience God even though we cannot really talk of God: "One can neither discuss nor understand the One" (DN 1.5 [593B; p. 53]). Koans halt the normal operations of our consciousness and bring about a death of the illusory self. As Zenkei Shibayama notes:

Master Dogen very aptly said, "Death: just death all through—complete manifestation!" When you die, just die. When you just die thoroughly and completely you will have transcended life and death. Then, for the first time, free and creative Zen life and work will be developed.[18]

While Dionysius does not discuss detailed methods of meditation, he does on occasion discuss methods of prayer in relation to theology (DN 3). Prayer makes us conscious of our relationship to what is higher than ourselves. In praying we do not bring God closer, but we become conscious of the God who has always been present. Dionysius compares this process to persons on a boat pulling a line attached to a rock. They do not pull the rock closer to them, but rather themselves closer to the rock (DN 3.1 [680C–D; p. 68]).[19]

For both Zen and Dionysius, the practitioner is to become identified with, respectively, the Buddha or the Christ, though the manner of this identification proceeds rather differently in each case. For Dionysius, this is an elevation to a divine nature which transcends us and is absolutely beyond our reach. For Zen, as expressed by Dogen, all things *are* the Buddha-nature, and practice manifests their true identity.

At the core of the process of salvation for Dionysius is the use of sacraments and symbols, perceptible realities that make present the divine and lift Christians up to a higher level of existence. The concrete spiritual practice that forms the context for Dionysius's journey of divinization is the Christian liturgy.[20] There is a descending movement from the One, from God, to the many things of the material world, some of which become symbols of God, and then a return movement upward, uniting and uplifting humans to the divine reality. Participation in Christian sacraments heals the fragmentation of human existence: "One cannot participate in contradictory realities at one and the same time, and whoever enters into communion with the One cannot proceed to live a divided life, especially if he hopes for a real participation in the One" (EH 2.3.5 [401A; p. 206]).

Where Zen uses zazen or koan practice to bring about the death of the illusory self, Dionysius turns to the symbolic actions of the liturgy to effect our initiation. He describes the transformation of human existence as a struggle leading to a death, modeled on the death of Jesus. Baptism gives Christians a share in the death of Christ (EH 2.3.6 [404A; p. 207]) as the way of imitating God: "This symbolic lesson therefore sacredly leads the one who is baptized into the mystery that by his triple immersion and emersion he imitates, as far as the imitation of God is possible to men, the divine death of one who was three days and nights in the tomb" (EH 2.3.7 [404B; p. 208]). Emerging from the waters of baptism, the newly baptized is clothed with bright white clothes which symbolize his newly bestowed likeness to God. The death of the Zen practitioner is the death of an illusory self that never really existed and the manifestation of one's true identity. The death of the Christian neophyte is, to be sure, the death of a false self, but it is also a participation in the death of Christ which transforms us and elevates us to a new level of existence.

In baptism the Christian imitates and shares in and identifies with the death and resurrection of Christ. In Ch'an and Zen Buddhism, the awakened Buddhist acts with the freedom and consciousness of a Buddha, and thus the actions of a Zen master are themselves the action of a Buddha. Lin-chi stressed to his students that they themselves *are* the Patriarch-Buddha and they should not seek him outside themselves:

Do you want to know the Patriarch-Buddha? He is none other than you who stand before me listening to my discourse. Since you students lack faith in yourself, you run around seeking something outside. . . . Followers of the Way, as I see it we are not different from Shakya[muni].[21]

As Bielefeldt has noted, this tradition of identification with the Buddha was taken up by Dogen and interpreted in light of his own stress on just-sitting. For Dogen all true practice *is* the behavior of a Buddha, and both the enlightened consciousness and the physical posture of sitting are reenactments of the example of the Buddha:

"Dogen explicitly links his *zazen* with the tradition that every act of the Ch'an master—whether holding up a finger or beating a student—represents the enlightened behavior of a Buddha, free from discrimination and beyond understanding."[22]

For Dogen, the concrete way in which one imitates the Buddha is through the practice of just-sitting, physically reenacting the behavior and the consciousness of the Buddha. Bielefeldt notes that in Dogen's interpretation the Buddha appears now less

as a symbol of pure consciousness than as example of liberated agent. If the model for Zen practice here is still the enactment of enlightenment, it is no longer simply the psychological accord of the practitioner's consciousness with the eternally enlightened mind; it is now the physical reenactment by the practitioner of the deeds of the historical exemplars of enlightened behavior.[23]

In baptism the Christian physically reenacts the descent of Jesus into the Jordan River and symbolically reenacts the death and resurrection of the Lord. Dionysius could agree that the consciousness and the deeds of Jesus Christ are both psychological and historical exemplars of enlightened behavior, examples for Christians to follow. For Dionysius, the action of the hierarch in the liturgy *is* the action of Christ upon the recipient of the sacrament, and the mind of the hierarch is modeled on the mind of Christ: "Jesus enlightens our blessed superiors, Jesus who is transcendent mind, utterly divine mind, who is the source and the being underlying all hierarchy, all sanctification, all workings of God" (EH 1.1 [372A; pp. 195–96]). The identification of the hierarch or of any Christian with Christ is, however, never total.

For both Zen and Dionysius, enlightened behavior heals the divisions of human life and overcomes the separation between the practitioner and the Buddha or the Christ, but the manner of this identification in each case is rather different. Zen challenges practitioners literally to become themselves a Buddha, an enlightened one. For Lin-chi, his students have only to open their eyes and believe in themselves to see that they are the Buddha. Dionysius, like most of the Christian tradition, distinguishes a unique sense in which Jesus Christ is the Son of God from the process of divinization through participation in the divine mysteries that all humans can share.

In both traditions there is a blending of decisional and gracious aspects in the experience of transformation. While the Christian tradition challenges people to turn from sin and seek God's saving love, it also accents the graciousness of God's gift in the experience of salvation, even in the decision to seek God. The reception of the gift of salvation becomes, in turn, the basis for new decisions. Zen awakening requires a decision to seek enlightenment, a decision to depart from one's illusions of the ordinary world. In Dogen's Soto Zen, as soon as one begins to practice meditation, one is enlightened, though the awakening of a beginning student is different from that of an experienced master. In Rinzai Zen, which characteristically looks to a sudden awakening, the experience of awakening, however diligently sought after, cannot be predicted or controlled. No set of exercises can guarantee enlightenment. The moment of awakening itself comes as gift.

For Zen, the enlightened awaken to the truth of their condition, of the Buddha-nature which they have been all along. As Dogen insisted, all things are the Buddha-nature, even though this is only manifested in practice. For Dionysius, Christians are transformed by a process of divinization which elevates them to a union with God which they did not possess by nature and which is beyond the power of human nature alone to attain.

Zen also negates the final distinction between ignorance and satori. As Shibayama notes: "There is still another barrier here for a Zen student to break through. The fact that he distinguishes satori from ignorance as if they were two different things just shows that his training is still immature."[24] While Dionysius would agree with the goal of abolishing any trace of spiritual pride or self-satisfaction from the spiritual ascent, he nowhere suggests that we should negate the distinction between those trapped in sin and the community of those being purified, illumined, and united to God.

Koans and zazen both express the consciousness of nonduality and also realize this nonduality. As Nagao commented on the twofold "realization" of enlightenment, the ascending path of wisdom makes one aware of nonduality, and the descending path of compassion realizes this in practice. For Dionysius, there is an analogous twofold "realization" of union with Christ in the sacramental life of the Church. Christians become conscious of their identity with Christ, overcome all duality between themselves and God, and in this process actualize their oneness with the divine.

The divinization into which baptism initiates the Christian is celebrated and perfected in the rite of "synaxis" or the Eucharist, the "sacrament of sacraments" (EH 3.1 [424C; p. 209]). Synaxis is a Greek word for calling people together for worship.[25] Like all sacraments, but in a preeminent way, synaxis "draws our fragmented lives together into a one-like divinization. It forges a divine unity out of the divisions within us. It grants us communion and union with the One" (EH 3.1 [424C–D; p. 209]). It is the overcoming of all duality and the realization of our true identity.

For Dionysius, the sacraments of baptism and Eucharist are the pre-eminent ways in which humans share in the incarnation of God in Christ. Zen practice aims at allowing the student to acknowledge and realize the Buddha-nature and thus overcome all traces of duality. Dionysius's description of the final moment of union with God in negative language can sound at times very similar to the language of Mahayana Buddhism: "here, being neither oneself nor someone else, one is supremely united by a completely unknowing inactivity of all knowledge, and knows beyond the mind by knowing nothing" (MT 1.3 [1001A; p. 137]). Such language could indeed be used by Buddhists in their own way, but the meaning of the language would remain quite different. For Dionysius, the sacraments do not simply awaken us to who we already are; they initiate us into the life of the eternal One who entered time for our sake. In becoming human, the Deity

> allowed us, as those of equal birth, to enter into communion with it and to acquire a share of its own true beauty. ... Beneficently it wrought a complete change in our nature. It filled our shadowed and unshaped minds with a kindly, divine light and adorned them with a loveliness suitable to their divinized state (EH 3.3.11 [441B; p. 221]).

5

Pure Land Buddhism

While the traditions of Ch'an and Zen have received much recent attention in the West, another very influential Mahayana Buddhist tradition has for centuries posed a powerful counterpoint to Zen: the tradition of Pure Land Buddhism. Historically, the Pure Land tradition has had great importance for East Asia, particularly for China, Korea, Vietnam, and Japan.

Where Ch'an and Zen have often challenged their followers to cast off their own entanglements through "self-power," Pure Land Buddhism rejects the assumption that humans can awaken themselves and emphasizes the grace that comes through reliance in faith upon a savior Buddha who sets humans free.

The Pure Land tradition focuses its primary attention not on the historical Shakyamuni Buddha who lived in the past, but rather on another Buddha, a transcendent figure who reigns in the present over another world located billions of Buddha-lands away to the west. This Buddha is known as Amitabha ("limitless light") and as Amitayus ("limitless life"). These two titles express his possession of the two central Buddhist virtues. Limitless light represents his wisdom, and limitless life represents his compassion. In Japanese, both these titles are combined in the name "Amida Buddha."

EARLY PURE LAND SUTRAS

THE STORY OF DHARMAKARA

One of the earliest and most important Pure Land sutras, *The Larger Sukhavati-vyuha*, probably composed in northwest India around 100 C.E., recounts the narrative of the central figure of this form of Buddhism.[1] This sutra tells us that one day when Shakyamuni Buddha was on the Vulture Peak, his face was radiant with a special glow of joy. His disciple Ananda asked him why this was. Shakyamuni responded by telling the story of a bodhisattva named Dharmakara (sometimes also called Hozo).

102

According to Shakyamuni, many ages ago a monk named Dharmakara went to a Buddha named Lokeshvararaja and asked to be instructed so that he could become a Buddha and save humankind from suffering, old age, and death. Having been instructed, Dharmakara meditated for ages and ages upon the perfections of the land he wished to establish. Deeply moved by the suffering of sentient beings in this world, he resolved to establish another land, a Land of Bliss (*Sukhavati*) where they could be free of pain, hear true preaching, and find enlightenment. Dharmakara made a series of forty-eight vows, resolving to postpone his own enlightenment until each vow had been accomplished.[2]

In the eleventh vow Dharmakara promised that all those who are born into his Land of Bliss will attain nirvana. In the twelfth and thirteenth vows, Dharmakara vowed to achieve such merit that his light (that is, his wisdom) and his life (that is, his compassion) would be infinite, filling the entire universe. The seventeenth vow promised that his name would be proclaimed in every land and that his offer would be universally known.

The most famous of his vows was the eighteenth, in which he vowed that all sentient beings—except for those who committed the five grave offences and those who abused the true dharma—should be born in his Land of Bliss by thinking of him for ten times.

Shakyamuni further recounted that Dharmakara practiced the Buddhist virtues for immeasurable ages, accumulated enormous merit, and established a Land of Bliss in the Western part of the universe. Dharmakara has now become Amitabha Buddha, the Buddha of infinite wisdom and compassion, and reigns in his domain. Shakyamuni describes the land of Amitabha as free from hells, as filled with sweet-smelling scents and trees bearing gems (*Larger Sukhavati* 15; II, 33).

Anyone who trusts in the compassionate vow of Dharmakara and calls upon his name in faith will be reborn in his Land of Bliss, the Western Paradise. In this land beings will be free from all suffering and will be able to hear the dharma, the true Buddhist teaching, preached clearly. They will then become enlightened and be able to enter into nirvana.

THE LAND OF BLISS

In another early Pure Land sutra, *The Smaller Sukhavati-vyuha*, Shakyamuni Buddha again describes Sukhavati, the Land of Bliss, the ideal land which would later be called the Pure Land.[3] Shakyamuni portrays Sukhavati as a state of peace and joy, a land in which there is no cause of suffering and in which everything leads to the realization of the true dharma. "The very name of hells is unknown in that Buddha country" (*Smaller Sukhavati* 6; II, 97).

This sutra also emphasizes the practice of bearing the name of Amitabha Buddha in mind as a spiritual exercise. Shakyamuni explicitly denies that rebirth in this land is due to any reward for good works in this life. He promises that if anyone hears the name of Amitayus Buddha and bears it in mind for one to seven nights before death, Amitayus Buddha and a host of bodhisattvas will come to greet that person in the hour of death and welcome the person into the Pure Land (*Smaller Sukhavati* 10; II, 98-99). The practice of bearing the name of Amitayus Buddha in mind later developed into the oral recitation of the name of Amitabha Buddha and became the most characteristic mark of later Pure Land practice.[4]

MEDITATION ON AMITAYUS

The third sutra on which the Pure Land tradition is based is the *Amitayur-Dhyana Sutra*, the Sutra of the Meditation on Amitayus. According to later tradition, Shakyamuni Buddha preached this sutra to Queen Vaidehi when he was between seventy-one and seventy-nine years old.[5] The sutra begins with a dramatic episode from the life of Shakyamuni.

At the time the account begins, Devadatta, a rebellious cousin of Shakyamuni who had been his follower but later became his rival, has persuaded Prince Ajatasatru to imprison his father, King Bimbisara, with the intention of starving him so that the prince could reign. Queen Vaidehi is faithful to her husband and brings him nourishment and encouragement. When Ajatasatru learns of this, he plans to kill her, but his counselors appeal to his sense of honor and warn him of the terrible stain this would bring upon himself and his caste. Ajatasatru repents and begs for mercy, but he orders his officers to confine the queen in a hidden palace and not permit her to leave.

Queen Vaidehi, thus confined, is in great distress over the situation and prays for help from the Buddha, asking him to send his student Ananda to comfort and instruct her. In response to her prayers, Shakyamuni Buddha appears to her, and she addresses him directly: "My only prayer . . . is this: O World-Honoured One, mayst thou preach to me in detail of all the places where there is no sorrow or trouble, and where I ought to go to be born anew. I am not satisfied with this world of depravities" (*Amitayur-Dhyana Sutra* 5; II, 165).

She asks Shakyamuni to teach her how to meditate on the Land of Bliss of Amitabha Buddha. Shakyamuni gives her detailed instructions on how to meditate on Amitayus Buddha and the bodhisattvas who accompany him. He explains: "Now does thou not know, O Vaidehi, that Buddha Amitayus is not very far from here? Thou shouldst apply thy mind entirely to close meditation upon those who have already perfected the pure actions necessary for that Buddha country" (7; II, 167).

Shakyamuni explains that after she has meditated on the Buddha Amitabha and has visualized the Buddha's land, her mind will become calm. Visualization leads to samadhi, the state of concentration and tranquility, and it also brings about the expiation of past faults (11; II, 171–72). In visualizing the Buddha, Shakyamuni continues, one identifies with the Buddha: "In fine, it is your mind that becomes Buddha, nay, it is your mind that is indeed Buddha. The ocean of true and universal knowledge of all the Buddhas derives its source from one's own mind and thought" (17; II 178).

Shakyamuni goes on to list the different levels of beings who will be born in the Land of Bliss: those who have practiced compassion and virtue, those who have studied the Mahayana sutras, and those who have practiced the Buddhist precepts (22; II, 188). After listing the various ranks of these beings, Shakyamuni later promises that even if someone commits many terrible crimes, that person will be instructed to say "Adoration to Buddha Amitayus." On doing this, the person will be freed from all sins and welcomed into the Land of Bliss to hear and understand the preaching of bodhisattvas and begin the path leading to becoming a bodhisattva oneself (28; II, 195). Even the worst of criminals who have committed the five deadly sins will be advised to utter the name "Buddha Amitayus," and will be free from sins and born in the Land of Bliss (30; II, 198). On hearing the teaching of Shakyamuni Buddha, Queen Vaidehi rejoiced and became fully enlightened.

THEMES AND PRACTICE OF PURE LAND BUDDHISM

ORAL RECITATION

The custom of calling upon Buddha Amitayus would have a long and important history in the Pure Land tradition. In the late fourth century C.E. the Sutra of Visualization on the Buddha of Immeasurable Life (commonly known as *Kuan-ching*) proposed the practice of orally reciting the name of the Buddha as a more accessible means of eliminating karmic punishment for past failings.[6] While the Visualization Sutra proposed this as an easier technique for inferior persons who could not do the more difficult visualization exercises, the practice of reciting the name came to be highly valued in its own right.

Pure Land Buddhists chant "Namu Amida Butsu," which literally means "Adoration to Amida Buddha." The word *Namu*—"adoration"—has been interpreted in various ways. Namu is sometimes translated as "I take refuge,"[7] and thus the chant expresses the act of taking refuge in Amida Buddha's compassionate vow. Hozen Seki, who was the President of the American Buddhist Academy, translated Namu as "myself." According to Seki, "*Namu Amida Butsu* is an expression of oneness"—the oneness of myself and Amida Buddha. In a similar vein, D. T. Suzuki explains that "*Namu* represents self-power"; "Amida is . . . other-power. *Namu Amida Butsu* symbolizes the unification of . . . self-power and other-power."[8]

SELF-POWER AND OTHER-POWER

Since the time of T'an-luan (476–542), the Pure Land tradition has made an important distinction between self-power and Other-power. Self-power represents our own efforts to practice the Buddhist virtues and meditation; the term has often referred to the methods and strategies of Ch'an and Zen Buddhism such as zazen and koan practice. Other-power is entrusting ourselves to the working of the gracious vow of Amitabha Buddha. These terms have often marked out the lines of differentiation between the Ch'an/ Zen and Pure Land traditions. In their early developments in China the Ch'an and Pure Land traditions often borrowed freely from each other. A figure like Tsung-tse in the late eleventh century could be a leader in both Ch'an and Pure Land traditions, and the Pure Land leader T'an-luan believed that any Buddhist practice could be done as Other-power.[9] In their later Japanese developments, however, these traditions tended to be more selective and more distinct from each other.[10] Other-power came to be associated exclusively with the Pure Land practice of recitation, and all the Zen methods came to be seen as forms of self-power.

Suzuki notes that both Zen and Shin Buddhism see the human journey as leading to an abyss which gapes before us. He contrasts the leap of Zen, which is straightforward to enlightenment through self-power, with the "crosswise leap" of Shin Buddhism, which is "really discontinuous, proving that the deed springs from the 'other power' which is Amida."[11]

The traditions of self-power and Other-power, while clearly different, are not absolutely opposed to each other in Buddhist tradition, for they both apply the twofold Mahayana movement of negation and negation of negation. Both approaches must negate both "self" and "Other" in order to realize the truth of nonduality. According to Suzuki, self-power and Other-power are united in the chanting of Namu Amida Butsu. This unification is not a static oneness, however, but a dynamic process of unity in difference that constitutes the basic twofold activity of ascent and descent of Mahayana Buddhism.

ASCENT AND DESCENT: T'AN-LUAN

The great sixth-century Chinese Buddhist, T'an-luan used the image of ascent and descent to express the dynamic of movement to and from the Pure Land. T'an-luan described the first activity of the practitioner as the "aspect of going forth." In this movement of ascent a person transfers all merits toward birth in the Pure Land. Once a person has attained enlightenment in the Pure Land, the person then descends to the world of suffering. Thus the second activity is the "aspect of coming back." Once awakened, the person returns as a bodhisattva filled with compassion for all sentient beings.

T'an-luan noted, however, that it is extremely difficult to gain sufficient merit on one's own for the arduous ascent to the Pure Land. T'an-luan believed that the world had become corrupt and that no Buddha or bodhisattva was present on earth to offer guidance. In these circumstances, T'an-luan warned against relying on our own efforts and stressed the importance of trusting the vow of Amitabha Buddha. T'an-luan probably began the practice of reciting and meditating on the name of Amitabha Buddha.[12] T'an-luan also made the distinction between self-power and Other-power that would be fundamental for all later Pure Land Buddhists.

T'an-luan viewed the path of self-power as both difficult and dangerous, for it can easily assume a dualistic view of reality. If we rely on our own strength and discipline in our ascent, he warns, we can easily increase the illusion of our clinging ego-self by cultivating spiritual pride and arrogance.

T'an-luan stressed the importance of the so-called "easy path" of Other-power. Anyone can follow this path simply by trusting in the power of the vows of Dharmakara and calling upon his name.[13] T'an-luan insisted that all beings, even those who have committed the five deadly sins, can be born in the Pure Land if they recite the name of Amida Buddha ten times with faith. Anyone who does this practice is freed from the burden of sin and is assured of rebirth.

T'an-luan stressed that the ultimate cause of our salvation is not our own efforts but the compassionate vow of Amitabha Buddha. Thus we should not look to our own strength but to Amitabha's compassion. According to T'an-luan, the name of Amitabha Buddha embodies the reality of the Buddha, and thus to invoke the name of Amitabha Buddha is to become one with the reality of Amitabha Buddha.

Any dualism between self-power and Other-power is overcome in the realization that Amida Buddha is realizing his vow in our own actions. Pure Land Buddhism applies the twofold negation of the Mahayana tradition to its own path. There is a first negation when the ego-self realizes its inability to save itself. Self-power reaches its limit and collapses, surrendering to the Other-power of Amida Buddha. But then there comes a second negation when we realize that Other-power is not simply other than ourselves: self-power is one with Other-power.

The second negation also overcomes the separation between this world and the Pure Land. Realization brings the awareness that the Pure Land of Amida Buddha is not another world reached after death but is this world right now, transformed by the power of Amida's compassionate vow. As Suzuki explains, "Pure Land is not many millions of miles away in the West. According to my explanation, Pure Land is right here, and those who have eyes can see it around them. And Amida is not presiding over an ethereal paradise, but his Pure Land is this dirty earth itself."[14]

As we saw earlier, the two-directional activity of ascent and descent leads to the negating of any dualism between the two paths themselves. Nagao stresses the importance of this final negation for Pure Land Buddhism. Faith realizes there is no difference between the ascent to wisdom and the descent in compassion. In one sense, for Pure Land Buddhists, the ascent is the descent and the descent is the ascent. Wisdom and compassion are two aspects of one experience. But in another sense, Nagao comments that "it is equally true that ascent is not descent; descent is different from ascent.

... Therefore, we can say that the two directions, ascent and descent, are simultaneously identical and not identical."[15]

The two directions unite in a single experience but nonetheless retain their distinct characteristics. Nagao insists upon the importance of the aspect of return for Pure Land Buddhism and for any religion: "[U]nless concern is directed to the world once more, the ultimate goal of religion cannot be fulfilled."[16]

AMIDA BUDDHA

The trust of Pure Land Buddhism in Other-power has led some to claim that it is closer to Christianity than to authentic Buddhism. Pure Land Buddhists strenuously reject this interpretation. Ryojin Soga (1875–1971) insists that

Amida is not a transcendent Other standing opposed to, and independent of, sentient beings. Amida is inherent in all sentient beings in his Bodhisattva manifestation as Dharmakara. Amida therefore is at once innate and transcendent. . . . To be awakened to the depth of the Original Vow then means to attain the enlightened wisdom to know who one really is.[17]

According to Soga, Dharmakara is not an historical savior, but a personification of what earlier Buddhists called the "storehouse consciousness," the underlying basis of all human subjectivity. The storehouse consciousness is the basis for all forms of awareness, both ignorance and enlightenment. It is not a transcendent creator but the primordial subjectivity of every person. It is the "storehouse" from which all forms of consciousness emerge; it stores both the seeds of all future realities and also it stores up and preserves the results of all past actions. Soga notes that *akara* means "mine" or "storage," and thus *Dharmakara* means literally "storehouse of Dharma."[18]

The career of Dharmakara, for Soga, is a myth that dramatizes the situation of every sentient being. Dharmakara represents the Buddha-dharma prior to Shakyamuni Buddha which made his historical teaching possible. Dharmakara is the primordial reality of Shakyamuni and of every other person, and the narrative of Dharmakara's vow and practice and realization illustrates the relation of our own primordial subjectivity to ourselves. Thus Soga distinguishes sharply between the real savior, Dharmakara, who is the primordial, true self of each of us, and a historical teacher like Shakyamuni Buddha:

Shakyamuni is our teacher, master, father, and ideal. Dharmakara Bodhisattva, however, is the real person whom we can directly experience, for he is our own eternal actuality. The preaching of our teacher Shakyamuni urges us to hear the voice of Dharmakara Bodhi-sattva, that clarifies for us the way by which we are to return to the undefiled, pure self.[19]

SHINRAN

LIFE OF SHINRAN

One of the most influential interpreters of the Pure Land tradition is the founder of the Jodo Shinshu tradition in Japan, Shinran (1173–1262). While the details of his early life are uncertain, he was probably born into a distinguished noble family, the Fujiwara, and his parents died when he was young, leaving him to be raised by an uncle. He was trained as a monk in the Tendai school of Buddhism on Mount Hiei near Kyoto, the same monastic complex where Dogen would study slightly later.

Although Shinran practiced most diligently, he did not find enlighten-ment or peace. The harder he practiced, the more frustrated he became, and he was troubled by a deep sense of inner conflict over his own passions. In 1201 he left Mount Hiei and abandoned the "difficult path" of Tendai meditation. According to a letter of his wife, Eshinni, he received a vision in the Rokkakudo temple in Kyoto which influenced him to abandon his earlier meditation practice and to study under Honen (1133–1212), one of the leaders of Japanese Pure Land Buddhism and founder of the Jodo sect in Japan. This meant embracing the "easy path" of Honen's Pure Land Buddhism. Instead of striving to attain enlightenment through his own efforts, Shinran placed his trust in the mercy of Amida Buddha.

The influence of Honen was decisive and lasting. In place of the strict discipline of Mount Hiei, Shinran placed his entire faith in the compas-sionate vow of Amida Buddha. After six years, Honen and Shinran and other disciples were banished from Kyoto on charges of irreligious behavior. Shinran left Honen's company and lived in exile for five years, during which time he married and had children. He had to struggle to adapt to the life of an ordinary villager, for which he was not at all prepared.

As Alfred Bloom has noted, Shinran's view of human passions was trans-formed by this experience. He came to see that passions are not to be uprooted or rejected. Passions themselves are signs of the compassion of Amida Buddha.[20] After he was pardoned in 1211, he did not return to Kyoto but rather settled in Inada in eastern Japan. In 1235 he finally returned to Kyoto and lived there, writing and teaching until his death in 1262.[21]

THE HUMAN CONDITION

Shinran saw the human condition as a house on fire with passions burn-ing out of control, and he was profoundly skeptical of the ability of humans to free themselves from this condition by the traditional meditation exercises. Shinran's own experience of failure on Mount Hiei and his constant awareness of his own ignorance and attachments led him to call himself "Gutoku," literally, "foolish, bald-headed old man."[22] He recognized, and eventually accepted, his own impotence to free himself through his own power.

For Shinran, religious practices can actually deepen the human predicament when they contribute to a sense of pride and satisfaction in one's own power and attainment. Even the practice of reciting the Nembutsu is vulnerable to this danger. The desperate character of the human condition eliminates any possibility of saving ourselves, even through the best of religious observances. Apart from the vow of Amida Buddha, all humans inevitably fall into hell. Not to recognize this is to be foolish and to rely on self-power.

We are so blinded by ignorance and attached to our present condition that we do not even long for the Pure Land:

> The working of blind passion also causes us not to want to go to the Pure Land and makes us feel uneasy worrying about death when we become even slightly ill. Impossible it seems to leave this old house of agitation where we have wandered aimlessly since the beginning of time, nor can we long for the Pure Land of peace which we have yet to know.[23]

FAITH

The seriousness, indeed, the hopelessness of the human predicament in view of our own resources means that the role of Amida Buddha has to be more than simply that of a pathfinder or an example to imitate. Amida Buddha has to offer us the power of salvation itself, and so Amida Buddha, for Shinran, is the absolute source of salvation. The center of Shinran's perspective was the act of faith as the only possibility of salvation. Earlier Buddhists had often seen faith as an initial act of trust in the Buddha's teaching, a beginning moment of the process of testing and affirming the teaching as true in light of their own experience. Shinran reversed this understanding and saw the act of faith as made by Amida Buddha in the individual. Even the act of faith itself is a gift of the Buddha.

Faith means entrusting oneself and one's salvation to the vow of Amida Buddha, relying only on the Buddha's resolve and power to save. While this had often been viewed as the "easy path," Shinran felt that this was actually the more difficult path, since humans almost inevitably strive to secure their own salvation. In response to this difficulty, Amida Buddha gives even the power to trust in his vow. Amida transfers all his merit to humans so that they can pass over to the Pure Land.

For Shinran, the experience of crossing over to faith is not the gradual result of long-term discipline, nor is it a gradual deepening of trust. It is rather a sudden experience, a negation of all our earlier efforts, happening in an instant because it does not come from ourselves.[24] Conversion is a reversal of the attitude of self-reliance and a sudden entrusting of oneself to the power of Amida Buddha.[25] Shinran's own experience of rejecting the disciplines of meditation of Mount Hiei in favor of the trusting faith in Amida became the center of his religious worldview and the paradigm for the journeys of his followers.

Shinjin, Birth, and Nirvana

Shinran described this experience as realizing *shinjin*, realizing the mind of Amida Buddha. *Shin* means "to understand" or "to trust." *Shinjin* means "understanding-mind" or "trusting-mind." Shinjin is the twofold awakening to the ignorance and impotence of the self and to the infinite compassion of Amida Buddha.[26] In the experience of shinjin, the person realizes the impossibility of any form of self-salvation and places all trust in the compassionate vow of Amida Buddha. The Nembutsu is the external expression of this act of understanding and trust.

In this act of trust the blind passions of the person's mind become one with the mind of Amida Buddha. Even though the passions remain, they are negated by the power of Amida Buddha, and the person reaches the stage of non-retrogression of a bodhisattva, the stage where enlightenment is assured. This is also called the stage of being truly settled. Shinran writes: "When we are grasped by Amida, immediately—without a moment or a day elapsing—we ascend to and become established in the stage of the truly settled; this is the meaning of *attain birth*."[27]

Earlier Pure Land Buddhists had placed great stress on bearing the name of Amida in mind at the moment of death. Shinran rejected this approach, stressing that if Amida has already grasped us in the present we do not need to be anxious over the state of our mind at the moment of death: "The moment of death is not the crucial matter; from ordinary times [the person who has realized shinjin] has been constantly grasped and protected, never to be abandoned."[28]

Earlier Pure Land Buddhists had seen "birth" as being born in the Pure Land at the end of one's earthly life. While the Pure Land was not itself immediately full enlightenment, it was to be a perfect environment free from temptations and illusions. In this Pure Land one would be perfectly prepared to hear the dharma and attain enlightenment.

Shinran profoundly transformed the meaning of "being born" by using it in two senses: (1) as the attainment of shinjin and the stage of being truly settled in the present life through conversion and (2) as the birth in the Pure Land at death. Moreover, Shinran, in contrast to the earlier tradition, identified the birth in the Pure Land with supreme enlightenment.

As Yoshifumi Ueda comments, this interpretation of birth as a present experience was "an epochal development in the history of Pure Land Buddhist thought. It might even be said that the core of Shinran's thought is manifest in it."[29] This is one application of the Mahayana Buddhist principle that samsara, impermanence, is nirvana in simultaneous identity and transformation. In entrusting ourselves to Amida Buddha, we experience nirvana in the present.

Shinran identified shinjin with true reality, variously called the Buddha-nature, the dharma-nature, dharmakaya, or suchness. He can distinguish and relate shinjin to nirvana as cause to result, but seen from the perspective of suchness, the two are not different:

> When a sentient being realizes the mind (shinjin) and practice directed to him for his going forth, he immediately enters the group of the truly settled. Because he dwells in the stage of the truly settled, he necessarily attains nirvana. To necessarily attain nirvana is eternal bliss.[30]

On the one hand, nirvana is the ultimate fruit of shinjin and remains a future experience; but on the other hand, the future experience is already present in this life. From one perspective, shinjin and nirvana can be distinguished, but from another, they cannot. As Ueda comments: "We find that the one who has been born has not been born, or that one who has in the present already been born will be born in the future."[31] This is related to the more general Mahayana Buddhist principle of original enlightenment or the Buddha-nature as the ground for practice and as already present at the beginning of practice, but as requiring practice for manifestation.[32] Thus Shinran addresses in his own way the same question that had puzzled Dogen.

Nirvana is the timeless, what transcends time. The experience of shinjin is an awakening from the temporal world of samsara to the timelessness of nirvana. Nirvana is neither past nor present nor future. Shinran states: "The realm of nirvana refers to the place where one overturns the delusion of ignorance and realizes supreme enlightenment."[33] The timeless, nirvana, is both other than the world of time and not other than it. Nirvana fills the world of time, allowing all beings to attain enlightenment, and nirvana is also beyond the world of time.

On our own, humans have no way of awakening to nirvana. Nonetheless, shinjin *is* the experience of nirvana in the present world, for nirvana *is* the great wisdom and compassion which manifests itself as Amida Buddha.[34] In entrusting ourselves to the compassionate vow of Amida Buddha, we enter the realm where all oppositions between time and the timeless are negated.

PASSIONS

Identity with the mind of Amida Buddha does not simply eliminate all the passions of a person's mind, however. These remain as long as one is in this world, and so the identity of the Pure Land Buddhist with Amida Buddha is paradoxically also a non-identity, indeed, a mutual contradiction. The opposition between identity and contradiction gives rise to a process of transformation in which the blind passions are transformed into the virtues of compassion.

Shinran expresses this process in directly conflicting images, some affirming the overcoming of all obstacles and others acknowledging the perduring evils that hinder enlightenment. On the one hand, he tells us: "Unfailingly the ice of blind passions melts and immediately becomes the water of enlightenment." On the other hand, he insists: "The more ice, the more water; The more hindrances, the more virtues."[35] The more one becomes aware of oneself, the more one becomes aware of evils, and so hindrances increase; but the awareness of evils leads one to repent and be grateful for Amida Buddha's mercy, and thus helps transform the evils into virtues. Again the basic structure of Mahayana thought is expressed in the identity of mutually contradictory elements. The sinful person is one with Amida Buddha and is not one. We see ourselves as foolish sinners, and also as saved by the working of the primal vow.

DHARMAKAYA

Shinran also describes the experience of shinjin in terms of the twofold dharmakaya: (1) dharmakaya as suchness, which is absolute reality itself completely transcending time and which we are incapable of knowing, and (2) dharmakaya as compassion, the manifestation of absolute reality in this world. Shinran, like T'an-luan before him, both identifies and distinguishes these two aspects of dharmakaya: they are paradoxically one but also different.[36]

Shinran identifies dharmakaya as suchness with nirvana, and dharmakaya as compassion with Amida Buddha. Dharmakaya as suchness or nirvana is totally beyond time. Nonetheless, it is not other than Amida Buddha, dharmakaya as compassion which becomes present within time. The timeless appears in time, and humans experience the timeless as grace, as salvation, as the compassionate vow of Amida Buddha. In the experience of shinjin, we are already beyond time, even though we remain in time.

The proper religious response to the gift of shinjin or faith is gratitude. Shinran deeply distrusted any sense of religious self-confidence or self-reliance, and stressed the importance of joy and gratitude, leaping and dancing for joy at the compassionate mercy of Amida Buddha. Precisely because Shinran does not rely on his own efforts, even for the act of faith itself, he is assured of salvation. He acknowledges that his own joy and gratitude is far from perfect and often is blocked by the continued operation of blind passions, but he trusts the power of Amida's vow, since the vow was designed specifically for Shinran and beings like him.[37] Even though evil remains at work in himself, "evil need not be feared, for there is no evil which can obstruct the working of Amida's Primal Vow."[38]

Christian descriptions of the experience of grace suggest both similarities and differences to the twofold movement of Pure Land Buddhism. While the contexts of the two religious traditions differ markedly, the themes of reaching the limits of one's own power, of abandoning all efforts to save oneself, and of the death of the self have had a long history in Christian traditions of spirituality. The next chapter will explore the journey of Augustine in relation to the Mahayana tradition. Any genuine Christian experience of grace must involve both a moment of wisdom, of transforming insight into the ultimate reality of God's redeeming love, and also a moment of compassion and concern for others.

6

Augustine and Mahayana Buddhism

A late fourth- and early fifth-century Christian bishop in North Africa would have agreed with Shinran that the heart of religion is gratitude for undeserved grace received. The African bishop shared Shinran's scepticism about our ability to save ourselves from our passions and illusions and sins. He also shared Shinran's insistence that we place our faith in the power of a savior greater than ourselves. The North African's interpretation of these themes, however, differed profoundly from Shinran's use of them.

In Western Christianity the most influential single model of both theology and spirituality from the early Middle Ages to the twentieth century has been Augustine. The narrative of Augustine's life as recounted in the *Confessions* became a dominant model for later Western Christian explorations of the relation between humans and God. Later generations of Christians often read the narratives of their own lives in light of Augustine's account of his own journey. Moreover, Augustine's strategies of approaching theological issues such as the Trinity, anthropology, ecclesiology, and the theology of time and history have dominated Western Christian discussions for centuries.

This chapter will compare themes of Augustine with those of Mahayana Buddhism, beginning with Augustine's reflections on the interpretation of signs in relation to Mahayana perspectives on language and truth. For Augustine, the interpretation of signs was intimately related to his deciphering of the signs of God's love in the narrative of his own life. I will explore the transformation of Augustine's awareness in the *Confessions* in relation to the transformation of consciousness in Zen and Pure Land Buddhism. Augustine's reflection on his own personal experience was, in turn, influential in shaping his later doctrine of grace in the controversy with an Irish monk named Pelagius over grace and free will. I will examine this debate in light of Pure Land discussions of self-power and Other-power.

As in the case of Dionysius, many themes of the Mahayana tradition find analogues in Augustine: the search for wisdom, the importance of love or compassion, the images of ascending and descending, the necessity of negating one's ordinary consciousness, and the experience of powerlessness, of relying on a greater power, and of transformation. Nonetheless, as with Dionysius, powerful differences in the context of Augustine's thought give these themes very different meanings. While the Buddhist themes presuppose the universe of dependent co-arising, for Augustine, all these themes, including the experience of salvation, presuppose the prior relationship of creation. The God who redeems us is the God who created us. The search for the proper understanding of creation was an important aspect of Augustine's early quest for wisdom. While in many ways Augustine's perspectives conflict sharply with Buddhist perspectives, the play of similarity and difference can be illuminating for both traditions.

THE INTERPRETATION OF SIGNS

As we have seen, Mahayana Buddhism is sensitive to the inadequacy of language to express ultimate truth and considers all doctrines to be skillful means. Augustine was also acutely aware that our language cannot express ultimate reality, and he developed a sophisticated and influential theory of signs in order to clarify the task of preaching and teaching the Christian faith.

Augustine sets forth his method of interpretation in *On Christian Doctrine*, a handbook of interpretation that he began in 397, when he was bishop of Hippo. In the middle of writing Book Three of this work, however, he stopped writing and began composing his famous *Confessions*. Thus the principles for interpretation that he sets forth in *On Christian Doctrine* received their first application in his telling of his own life story and in the reflections on the human person, creation, time, and the interpretation of scripture in the closing books of the *Confessions*. To understand the meaning of his own life, both his past wanderings and his present task as a Catholic bishop, Augustine found that he had to learn to decipher a variety of signs: the signs of the scriptures, the signs of others' behavior, the signs of fortuitous events, and the signs of his own moods and feelings.[1] In deciphering these signs, he had to learn to discern which revealed the will of God for him.

For Augustine, the interpretation of signs is crucial to following the path of the Christian life. Our immediate understanding of ourselves and our world is systematically distorted by sin, which prevents us from seeing the signs of God's love around us. If we misinterpret signs, we inevitably misread the meaning of our emotions, as well as the true significance of the persons and objects around us. Deceived in our self-understanding, we misdirect our energies and desires, making some finite object our ultimate goal. Knowing how to interpret signs offers us the key to knowing ourselves, to seeing the temptations that deceive us, to deciphering the activity of God in our lives, and to finding the true path to wisdom and happiness.[2] For Augustine, knowledge of self and knowledge of God are inseparable, but we only know God and ourselves through the interpretation of signs.

On Christian Doctrine is an educational handbook to instruct Christian teachers and preachers and bishops to interpret signs properly so that they in turn can lead the entire Christian community. The work sets forth a system of Christian eloquence and rhetoric, a way of interpreting the scriptures to clarify the meaning of human existence. To accomplish this end, it also offers us a theory of language to clarify the way we speak of God and human existence. Throughout this work Augustine assumes that the signs of the Bible come from God and are God's gracious gifts to illumine our path.

LANGUAGE AND THE ULTIMATE

For Augustine, we can never directly describe the reality of God. The incomprehensibility of God is a basic principle that guides all interpretation of language about God. As he proclaimed in his own preaching: "If you have comprehended, what you have comprehended is not God" (*Si comprehendis, non est Deus*).[3] If we think we understand literally what our words about God mean, we have mistaken our own finite thoughts for the infinite divine reality. The literal meaning of any human concept or image or analogy must be negated when applied to God. Despite this radical limitation on all language about God, human words can be used by God to transcend themselves and communicate knowledge of the eternal Word which is the ground of all knowledge and language. The narratives and images and hymns of the scriptures are so many gifts of God to us, to call us out of illusion and sin to the road home. Even though we never fully comprehend their significance when applied to God, the words of the scriptures can transform our lives and guide us to salvation.

As we have seen, Mahayana Buddhists affirm that ultimate truth cannot be captured in words, but conventional truth expressed through skillful means can transcend itself and lead us to the ultimate truth. No words can literally state the meaning of shunyata or nirvana or dharmakaya, but skillful means can lead us to the experience of ultimate truth which is beyond words. The skillful means of the Buddha are not gifts of a creating and redeeming God, but they do manifest the graciousness of the Buddha, the bodhisattvas, and thus of dharmakaya, of absolute reality itself. The Buddhas know reality as it is, and they also understand the different forms of ignorance that hinder humans from knowing reality. The skillful means of the Buddhas and bodhisattvas awaken us from ignorance, separate us from our attachments, and aid the process of becoming who we are. For both Mahayana Buddhism as well as for Augustine, no language can literally convey ultimate truth, but language properly used and understood can guide us to a true vision of ourselves and our world. For both, true language about ultimate reality comes as a gracious gift.

Even in making such distinctions and comparisons, the problem of language immediately presents itself, however. Augustine warns us that we cannot really talk about the one reality that we should enjoy because God is ineffable, and thus Augustine has not said what he wished to say (1.6.6). This places a strong negative limit on the entire project of theological reflection. In talking about God we do not know what we are talking about. If we think we have captured the reality of God by stating that God is ineffable, we have missed the point, and thus God should not be said to be ineffable: "If what I said were ineffable, it would not be said. And for this reason God should not be said to be ineffable, for when this is said something is said" (1.6.6.; p. 11).

Augustine finds a dialectic between the said and the unsaid which leads into a seeming contradiction, a paradox which he advises us to pass over in silence rather than trying to resolve it in words. God both is and is not ineffable. The unsaid ineffable reality of God is not what is said by the word *ineffable*. The reality of God (like nirvana or dharmakaya or absolute truth of Mahayana Buddhism) is never what is said. The reality of God is not the same as the sign, but the reality can only be known and make itself known through signs. Where Dionysius and the Mahayana tradition explicitly acknowledge a twofold negation, there is a double negation implicit in Augustine: (1) a negation of everything we say of God, since God is ineffable; and (2) a negation of the negation, since calling God "ineffable" does not resolve the problem, and thus God is not ineffable. We have to negate even our negations to communicate truthfully concerning God.

In Buddhism the notion of skillful means has sometimes allowed for the mutual acceptance of differing Buddhist traditions which conflict and even directly contradict each other. Tendai Buddhism in China and Japan adopted this conciliatory approach, interpreting a wide variety of Buddhist doctrines as equally legitimate skillful means. A number of major Buddhist figures, however, including both Dogen and Shinran, saw their own respective approaches not merely as one among many possible skillful means, but as "the only true ways to express the highest teaching of the one vehicle."[4]

Augustine's recognition of the incomprehensibility of God does not go as far as Tendai Buddhism in accepting alternate formulations of the truth. Augustine remains rather closer to the selective approaches of Dogen and Shinran in his insistence on the language of the Catholic Church. Augustine's insistence on the literal inadequacy of human language to express the divine does not mean that all formulations are equally acceptable: some are relatively more adequate than others, and some expressions are officially sanctioned by Church teaching. Augustine clearly affirms the necessity of the proper language, as in trinitarian doctrine, even though he knows this language is only relatively, never absolutely, adequate. Where Dogen and Shinran were profoundly sceptical of alternate interpretations of the

Buddhist dharma, Augustine would never admit that the formulations of the heretical Arians or Donatists or Pelagians were equally acceptable alternative construals of the divine mystery beyond language.

PRINCIPLES OF INTERPRETATION

Augustine begins his discussion in *On Christian Doctrine* by offering some fundamental principles of interpretation. He anticipates the objections of his opponents and blames them for misunderstanding him, in effect launching a preemptive strike to silence his critics before they can attack him. Behind the rhetorical device is a somber recognition of how fragile human communication is: Augustine is a professional rhetorician beginning a work on how to communicate, and he admits that he cannot communicate without the illumination of God (Prologue, 2–3; pp. 3–4). Communication concerning the most important matters in life is not within the reach of humans by our own power alone. Ignorance and misunderstanding are pervasive in human life, and we cannot free ourselves from them on our own.

In response to this dilemma, Augustine appeals to the fundamental principle of divine illumination that he had set forth in his earlier dialogue with his son, Adeodatus.[5] No human being can teach another human being anything in the true sense of the word. We can point out signs which point to realities, but we cannot force people to see the realities themselves, nor can we give them the power to see. The only true teacher is God, whose illuminating light is directly present to every human mind.

In light of this principle, Augustine chides his critics, warning that they "should stop blaming me and ask God to give them vision. Although I can lift my finger to point something out, I cannot supply the vision by means of which either this gesture or what it indicates can be seen" (Prologue, 4; p. 4). Augustine uses the image familiar to Zen: a finger pointing to the moon. The context is very different, however: He remarks rather sarcastically that if his foes want to see the moon and they cannot even see his finger which points to the moon, they should not become angry with him because he cannot give them eyesight (Prologue, 3; p. 4)! For Augustine, as for Zen, what matters is to see the moon, and all religious language, including the "finger" of his interpretation of Christian doctrine, is a means to the end of true seeing.

Even though human instruction alone is never adequate, Augustine advises us that we should try to learn whatever we can from humans, because God can illumine us in this way, too. In Augustine's thought there is a "double" agency throughout human life which is not simply "double" in a direct, dualistic sense. God alone enables us to know the true and to will the good, but God also acts through other persons without destroying their own power to act. Augustine even tells us that "charity itself, which holds men together in a knot of unity, would not have a means of infusing souls and almost mixing them together if men could teach nothing to men" (Prologue, 6; p. 6). This principle coheres with Augustine's later principle on grace and free will: only God's grace can save us, but grace can come to us through the mediation of other human beings. The action of God and the action of humans is not simply the same but not completely separate. In and through human words and deeds, the love of God can be at work. Both the distinction of creatures from their Creator and the oneness of creatures with their Creator are overarching hermeneutical principles for Augustine, and much of the tension of his thought comes from the inter-relation between these two principles.

In Mahayana Buddhism the concrete words and actions of Buddhist teachers are also the skillful means of absolute reality, dharmakaya itself, which appeared in Shakyamuni. For Ch'an and Zen traditions, the teachings and actions of the Ch'an or Zen masters *are* the teachings and actions of the Buddha. For Shinran, the experience of shinjin *is* the experience of dharmakaya as compassion appearing as Amitabha Buddha. In whatever form of Mahayana Buddhism, the human teachers present insight into absolute reality and truth through the language of conventional truth, and dharmakaya manifests itself. While the question of double agency in Augustine's sense never arises, nonetheless there is a dialectic of self-power and Other-power which is overcome in the realization of Mahayana wisdom.

While Augustine would not accept the Buddhist principles of nonduality and dependent co-arising which negate a creating God, neither would he affirm a naively dualistic understanding of God as a being external to the world. As the infinite source of all that is, God is not simply opposed to the finite: God is within the finite, and the finite is within God. Indeed, for Augustine, it is impossible to state clearly and directly what the act of creation is, for it is a unique relation, quite different from our relationship to all finite realities. In the end, Augustine will only understand creation properly from the perspective of grace.

Where Vimalakirti expressed the Buddhist principle of nonduality with a thundering silence, Augustine knows that no words can express the reality of God. He would prefer to be silent, but the responsibility of his public position as bishop and the needs of his audience demand that he write and speak. He preaches and writes out of compassion for his people.

Augustine's reference to charity (*caritas*) introduces his most fundamental principle for all interpretation and the key to the reading of all of scripture: Scripture teaches nothing but the double love of God and neighbor. Anyone who finds a different meaning in the Bible does not understand it at all (1.36.40; p. 30). Anyone who finds a meaning in scripture that coheres with caritas has found a true interpretation. Even if this was not apparent to the human author of the text, it was foreseen and intended by the divine author, who is love itself. Thus one sentence can summarize the message of the entire Bible: "Scripture teaches nothing but charity, nor condemns anything except cupidity, and in this way shapes the minds of men" (3.10.15; p. 88).

Where Augustine turns to caritas, the Mahayana tradition has turned to the principle of compassion as the overarching hermeneutical principle for reading all the sutras and all of Buddhist teaching. *The Awakening of Faith*, an important text of Mahayana Buddhism attributed to Ashvaghosha, presents the freedom of the bodhisattvas in teaching the Buddhist way to their followers. In order to be of maximum help to all sentient beings, the bodhisattvas "do not rely on words"; they are not confined to a literal interpretation of the Buddhist scriptures but, as Yoshita Hakeda comments on this text, "are ready to interpret them freely, accommodating their interpretation to all possible situations of suffering beings, with the single aim of helping them to advance to the way of salvation."[6] Where Augustine finds his basic principle of interpretation in caritas, the fundamental hermeneutical principle for the bodhisattva is compassion. In each case, the underlying value — Christian love or Buddhist compassion — provides the key to interpreting the words of the scriptures.

SIGNS AND REALITIES

Augustine develops his theory of communication by distinguishing between realities (*res*) and signs (*signa*). Realities are learned by signs, and so a sign is a means to an end.[7] We need signs, but we should not cling to them for their own sake. In the case of signs of God, signs should point beyond themselves to God, the ground of all true communication. Since it is not the sign that matters but the reality to which it points, to cling to the sign is to misunderstand its meaning. Elsewhere he compares even the words of scripture to clouds against the face of heaven: they can be luminous with the light of heaven, but they can also be concealing.[8] Without a consciousness illumined by God, even divinely revealed words fail to convey their message. Where the Mahayana tradition insists on the dynamic of negation to understand Buddhist teachings, Augustine knows that we must not cling to signs, mistaking them for God, but we must negate them by moving through and beyond them into God.

The dialectic of sign and reality in communication is one of the most fascinating and paradoxical relationships in Augustine's thought. We need to have some sense of the reality we are interpreting in order to interpret the signs. If we do not know a reality at all, words about the reality will not help us very much. But we learn realities through signs (*On Christian Doctrine*, 1.2.2; p. 8). So we can only learn and communicate the reality intended through signs.

This leaves us with the puzzle: Which comes first? We can only understand the reality through the signs, but we can only make sense of the signs if we understand the reality. The power that undergirds this dialectic and makes it fruitful is the illumination of Christ. On our own we cannot understand either the reality or the sign, but the eternal Word establishes the signs which lead us to itself. The reality we are to understand is God, who is love, and the signs that reveal God are expressions of the divine love.

This means that for Augustine, theology and rhetoric must proceed indirectly through the interpretation of signs, while relying on the assistance of the divine reality which is being interpreted. Where Mahayana Buddhists acknowledge that we cannot state ultimate truth directly and must use the conventional truth of skillful means to communicate, Augustine warns us that we cannot state directly what God is, and thus we make a detour through signs. Where Augustine interprets the signs of the scriptures as gifts of God, the Mahayana interprets the teachings of Buddhism as manifestations of dharmakaya as compassion. For both Augustine and Mahayana Buddhists, we have to be illumined by the reality of which the text speaks if we are to understand the text.

The Zen tradition warns that we do not understand the meaning of its teaching without the experience of inner awakening, the direct transmission from mind to mind. Unless we have awakened to reality as it is, all the skillful means of Zen teaching, whether sutras or koans or zazen, will not help us. To use words or imitate actions without the direct transmission from mind to mind is simply to persist in delusion. Yet it is through the different practices of Buddhism that we come to awaken. To interpret the skillful means, we need to know reality as it is, but we come to know reality as it is through skillful means.

Where Augustine turned to the theory of illumination from the power of God to resolve the dilemma of learning what cannot be said directly, Mahayana Buddhism developed the notion of the Buddha-nature which is always present as the ground of practice and awakening.[9] For Augustine, the illumination of Christ allows us to see signs as pointing to the divine reality; for Mahayana Buddhism, the Buddha-nature which we already are allows us to awaken to the reality communicated through skillful means. Yet, as Dogen insisted, the Buddha-nature is not manifested apart from practice. It cannot be abstracted and idealized as an essence apart from the universe. For Dogen, manifestation and practice are inseparable. For both Augustine and the Mahayana, we must seek in order to find, but the reality we seek is in some way present to us as the ground of our seeking from the beginning.

Two Loves

Augustine further develops his principles of interpretation through a far-reaching distinction between the types of realities we interpret: (1) realities that are to be enjoyed and (2) realities that are to be used. He explains: "To enjoy something is to cling to it with love for its own sake. To use something, however, is to employ it in obtaining that which you love, provided it is worthy of love" (1.2.4; p. 9). The only realities to be enjoyed in the strict sense of the term are the Persons of the Trinity: Father, Son, and Spirit (1.5.5; p. 10). Everything else should be used.

Thus we should use this world and not enjoy it, so that we may enjoy God (1.4.4; p. 10). Even other people are not to be enjoyed for their own sakes, but only in God. When we enjoy others in God, it is God rather than the people that we enjoy (1.33.36; p. 28). To cling to another person as our final goal is a form of illusion and idolatry.

In light of this distinction, Augustine organizes all human experience around two loves: (1) the true love (*caritas*) which is centered on God and "uses" every other reality on its path of return to God; and (2) the false self-centered and self-destructive love (*cupiditas*), which loves and clings to finite realities for their own sake and thereby falls into idolatry. In Augustine's theology of history, these two loves build two cities, the City of God, consisting of those being saved, and the City of the Devil, consisting of those on the path to damnation.

Where Mahayana Buddhism finds the central problem of human existence in the ignorance of deluded, discriminating consciousness that believes in an illusory self and world waiting to be dominated, Augustine locates the fundamental problem in cupiditas, the choosing of some creature instead of the Creator. For both Augustine and the Mahayana, this deluded decision disorients our entire perception of the world and prevents us from knowing who we are. The illusory self that makes itself or some concrete object the center cannot see reality and cannot interpret language properly.

For Augustine, the only way we can escape the prison of cupiditas is through the grace of God. The love of God uses human words, allows them to refer to the divine reality, and empowers them to transform our consciousness and our lives. Again there is a dialectic between reality and sign. The reality of God chooses to allow the sign to refer to God, even though the sign is radically inadequate to the task. For Augustine, every sign is a means to an end, and the signs that God establishes are always means to the end of knowing and loving God.[10]

Where the Buddhist tradition sees its language as a help on the path of wisdom and compassion, Augustine sees language about God as part of a journey or a voyage home (1.10.10; p. 13). For Augustine, as for Mahayana Buddhists, language about ultimate reality is not neutral, objective, or objectifying language. Augustine warns us that religious language cannot be used properly if our consciousness is not prepared to use it: "the mind should be cleansed so that it is able to see that light and to cling to it once it is seen" (1.10.10; p. 13). The use of language about God is self-involving and transformative of the self.

THE PATH OF THE CHRISTIAN LIFE

The interpretation of signs is a guide to the path of the Christian life, and for Augustine, this path is a search for wisdom. Augustine assumes that we cannot follow this path without divine assistance. Wisdom incarnate in Christ is both the goal (our native country) and also the Way to that country (1.11.11; p. 13). On this journey we should love others for the sake of God, not for our sake or their sakes. In this sense we should "use" other people, i.e., love them for the sake of God. We should not enjoy ourselves either, in the strict sense of the term, but should love ourselves for the sake of God rather than for our own sake.

The principle of the two loves means we must not cling to any temporal reality. We are on a journey, and "nothing should hold us on the road, for the Lord Himself, although He saw fit to become our road, did not wish to hold us upon it, but wished that we pass on, lest we cling in infirmity to temporal things" (1.34.38; p. 30). Augustine insists as firmly as the Buddhist tradition on the need for detachment, for not clinging to any finite realities. Only in detachment can we find ourselves and our God.

For Augustine, detachment does not mean the eradication of desires but their transformation. Feelings, strivings, desires are crucial to understand the religious journey. Augustine comments that we are on "a road of affections." The road of affections itself is not bad, but it is blocked "by the malice of our past sins," and we need someone to clear the road for us to pass (1.17.16; p. 16). For Augustine, moods and mood shifts can be profoundly revealing disclosures of who we are and of where God is calling us to go. Oriented by the fundamental value of caritas, our desires cease to be our tyrants and can become the pathway of our return to God. Augustine interprets the principle of the two loves to mean that "it is not the use of the things but the desire of the user which is culpable" (3.12.18; p. 90).

Caritas becomes, in Augustine's hands, a synthesis of *agape* (love as gift from God) and eros (striving, desire, and need).[11] Augustine's interpretation of *eros* comes from his reflection on his own life journey, expressed in his famous affirmation at the beginning of the *Confessions*: "The thought of you stirs him [the human person] so deeply that he cannot be content unless he praises you, because you made us for yourself and our hearts find no peace until they rest in you."[12] God's love (agape) in creating is the primordial gift which sets the stage for the search for God, the restlessness of our hearts that are always seeking (eros) until they find peace in God. Hans Urs von Balthasar has commented on the dynamic striving of eros in Augustine's thought and life:

> No-one has praised God so assiduously as the supreme beauty or attempted so consistently to capture the true and the good with the categories of aesthetics as Augustine in the period during and after his conversion. And this was not just in words, but also in action: the *eros* with which he seeks the true and wants the good is, in both Christian and Platonic terms, an active enthusiasm which . . . does not cease to press back unswervingly towards the point at which God had

unveiled himself to the enflamed heart of the young man as the supreme beauty.[13]

The Buddhist tradition has long been suspicious of desire as the source of suffering, and the awakened Buddhist is no longer dominated by the desires of a discriminating consciousness. Freed from the tyranny of desires, the bodhisattva can move freely in the world, affirming the desires that were negated in the path of the ascent without being driven by them. As we have seen, Shinran viewed blind passions themselves as the gift of Amida Buddha.

Augustine outlines seven stages on the path to God, a path which begins with fear arising from the thought of our mortality and our future death (2.7.9; p. 38). Augustine, like the young Prince Siddhartha, sees the path to wisdom as beginning with the awakening to the impermanence of human life. In Augustine's own life the awareness of evil as impermanence leading to death was an earlier and more fundamental problem than that of moral evil. For Augustine, recognition of our own mortality starts us on a journey which leads to piety and meekness and then to knowledge.

The Mahayana tradition insists that wisdom express itself in a compassionate return to the world; Augustine begins his journey with knowledge, but genuine knowledge leads beyond itself and expresses itself in action, which Augustine describes as fortitude, a hunger and thirst for justice. Fortitude, in turn, leads beyond itself to mercy, to the cleansing of the eye through which God may be seen, and finally to the peace and tranquility of wisdom (2.7.9–11; pp. 38–40).

In Mahayana Buddhism, the outcome of the process is assured, for, as Michael Pye points out:

> The release of all sentient beings is guaranteed in the nirvana of any one bodhisattva, a nirvana postponed and yet assured. . . . [A]s the Lotus Sutra puts it, all things are nirvanic from the beginning. The path of a bodhisattva is to know this, and at the same time to keep on playing the game of skillful means to save people from themselves.[14]

For Mahayana Buddhists, there is no division of the human race into two cities, and there is no everlasting hell or risk of eternal separation from ultimate reality. In the Mahayana universe, no one is lost forever. The failure to awaken prolongs the cycle of suffering, but does not condemn us to everlasting ignorance, for the skillful means of the Buddhas and bodhisattvas are ultimately efficacious. For Augustine, the risk in interpreting signs is far more dangerous: we can fail, and our own eternal destiny is at stake. Indeed, apart from the grace of God, we inevitably do fail. As he would later affirm more explicitly, only the predestining grace of God can reorient our lives.

This is one of the most far-reaching differences between Augustine and Mahayana Buddhism. Where Origen had earlier expressed the Christian hope that all humans and even the devil would be saved in the end, Augustine disagreed. To misunderstand the signs of God is to misunderstand ourselves and God and to choose some finite reality in place of God. Unless God intervenes, this leads inevitably to everlasting separation from God. For Augustine the interpretation of signs is crucial to living the Christian life, but it is ultimately only the power of God that allows us to interpret signs correctly.

THE *CONFESSIONS*

Augustine interrupted the writing of *On Christian Doctrine* to compose his most famous work, the *Confessions*. The first nine books of the *Confessions* recount Augustine's series of conversions in his own personal search for wisdom, happiness, and truth. Books 10–13 complement the narrative of Augustine's life by meditating on the human person in relation to memory, time, and creation. The entire work is a profound meditation on the human person in relation to God, both in Augustine's personal struggles and in the more theoretical discussions of the closing books.

In this work Augustine is trying to find words to praise God for God's grace to him, and he is trying to appropriate his own identity more profoundly by confessing his sins and exploring the meaning of his process of conversion. Through reflection on his own experience, Augustine was convinced that God's grace was absolutely necessary for the process of returning to God. God is constantly acting through the persons that Augustine meets and through Augustine's own inner experiences. The free, gratuitous intervention of God is indispensable for genuine knowledge and for conversion. Everything that Augustine has learned about himself and God is from the light of God's truth (*Confessions*, 10.40).[15]

GOD AS AUDIENCE

Augustine addresses the *Confessions* to God, and begins by noting the paradox of addressing this audience. There is nothing of Augustine that God does not know, even though there is much of Augustine that Augustine himself does not know and God does. Where Augustine has hidden from himself, God acts through other persons to force Augustine to face himself, to see himself in all his sinfulness (e.g., 8.7). Augustine can tell God nothing new about himself, and so his confession is not a revelation to God, but it may be an occasion of self-knowledge for Augustine himself and for his human readers.

In recounting his life before God in the implicit presence of human readers, Augustine is coming to know himself. From the first page of the *Confessions* to the last, knowledge of God and knowledge of self are tightly interwoven. As our knowledge of God is transformed, so too is our knowledge of ourselves, until we come to know ourselves as absolutely dependent on God for every good. Our knowledge of ourselves is so warped and twisted by sin that the only way we can truly know ourselves is through God's grace, and this means that genuine knowledge is only possible in love.[16]

Augustine's addressing his *Confessions* to God is in stark contrast to the Buddhist tradition. Where Mahayana Buddhists such as Yoshifumi Ueda affirm that "Buddha is none other than the sentient being who has awakened to his true self,"[17] Augustine distinguishes sharply between all created reality and God: "I scrutinized all these things and stood back in awe, for without you I could see none of them, and I found that none of them was you."[18] Augustine recognizes the transience, the impermanence, the contingency of all the things of the universe, but he interprets impermanence not as a sign of co-dependent arising but as the mark of the dependence of all created things upon God. For the Mahayana tradition, impermanence is ultimate reality; for Augustine, impermanence is absolutely dependent on ultimate reality for its very being.

Where Mahayana Buddhism sees the true identity of the human person and of all reality as the Buddha-nature, Augustine sees the true identity of the human person in the image of God within. For the Buddhist tradition, the meaning of the Buddha-nature manifests itself in the concrete experience of wisdom and compassion; for Augustine, the activities of knowing and loving are the image of God within us, a reflection of the triune God.[19] As intended by God, the image of God within us should have allowed us to know and love in imitation of God and to accept God's love. The ravages of sin, however, both original sin and our own personal sinning, have destroyed the salvific capacity of the image of God. While the image is always present from our creation, it has been so damaged and distorted by sin that humans are powerless to know and love truly apart from grace. Where Dogen saw all beings *as* the Buddha-nature, he also insisted that practice was necessary to manifest their true identity. For Augustine, we always *are* the image of God, but we must be saved from sin in order for this to become manifest and efficacious.

For Augustine, salvation involves coming to know who we really are, but this breakthrough is only possible through the grace of God allowing us to become one with God. If we know ourselves truly, then we know ourselves as created in the image of God, but as warped by sin and in need of redemption. Full recognition of the image of God within will allow us to live out the trinitarian image of God in human knowing and loving. If we truly love another human being, Augustine will also insist, then at least implicitly we know and love the triune God.[20]

A Paradigmatic Life Story

Augustine tells his own life story as a paradigm of God's plan for every person. While God's care for him is most personal, the pattern of God's love is universal. Thus Augustine's own journey reveals the pattern of every human life as a prodigal child, a lost sheep.[21] In the experience of his own life, Augustine finds revealed the archetypal journey of the human race: Augustine himself is Adam and Odysseus and the Prodigal Son. Every human person has a unique history, and the real meaning of this history is the relation of the soul to God, revealed in the universal struggle between the two conflicting loves of charity and cupidity. Where the narrative of the life of Shakyamuni Buddha became paradigmatic for the Mahayana bodhisattva ideal, Augustine understands the narrative of his life not directly on the model of the sinless Jesus Christ but more closely on the model of the sinful Adam or the Prodigal Son.

The life of Shakyamuni Buddha sets forth the paradigm of awakening from illusion to truth, followed by the manifestation of the goodness of all reality in the preaching of the dharma. Augustine's life story is also an awakening from illusion to truth and an exultation in the glory of all reality, but his paradigm concretely follows the rather different model of redemption from sin through the grace of a divine savior. Where the Buddha awakened by his own power, Augustine's experience is rather closer to Shinran's, for he finds himself powerless to free himself.

FINITE AND INFINITE

As Augustine begins his invocation of God at the very beginning of the *Confessions*, he notes that humans carry around our mortality and the testimony of our own sin (1.1). These are the two forms of nonbeing that threaten our very existence: death threatens our earthly life and sin our everlasting life. As fallen creatures we are mortal and sinful, and the meaning of human life will be discovered only by wrestling with both our mortality and our sinfulness before God.

Augustine also reflects on the paradoxical mystery of God's transcendence and immanence. This mystery dominates his discussion of both creation and grace and gives rise to ever new attempts to express God's omnipresence and God's otherness. Where Dogen had held that all things always already are the Buddha-nature, Augustine recognizes that even though he has wandered far from God, he has not strayed from God's presence at all, for God is always there:

> For I should not be there at all unless, in this way, you were already present within me. I am not in hell, and yet you are there too. . . . So, then, I should be null and void and could not exist at all, if you, my God were not in me. Or is it rather that I should not exist, unless I existed in you? (1.2; p. 22).

Augustine has been absent from the innermost reality of his own life. Augustine's God is clearly not one more being alongside of other beings or separate from the world, for then God would be finite. Creation in no way means that God is an external maker of the world, for the world is in God, and God is in the world with an intimacy so close to us that we do not know how to express it. All things cry out that they are made; they are in themselves insubstantial but can become transparent to God's glory.

The infinity of God is literally unimaginable, and so Augustine twists language to evoke some sense of the reality of God. Where the Mahayana tradition oscillates between viewing the universe as one and as many, as dharmakaya and as the ten thousand things, Augustine's language oscillates between a vision of God as omnipresent to the extent that God seems to be the only agent in all the universe and an affirmation of distinctions between the infinite God and finite realities through the image of creation and emanation.[22] On the one hand, the creature's actions risk being swallowed up by God; on the other hand, our ability to sin shows most clearly that we are not simply acting on behalf of God but can assert our own independence sinfully against God.

THE DESCENT

Augustine recounts his downward journey into the depths of hell. This is a journey away from God and away from himself. Augustine recognizes the paradox in even describing this senseless journey toward destruction. There is no reason for sin, and thus no knowledge of it in the proper sense. Sin has no efficient cause, but only deficient causes. As a form of nonbeing, sin cannot be comprehended. Augustine elsewhere poses the question: What is the cause of the movement of the will away from God? He answers: "If you ask this, and I answer that I do not know, probably you will be saddened. And yet that would be a true answer. That which is nothing cannot be known."[23]

Where the Buddhist tradition finds the origin of suffering in the cravings that come from ignorance, for Augustine the root of all sin is turning away from God; but this turning away is itself a form of ignorance of who we really are and gives rise to cravings very similar to those found in Buddhist descriptions. As Augustine comments: "[M]y sin was this, that I looked for pleasure, beauty, and truth not in [God] but in myself and his other creatures, and the search led me instead to pain, confusion, and error" (*Confessions* 1.20; pp. 40–41).

Augustine knows how powerful cravings can be in warping human life, and he describes his own experience of a triple concupiscence, a threefold lust for power, for gazing at spectacles, and for feeling sensual pleasure (3.6; p. 66), or, as he would later put it, pride, curiosity, and concupiscence. Conversion to God will strip these away and replace them with humility, charity, and wisdom. Where Augustine presents the main categories of sin as pride, curiosity, and concupiscence, the Buddhist tradition has described the three poisons of human life as ignorance, anger, and greed. The experience of Buddhist awakening transforms these poisons into the virtues of realization, wisdom, and compassion.

Augustine takes a seemingly trivial incident from his youth, the theft of pears from a garden, as a paradigmatic case which reveals the essential nature of the descent into sin (2.4–10; pp. 47–53). The very triviality of the incident is itself revelatory of the nature of sin as impotent before the ultimate power of God. As von Balthasar has commented, for both Dionysius and Augustine, evil and sin are powerless to destroy the divine order of the cosmos; "at best they contribute to its clearer revelation."[24]

The setting of the theft is also significant. The pear tree in a garden recalls and parallels the setting of the fall of Adam and Eve, the great archetype of sinful humanity. Gardens will recur throughout the *Confessions*, as places of temptation and falling, but also of conversion and of union with God. Augustine will experience his conversion to Catholic Christianity in a garden, and he and his mother will share the mystic vision at Ostia while overlooking a garden. The garden for Augustine plays a role analogous to the forest in the Buddhacarita or the desert in the Bible: it is a place of testing, of sin, but also of transformation and insight and union with ultimate reality.

Not only is eating the forbidden fruit common to the account of Adam and Eve and Augustine's theft, both acts are gratuitous: neither Augustine nor Adam and Eve were in need of food. Augustine's pleasure lay in the evil deed itself. Moreover, the sin was done in the company of others; his accomplices urged him on, and he protests that he would not have done it alone. The boyhood solidarity in sinfulness becomes a symbol of the solidarity of the entire human race in sin.

Augustine's act gave him and his companions a perverted sense of liberty. This false sense of freedom is a parody of the true freedom of God, and echoes the promise of the serpent in Genesis that humans shall be like gods if they eat the fruit. Thus sin appears as a gratuitous, communal act, which promises a false liberty. In effect, sin is an attempt to make oneself like God and involves a deluded self-consciousness and false notions of happiness and freedom.

Where the Buddhist tradition found cravings arising from the illusion of an independently existing substantial self, Augustine sees sin as arising from a deluded notion of who we are, a false sense of freedom, and a futile attempt to make ourselves into gods. Both the Buddhist tradition and Augustine see our illusions as rooted in a false notion of independence. The Mahayana tradition corrects this illusion with a vision of dependent co-arising; Augustine, by contrast, finds our true identity in our absolute dependence on the God who created us. Augustine finds the core problem of humans in the deluded efforts of a self trying to become God, while the unique character of the divine reality is precisely its independence. To attempt to become God is to be deceived by the illusion of one's independent existence.

PRELIMINARY CONVERSIONS

On his journey into sin and illusion, Augustine progressively destroys his own freedom to choose the good. He is troubled by the problem of evil, however, and this will become increasingly an obsession for him, and ultimately will be important for the road of his return to God. His dissatisfaction with his present condition serves as a spur to further inquiry. He experiences a conversion to philosophy, in the literal sense of the "love of wisdom," through his reading of Cicero's *Hortensius*. While this conversion is not yet the complete discovery of the truth, it is the beginning of his turning to the truth, and it will be a lasting conversion that will shape his entire life. In many ways, for Augustine, the soul is led by the thirst for wisdom and truth, which is inseparable from the quest for happiness.[25]

Augustine's search for truth does go astray, as it leads him to the Manichees; but the dynamism of the quest itself will, guided by God's grace, eventually lead him to God. After spending nine years with the Manichees, who posit evil as a separate power against God, Augustine has the opportunity to meet and question Faustus, one of their bishops and leading teachers. His disappointment with Faustus's answers leads to his disillusionment with the entire Manichean path, and he continues his search.

Next Augustine learns from the Platonists that evil does not exist of itself; it is not an independently existing reality, but only a twisting and warping of the good things God has made. Evil is a form of nonbeing, the absence of a good that should be present, and thus it does not require a creator to explain it. The Platonists teach Augustine to think of spiritual realities which he cannot imagine: not everything real is a body. This is another decisive breakthrough that will shape Augustine's entire life and thought, but it is not yet the final truth.

The understanding of good and evil is another far-reaching difference between Augustine and the Mahayana tradition. Mahayana Buddhism presupposes the ethical principles of the beginning of the eightfold path but then proceeds to apply the dialectic of negation and affirmation to the distinction between good and evil, in accordance with the basic structure of Mahayana thought. As Masao Abe explains:

> In Buddhism . . . what is essential for salvation is not to overcome evil with good and to participate in the supreme Good, but to be emancipated from the existential antinomy of good and evil. In the existential awakening to Emptiness, one can be master of, rather than enslaved by, good and evil.[26]

Where the Mahayana moves beyond the discriminating consciousness of good and evil to transcend the distinction in emptiness, Augustine insists firmly on the reality of the good and the ultimate unreality of evil. For Augustine, the interpretation of evil is set by his doctrine of creation: whatever God has created is good, and evil can only be the perversion of the will turning to a finite reality rather than to God. As we have seen, Mahayana Buddhism negates the path of ascending and descending itself, negating even the distinction between the ignorant and the enlightened. Augustine can transcend the distinction between good and evil in all the things that God has made (7.13; pp. 148–49), and he can certainly acknowledge sinful elements lingering in the forgiven Christian who is being healed by grace, but he would never negate the distinction between the sinner and the saved or between the City of God and the City of the Devil.

Even though Augustine accepts the Platonic philosophers' understanding of evil as a privation of the good, he soon discovers that the ethics of Socrates and Plato are impossible for him to practice. Where the Platonists promised that to know the good is to do the good, Augustine learns bitterly that his own experience is rather more like Paul's, and also like Shinran's: even though he can see the good, he is unable to do the good he wills to do.

DEADLOCK AND BREAKTHROUGH

Despite his best insights and intentions, Augustine is unable to master his passions and desires. Even though his mind has accepted a new understanding of the true and the good, he finds his own will bifurcated, and he feels powerless to resolve the deadlock. He wills to live as a celibate Catholic Christian in order to seek wisdom through contemplation and philosophical reflection, but he is still a slave of his desires and cannot bring himself to take this step. Even though he has the examples of Marius Victorinus and Anthony to inspire him, he cannot resolve the crisis. He learns that he cannot break through the deadlock of his own will and set himself free. Like Shinran, Augustine learns through bitter personal experience that to know the good is not sufficient; Augustine needs the grace of God.

O'Connell distinguishes three related notions of faith which are interwoven in the account of his conversion. Faith involves first of all an acceptance of the explicit beliefs of the Catholic Church and the scriptures, but faith is even more importantly the act of "childlike trust in God's maternal care."[27] A third understanding of faith, however, dominates the entire account: faith heals the mind's eye so it can see the truth. To accomplish this goal, God sends Augustine suffering, to free him from the attachments that blind him:

> Your goad was thrusting at my heart, giving me no peace until the eye of my soul could discern you without mistake. Under the secret touch of your healing hand my swelling pride subsided, and day by day the pain I suffered brought me health, like an ointment which

stung but cleared the confusion and darkness from the eye of my mind (7.8; p. 144).

In the famous scene in a garden, Augustine is exhausted from the struggle within him of the two opposing wills. He hears a voice chanting, *"Tolle, lege"* ("Take it and read" [8.12; p. 177]), and he reads the admonition of Paul to the Romans to stop living in drunkenness and rioting and strife and envy and to put on Christ (Rom. 13:13). With that, Augustine is freed from his struggle. Grace triumphs, and he need read no further. At about the same time, his friend Alypius has a similar experience, and the two are converted together, reinforcing the theme of the solidarity of humans in sin and in grace.

O'Connell finds three distinct notions of grace at work in the conversion. Augustine views grace in neo-Platonic terms as (1) a stripping away of a heavy weight which burdens the soul and (2) as the attractive power of a higher beauty. But Augustine transforms the neo-Platonic notion of conversion by uniting it to (3) a more interpersonal and biblically inspired image of God as personal, loving, and caring, indeed as maternal. The "chaste beauty of Continence" appears to Augustine in the garden as "not barren but a fruitful mother of children, of joys born of you, O Lord her Spouse" (8.11; p. 176). Augustine hears her advice: "Cast yourself upon God and have no fear. He will not shrink away and let you fall" (ibid.). God's loving care appears as a mother's love.[28]

Where T'an-luan and Shinran interpret the source of Other-power as Amida Buddha, who is a personification of dharmakaya as compassion, Augustine finds grace mediated through the revelation of God in Jesus Christ.[29] Christ must provide the strength that Augustine lacks in himself. Where T'an-luan and Shinran reject the claims of Zen to awaken through vigorous practice, Augustine rejects the claims of the neo-Platonic philosophers to have purified themselves through their own efforts. He later looked back on his own condition at this time: "I was full of self-esteem, which was a punishment of my own making. . . . But how could I expect that the Platonist books would ever teach me charity?" (7.20; p. 154). Elsewhere he later described the claims of the neo-Platonists as an illusion: "However, there are some people who think that they can purify themselves for contemplating God and cleaving to him by their own power and strength of character, which means in fact that they are thoroughly defiled by pride."[30]

For both Shinran and Augustine, the claim to be able to purify our own consciousness is itself a snare and a delusion; for both, the face of absolute reality is a personal and compassionate will to save, but we only experience this grace when we abandon our efforts to save ourselves. For both Shinran and Augustine, faith comes as a gift from beyond our own powers. Augustine's interpretation of his experience, however, is decisively guided by the understanding of a creating God who decides to intervene to save a lost human race. For the Pure Land tradition, dharmakaya as compassion or Amida Buddha is not the transcendent-immanent creator of the universe itself, but is our own primordial subjectivity, the way reality itself manifests itself.

VISION AT OSTIA

Shortly after his conversion experience, Augustine has a mystical experience with his mother, Monica, in another garden, this one in Ostia, the port city of ancient Rome. The vision of God at Ostia is a foretaste of the vision of heaven, an anticipation of the restoration of the soul to God in contemplation. As Monica and Augustine are discussing the happiness of the lives of the saints, they experience the love of God leading them beyond themselves to the eternal Wisdom. Augustine and Monica discuss what it would be like if all the tumult of creation were to fall silent so that they could hear God speaking directly, with no intermediary (9.10; pp. 197-98).

Augustine distinguishes three levels of the experience: (1) they are led from the material universe, (2) move into their own souls, and (3) then move beyond the soul to the realm of unending happiness, to the Wisdom that simply is and "for one fleeting instant we reached out and touched it" (9.10; p. 197).[31] As soon as they have the experience, it is ended, and they return to the sound of their own speech in the world of time. For Augustine, only a foretaste of full union with God is possible in this world.

While the language describing this experience is heavily endebted to Plotinus, Augustine differs sharply from Plotinus by acknowledging that Monica shares the vision with him. Because it is the grace of Christ and not our own efforts that makes possible the mystical vision, the experience is open to an uneducated woman like Monica. This would have been inconceivable for the neo-Platonic philosopher, who would have demanded a sophisticated process of education and training of one's consciousness. Monica herself appears as a paradigm of Christian discipleship, sharing in the vision of God without having traversed the path of philosophy. The decisive factor in union with God is not intellectual preparation or neo-Platonic meditation, but the grace of God, given in baptism to every Christian.

Augustine also transforms the neo-Platonic language by grounding it in creation: All things first cry out, "We did not make ourselves" (9.10; p. 198), and then fall silent. In the silence of creation, Augustine and Monica hear God directly, with no intermediaries. The notion of a direct, mystical union with the God who creates the universe is foreign to all branches of the Mahayana tradition. The moment of Zen awakening is true seeing of the universe just as it is, of seeing the One in the many and the many in the One, but the One is not a transcendent creator.

Nonetheless, there are similarities. Both Augustine and Mahayana Buddhists describe direct contact with absolute reality itself, beyond all concepts and all intermediaries. In both Augustine and the Mahayana, this is an experience of the timeless in this world of time, a point of oneness of the impermanent and the reality that transcends time. The experiences of realization for Dogen or of shinjin for Shinran are experiences of the timeless, of nirvana in the world of time. For Augustine, as for the Mahayana tradition, the sheer presence of absolute reality itself, the eternal, the unconditioned, cannot be described in words and involves a transformation of ourselves, a transcending of our ordinary consciousness, and a new experience of true freedom.

ASCENT AND DESCENT

We have seen the fundamental structure of Mahayana Buddhist experience in the ascent-descent motif. Augustine, often adapting the language of Plotinus, reads his experience more typically as a descent followed by conversion and ascent.

At the time of writing the *Confessions*, Augustine appears to have believed in the preexistence of the soul and its enjoyment of God's truth and beauty in the heavenly City of God. In this state we had spiritual bodies, unlike our present mortal bodies. While we were blissful in this condition, we were subject to temptation, especially the temptation of pride and its companions, concupiscence and curiosity. Succumbing to the temptation to be independent of God, we fell into the bodies in which we find ourselves in this world. Thus our birth into this world is a fall from that world which is our true home.[32]

Augustine's journey in this world begins with a further descent. First he descends into the region of want, into the cauldron of lust at Carthage, into the hell of sin. Then he experiences a series of turnings that reorient him to God, until finally he experiences the reality of God directly, apart from creation, at Ostia. Augustine's own experience of descent and ascent is made possible by the action of God in creating and redeeming, which itself can be read as a descent and ascent. All things flow forth from God's creative Word, but God's own Word must become the mediator that redeems humans and makes possible the way of return to God: "Our Life himself came down into this world and took away our death. He slew it with his own abounding life, and with thunder in his voice he called us from this world to return to him in heaven" (4.12; p. 82).

Augustine agrees with the Mahayana tradition that (1) our initial consciousness in this world is distorted by ignorance of our true identity and deluding desires that run out of control, and that (2) this initial consciousness must be negated so that we can appropriate our true identity, and that (3) our true destiny is a state of oneness with ultimate reality, which defies description. He also agrees with the Pure Land tradition that our own efforts to bring this about are futile. We must abandon our reliance on our own strength of will and place our trust in the will of a power greater than ourselves.

The dynamics of this movement, for Augustine, are determined by the relations of creation and grace, while for the Mahayana the dynamics follow from the interdependence of co-arising and the compassion of dharmakaya. For both Augustine and the Mahayana tradition, ultimate reality cannot be understood as a purely objective reality apart from the journey of transformation of our own life.

Augustine presents his early life as a life of delusion dominated by desires out of control, a life of estrangement from himself. Augustine must go through a series of disillusionments with himself, his values, his beliefs, his teachers, and his goals, before he can learn who he is. Successive negations of illusions make possible his early ascent to wisdom. The driving force in his ascent is his desire for happiness, which inextricably involves the desire for wisdom and truth. Augustine is always searching for the reality which will satisfy his restless heart, and every finite reality that he experiences leaves him still restless. His dissatisfaction with himself and his life is itself a positive force leading to God.

Where the ascending path of Mahayana Buddhism relentlessly attacks the illusion that things are substantial, Augustine's own ascent involves the recognition that all things cry out that they are made. Augustine could agree with the Buddhist tradition that things cannot support themselves: they have no independent, substantial being of their own. Augustine would also agree that the negating power of the awareness of contingency is not an objective theory about external reality. It is a religious insight which, if appropriated, will transform us and our relations to ourselves, to other creatures, and to God. Augustine's perspective, nonetheless, differs from the Buddhist by finding the support for realities in God. The Mahayana tradition sees dharmakaya as wisdom and compassion, the fountainhead of illumination; Augustine sees God as love, a love freely shared in the relationships of the inner life of the Trinity, a love which gives to creatures even to the point of Incarnation and the cross.

Augustine cannot find his way alone, and so he needs outward guides to orient his quest. Each of his conversions involves the reading of a book: The first conversion to philosophy comes through reading the *Hortensius* of Cicero, the second conversion to spiritual realities comes through reading the Platonic books, and the final conversion to Catholic Christianity comes after reading Paul's Letter to the Romans. Each of these books calls him to himself and closer to God. For Augustine, knowledge and turning to God go hand in hand. In a sense, the guides that Augustine encounters are so many means used by God to answer Monica's prayer that Augustine become a Catholic Christian. Where Mahayana Buddhists present the entire teaching and practices of Buddhism as the skillful means of the Buddhas to enlighten wayward beings, Augustine presents the positive moments of his entire life journey as guided by God.

Augustine, in his own way, does make a journey of ascent and descent. Starting from his sinful condition, one could read the narrative as an ascent from illusion to the vision at Ostia, followed by a descent, a return to the world and the acceptance of the responsibilities of caring for the Church as bishop. After his conversion in the garden, Augustine wants to live the life of a leisured scholar, a Christian neo-Platonic philosopher reflecting on philosophical and religious questions and not worrying directly about the affairs of the Church in the world. The climax of Augustine's ascent is the vision at Ostia, a moment of direct communication with God, with the eternal Wisdom. The moment of possessing God is the end of striving, the goal of the restless heart, and the transformation into God. As Etienne Gilson comments, for Augustine, "to love the eternal is to become eternal; to love God is to become God."[33] The union with God is the overcoming of the duality between ourselves and God, the actualization of the image of God within us.

But the moment is fleeting. As long as we are embodied in this world, we cannot enjoy the lasting vision of God in heaven. Augustine must make another descent into the world, but this time as a transformed man. He would later become priest and bishop and, somewhat against his own preferences, would become involved in the daily concerns of administration and of church conflicts. Where the Mahayana Buddhist tradition insists on the descent of the bodhisattva from the mountain peak of shunyata, Augustine in his own life had to leave the bliss of the vision at Ostia and immerse himself in the world of the Church of North Africa.[34] The rest of Augustine's life would be dominated by the oscillation between the pursuit of wisdom and the demands of love, of active involvement in the life of the Church, expressed in his activities as a bishop, in his sermons, and in his pastoral and polemical writings.

GRACE AND FREEDOM

Where much of the Buddhist tradition, in particular the Zen tradition, claims that one can awaken to reality as it is by oneself, Augustine's perspective is rather closer to Pure Land Buddhism and Shinran. To explore this relation we turn to Augustine's more explicit reflections on grace and human freedom.

Augustine's reflection on his own personal experience was decisive in his development of his doctrine of grace and freedom in his debate with the Irish monk, Pelagius. Pelagius was a spiritual director to Christians who advised them to think highly of human nature as created by God and to use their freedom to do the will of God. The fundamental concern of both Augustine and Pelagius was the pressing existential question of how we are to be saved. Both Augustine and Pelagius believed in the freedom of the human person and the necessity of God's grace for salvation. Yet their understandings of the meaning of freedom and grace diverged most radically.

Buddhism has never wrestled with the problem of free will in the sense that Augustine posed it. Where Augustine experienced his will as fallen and bound in a horizon of sin, in rebellion against God, Buddhism sees the will as bound by karma, by the fruits of past evil actions which imprison us. As Abe comments, "emancipation from karma does not lead us to the Will of God (as in Christianity), nor to the will to power (as in Nietzsche), but rather to Shunyata, which is entirely beyond any kind of will. It is *jinen*, that is, naturalness, or spontaneity without will."[35]

Pelagius agreed strongly with Augustine's early work *On Free Will* and later claimed to be following Augustine's own teaching. Pelagius argued that human nature, created by God, is good. It has been led astray by the custom of sinning, but it is not fundamentally corrupt.[36] Scripture urges us to do the good, and God cannot in justice command what is not possible. Therefore, Pelagius concluded, it must be possible for us to do the good from the resources of human nature. Moreover, God has given us a conscience which rebukes us when we do wrong. It would be irrational and unjust to rebuke us for what we cannot avoid. Thus Pelagius urged his followers to have a high estimate of the possibilities of human nature. By striving for the good, we can overcome the power of custom and be saved.

Much of the language of Buddhism and of the Zen tradition in particular appears similar to that of Pelagius. The Dhammapada assures us that we can control our mind and our emotions and cast aside our illusions; Zen masters warn that no one else can cut through our entanglements. While the Buddhist tradition would not base its confidence in self-power on the goodness of God's creation, its reliance on religious practice and refusal to look to a savior brings it close to the approach of Pelagius. Moreover, Pelagius's interpretation of Christ as a teacher who points out the way of virtue bears similarities to the Buddhist view of Shakyamuni as a pathfinder and teacher of wisdom.

Augustine argued vigorously against Pelagius in *The Spirit and the Letter* in 412 and in a series of later writings, and his arguments have had an immeasurable influence on both Roman Catholic and Protestant theology.[37] The letter of the law kills, Augustine insisted, because we cannot fulfill it. He argued from Paul's Epistle to the Romans that we cannot be saved by good works. Striving for our own righteousness leads to death. Only God's grace, received in faith, makes us righteous. Augustine insists: "Even our believing is a thing that God has granted to us."[38] Without grace, our freedom is a freedom to choose within a horizon of evil. We cannot save ourselves by our own resources.

As the dispute went on, Augustine became more vitriolic in his attacks on Pelagius. In *On the Grace of Christ* in 418, Augustine clarified the meaning of grace.[39] The capacity of nature is not grace. Nor is teaching and the law, external assistance to the will, or even the moral example of Christ.

Grace is a special gratuitous gift from God, beyond the capacity of nature which moves the will internally to do the good. This grace is given apart from any merits foreseen by God, and it is absolutely efficacious.

The *Confessions* reflects Augustine's early understanding of grace by showing Augustine's inability to save himself. By Book 8 Augustine knows what he should do, and he wants to do it, but he is unable to put into practice his resolution. This experience meant a radical break with the Platonic tradition, which held that to know the good leads to doing the good. Augustine found his own will radically bifurcated and felt impotent to break the deadlock himself. God's gratuitous grace had to set him free. Without grace, he could choose only within a horizon of cupidity, of self-centered love. The insistence on the impotence of the unaided will would remain at the center of Augustine's thought throughout the Pelagian controversy and beyond.

For Augustine, to know ourselves as we are is to know ourselves as fallen souls redeemed by God in Christ. The neo-Platonic motif of descending and ascending dominates his anthropology. The descending motion refers both to the procession of all creation from God and also to the specifically human descent into sin. The grace of Christ intervenes, turning us around so that we can ascend to God and see ourselves and God.

In Augustine's interpretation of grace, the will of God establishes our will in freedom so that it can do the good. While this perspective contrasts sharply with much of the Buddhist tradition, it bears strong similarities to Pure Land Buddhism, and to T'an-luan and Shinran in particular. Both T'an-luan and Shinran sharply rejected any reliance on our own efforts to free ourselves from ignorance. As we have seen, in Shinran's interpretation, shinjin (true entrusting or faith or conversion) is not the work of an autonomous human subject but is itself the work of Amida Buddha accomplishing the inconceivable Vow in humans. For Augustine, faith itself is a gift of God.

For Pure Land Buddhists, the opposition between the foolish human being and Amida Buddha is overcome: "Thus, shinjin makes possible the complete entrusting to the Buddha as the ultimate liberation from attachment to a fixed self. The act of true entrusting is none other than the freedom realized in 'birth in the Pure Land.' "[40] For Augustine, our will cannot reorient itself and turn to God apart from God's grace. His vision of grace as an internal motion of the will coming from God which cannot be resisted leads to a close identification of our good actions as actions of God. When we will the good, it is because of the power of God willing in us.

While their descriptions of their experiences of faith or conversion bear obvious similarities, Augustine and Shinran differ profoundly in their interpretation of the reality that saves them. For Augustine, God is absolute reality, perfect and eternal, apart from all creation. It is true that for Augustine we become one with God in grace, but Shinran negates the distinction between ourselves and Amida more radically than Augustine ever overcomes the distinction between God and ourselves, and thus Shinran can make statements about Amida Buddha that Augustine could never have made about God. For Shinran, the Other-Power of Amida Buddha is not a divine creator on whom all things are absolutely dependent. As Suzuki comments: "Amida is really ourselves. . . . Amida *is* our inmost self, and when that inmost self is found we are born in the Pure Land."[41]

While Shinran's and Augustine's descriptions of the experience of the impotence of the will and the power of grace appear very similar on one level, the relations of dependent co-arising and the negation of all duality form the context for Shinran's faith in Amida Buddha; and the relation of creation and the historical event of the Incarnation form the context for Augustine's faith in Jesus Christ. For Shinran and Pure Land Buddhism, Amida Buddha is dharmakaya as compassion, ultimate reality manifest in our world as grace. But from the beginning we are not other than Amida Buddha. For Shinran and the Pure Land tradition, the words of Shakyamuni Buddha to Queen Vaidehi remain true: "In fine it is your mind that becomes Buddha, nay it is your mind that is indeed Buddha."[42]

For Augustine, we become one with God in grace, but we are from the beginning contingent creatures absolutely dependent on God. Our salvation is dependent on a historical process played out in time – The divine Word through whom all things were created became flesh:

> Our enlightenment is to participate in the Word, that is, in that *life which is the light of men* (Jn. 1:4). Yet we were absolutely incapable of such participation and quite unfit for it, so unclean were we through sin, so we had to be cleansed. . . . [T]o contemplate God, which by nature we are not, we would have to be cleansed by him who became what by nature we are and what by sin we are not. By nature we are not God; by nature we are men; by sin we are not just. So God became a just man to intercede with God for sinful man. . . . So he applied to us the similarity of his humanity to take away the dissimilarity of our iniquity, and becoming a partaker of our mortality he made us partakers of his divinity.[43]

PART III

Contemporary Paths

Engaged Buddhism and Theology of Liberation

Introduction

Jesus Christ and Shakyamuni Buddha continue to inspire Christians and Buddhists to follow their respective paths, and the classic interpretations of these traditions by Augustine and Dionysius, and by Zen and Pure Land leaders, continue to shape the lives of Christians and Buddhists throughout the world. The contemporary world, however, presents new challenges to any religious tradition; the massive suffering of the twentieth century presses most powerfully the ancient question of understanding and responding to evil.

The transition to the contemporary world has profoundly affected every religious tradition. Through the European conquests from the sixteenth to the nineteenth centuries, modern Western culture has affected every other culture and every religious tradition. Modern Western culture itself has been uniquely marked by secularizing tendencies that have led influential figures and sectors in society to dismiss religion in any form as an illusion or a by-product of other aspects of human existence. The rise of modern science has brought wide-ranging power to control nature. The rise of modern historical consciousness has brought powerful relativizing tendencies. The modern awareness of the contingency of historical, social, and political structures has given birth to new forms of the ancient quest for justice in movements which seek to reshape society in radical ways.

Both Buddhism and Christianity have been profoundly challenged and transformed by these developments. Christian theologians since the Enlightenment have pondered strategies to respond to and critique modernity. While Buddhists sometimes note the similarity of contemporary physics to classical Buddhist notions of the universe, Buddhists are also aware of the serious threat posed by anti-religious ideologies to any religious tradition in the world today.[1] While many Christian theologians and some Buddhist thinkers have sought to interpret their traditions in response to the challenges of modern Western thought, many Christians and Buddhists, especially from areas outside of Europe and North America, have been deeply aware of the ambiguities of modern "progress," and have been less impressed by the successes of modern Western culture than by the tremendous suffering it has caused.

If modern Western culture poses a powerful challenge to religion in any form, the reverse is equally true. The major religious traditions of the past possess resources to question central assumptions of the modern West, especially in light of the widespread suffering in the world.[2] Two of the most creative and influential figures in responding to the contemporary world from the resources of their religious traditions are the Vietnamese Buddhist monk Thich Nhat Hanh and the Peruvian Catholic priest Gustavo Gutiérrez. Each figure is steeped in the classical wisdom of his tradition and interprets his tradition in light of his own experience of the contemporary world. Gutiérrez is a parish priest in Lima, Peru, who does theology from the perspective of the poor of Latin America. Nhat Hanh, having lived through the terrible violence in Vietnam in the 1960s, writes from the perspective of having lived more than twenty years in exile from his homeland. Both authors assume that their religious practice is primordial and fundamental for their respective religious visions. Much of the persuasiveness of each writer comes from his ability to reinterpret classical perspectives in light of the contemporary experience of his people.

The ancient contrast between creation and dependent co-arising reappears in a new form in these figures, with Gutiérrez organizing much of his thought from the perspective of a theology of creation and Nhat Hanh from the perspective of dependent co-arising. Both figures use these classical understandings of the universe to cast suspicion on modern notions of the self. Both suspect that the self-understanding of modern Western culture has been systemically distorted by illusions that prevent a genuine experience or understanding of oneself or others. Gutiérrez applies the ancient critiques of idols by the prophets of Israel to contemporary social and economic structures. Nhat Hanh applies the ancient Buddhist suspicion of the illusory self to modern Western notions of identity, and writes of a self composed of "non-self elements." For both, the dominant Western notion of a self, especially the independent, grasping, greedy self of modern capitalism, is an illusion to be identified and destroyed.

Part III will explore these two contemporary paths of living out the Buddhist and the Christian life in a world dominated by competing rivalries, a world of suffering, but also a world of life and joy. The next chapter will explore the engaged Buddhism of Thich Nhat Hanh, and the following chapter will study the theology of liberation of Gustavo Gutiérrez.

7

The Engaged Buddhism of Thich Nhat Hanh

LIFE OF THICH NHAT HANH

Thich Nhat Hanh was born in Vietnam in 1926. At the age of sixteen he entered a Zen monastery and began the practice of the Buddhist monastic life. The Vietnamese Buddhism in which he was trained is a unique blending of various Buddhist traditions. Buddhism originally came to Vietnam from India by sea routes and from China by overland routes.[3] Because of its dual origin and its geographical setting between the Theravada Buddhist traditions of Thailand, Burma, and Sri Lanka and the Mahayana Buddhist heritage of China, Vietnamese Buddhism has been shaped by the intertwining of both of the major Buddhist traditions.

The most important tradition in Vietnamese Buddhism has been *Thien*, the Vietnamese term for Sanskrit *dhyana* or Chinese Ch'an or Japanese Zen. In Vietnam, however, Thien or Zen has itself been heavily influenced by Pure Land Buddhism, and so almost all Vietnamese Thien monasteries and temples include a synthesis of Zen and Pure Land teachings and practices. As Nhat Hanh explains, the main emphasis in Thien monasteries is not on beliefs: "Thien is an attitude or a method for arriving at knowledge and action. For Thien the techniques of right eating and drinking, of right breathing and right concentration and meditation are far more vital than mere beliefs."[4]

Nhat Hanh traveled to the United States in 1961, studying and teaching comparative religion at Columbia and Princeton universities. He returned to Vietnam in 1963 at the request of other monks, who sought his leadership in resisting the violence in Vietnam after the fall of Diem.[5]

During the Vietnam War in the 1960s, Nhat Hanh and other Buddhist monks decided that the demands of compassion called them to move beyond the usual rhythms of monastic life and become actively involved in aiding the victims of the war and in working for a peaceful end to the conflict. Concerned to interpret Buddhism as a dynamic response to the sufferings of his people, Nhat Hanh developed a contemporary form of the ancient path of compassion, which he called "engaged Buddhism." Engaged Buddhism brings the resources of Buddhist wisdom and meditation to bear on re-envisioning and addressing contemporary conflicts. The first step in making peace in the world is to be this peace ourselves.

The years following his return to Vietnam were filled with intense activity and engagement with social and political problems. In 1964 Nhat Hanh founded the School of Youth for Social Service in South Vietnam in order to teach the path of compassion to others. Members of the school helped victims of the war, aiding Vietnamese in rebuilding villages and resettling wartime refugees. The foreign press named them "the little Peace Corps." In 1964 he was involved in establishing the La Boi ("Palm Leaves") publishing house. During this same period he was instrumental in founding and teaching at Van Hanh University, the Buddhist university in Saigon.

He also founded the Tiep Hien Order, or the Order of Interbeing, in 1964. As he explains, "*Tiep* means 'to be in touch.' The notion of engaged Buddhism already appears in the word tiep."[6] Meditation allows one to be in touch both with oneself and also with modern society. *Tiep* also means "to continue": "It means that the career of understanding and compassion started by Buddhas and Bodhisattvas should be continued."[7] *Hien* means "the present time, because we practice the Buddhist precepts for the sake of being peace and compassion in the present." *Hien* also means "to make real, to manifest, realization."[8] Nhat Hanh translates the two words together, *Tiep Hien*, as "interbeing," referring to the interconnectedness and interdependence of all reality in the vision of dependent co-arising. The Tiep Hien Order is a continuation of the Lin Chi School of Ch'an Buddhism and applies the wisdom of this tradition to contemporary life.

In 1966 he traveled to the United States, where he gave many talks explaining the conflict in light of the history and views of the Vietnamese people and proposing a plan to end the fighting. He traced the history of his people both religiously and politically from the more distant past, through the French colonial period, up to the present. He offered a concrete interpretation of the historical, political, and social background of the agony of Vietnam and set forth his own proposal for peace. After speaking widely and meeting with Secretary of Defense McNamara, Dr. Martin Luther King, Jr., and Thomas Merton, he traveled to Europe, where he continued to speak about the war and met Pope Paul VI.

Nhat Hanh refused to side with either side in the conflict in Vietnam, and his plan called for a non-Communist interim government representative of the major religious traditions of Vietnam, which would work for democratic elections. His efforts were opposed by both sides, including the Communist North and the government of South Vietnam. Unable to return to his homeland, he remained in exile and continued working for peace in Paris. He later became the Chair of the Vietnamese Buddhist Peace Delegation at the Paris Peace Conference. In 1967 Dr. Martin Luther King, Jr., nominated him for the Nobel Peace Prize.

After the Peace Accords were concluded, Nhat Hanh was still unable to return home, and so in 1973 he founded a community southwest of Paris which he named "Sweet Potato." A few years later he became involved in efforts to assist the boat people fleeing Vietnam. He traveled to Singapore to organize relief operations, arranging for boats to take the refugees to safety. His efforts were opposed by the governments in the area.

In the late 1970s Nhat Hanh began a five-year retreat at his residence in France. Since 1982 he has accepted invitations to attend conferences, lead retreats, and speak to groups engaged in work for peace. He currently lives at Plum Village, a community he founded in 1982 in the south of France near Bordeaux, where he continues to meditate, garden, teach, and work on behalf of the Vietnamese people and refugees worldwide.

Nhat Hanh has expressed his teaching in a variety of forms: in a one-act play, in short stories and poems, in a retelling of the life of the Buddha, in commentaries on Buddhist scriptures, and in books on meditation and Buddhist life.[9] Perhaps the most accessible path to enter his vision of life is through his one-act play and his short stories.

STORIES OF SUFFERING AND SEEING

THE PATH OF RETURN CONTINUES THE JOURNEY

Shortly after midnight on July 5, 1967, five of the young men who worked at the School of Youth for Social Service were taken from the village of Binh Phuoc to the bank of the Saigon River and shot. Four died at once, but the fifth survived and was left for dead. Thich Nhat Hanh's one-act play, *The Path of Return Continues the Journey*, presents the journey of the dead across the river that night and their conversation with one another and with their guide, a young woman named Mai, a Buddhist nun who had immolated herself for peace on May 16, 1967.

As the play begins about 1:00 A.M. on the night of the murders, a sampan approaches the shore. Mai arranges the four young men in the boat and instructs them to row with their hands. Because they are dead, they weigh very little, and the gentle motion of their hands propels the boat on its way. The young men ask if they will be able to see two young women from the School of Youth for Social Service who had been murdered during a night raid in April of that same year. Mai assures them that they will and introduces them to what life in the world of the dead will be like.

Vui, one of the young women who had been killed, still cares for the villagers as she did in this world. Lien, the other young woman, studies the *Prajnaparamita Sutra*, and draws, and teaches Vui to draw. In the world of the dead, each person is free to do as she or he pleases. When asked why Vui has to continue working for villagers as she had in this world, Mai

explains: "If Vui wants to do that, then there are simply villages and villagers for her to work for. The universe of the dead changes according to
one's wishes. And, as I see it, the universe of the living does, too."[10] On
hearing this, Tuan, one of the young men who had been a Buddhist seminarian, murmurs to himself: "The mind is like a painter, it can paint anything it wants" (10). Another young man asks if they are in heaven or hell,
and Mai explains that it is neither: "And it's not a world so far apart from
the world of the living as is generally believed" (10). Another of the young
men notes the paradox that life and death are intimately united: even
though they are now dead, they are still alive, and when they were living,
they were already dying. Though one young man notes that he feels as if
in a dream, they all become able to see more clearly the meaning of life
and death.

With their new vantage point, they no longer are trapped by sorrow or
pain or bitterness or any desire for revenge. Instead they are filled with
compassion for the living, even for those who killed them. Tho observes:

> I feel now that if I were still alive, I would be going to the house of
> the man who shot me, to ask him what in the world made him drag
> me to the river bank in the dead of the night and shoot me. But now,
> I really do not feel any grudge against him, none at all. Perhaps the
> dead are more forgiving (13).

Another of the young men, Hy, tells Mai what had happened that night:
about eleven armed men had captured and bound them, burned the Health
Aid Post, and then had taken them to the bank of the river. Their captors
were young, some only teenagers, and the oldest no more than twenty-
seven or twenty-eight. The armed men were quite friendly in talking on the
road, and they appeared reluctant to kill their young captives, apparently
having to struggle with themselves to shoot them. The captors asked the
young men repeatedly if they worked for the School of Youth for Social
Service. Finally, the leader said he had to kill them. After the first victim
was shot, the second began reciting the name of Amita Buddha, and was
quickly shot down as well. A third fell into the river as soon as he was shot.
Even though his arms were bound, he tried to swim, only to be shot repeatedly as he struggled to rise to the surface.

The dead regret the pain this will cause to the living, but they feel no
pity for themselves and no anger toward their killers. As they move up the
river, flarebombs explode in the night darkness. Hy asks why the suffering
of Vietnam must continue so long, and Mai assures him: "Be calm, brother.
Our country will be destroyed and our people will suffer even more than
they already have. The cycle must be completed. Life and death are in the
course of things. In the end there will be peace" (18).

Mai recounts her own death by fire. She had remained calm, as she had
hoped, and sat very still amid the flames. After she was dead, she watched

the crowd around her body, and her father fainting, regaining consciousness, and fainting yet again. Only when an army officer came to remove the body did her father's anger banish the sorrow. Mai herself has been peaceful since her death. She is confident that peace will come to Vietnam, and she affirms that she really still is at work in the land of the living.

The young men are puzzled, and so Mai explains the meaning of dependent co-arising: "Nothing can be lost; yet at the same time, nothing that remains static can keep its nature intact" (21). Every moment, every thing, every energy leaves an effect on all other realities in the world. The process of transformation continues forever. Even death is part of the process of change and transformation. In life we are constantly changing and evolving, and in death, the evolution moves into a new period or cycle. The living live only by receiving countless realities into themselves: air, food, education, love, parents, grandparents, friends. Thus the dead are still present in the land of the living, especially in those whom they loved. Nothing is ever lost: "All that you have said and done has already begun its journey. You are present everywhere" (22).

One of the young men reflects that their journey this night to find Lien and Vui is not really an external journey, but an internal voyage. Lien and Vui are all around them, but they must struggle with themselves to search for the Lien and Vui of their feelings and habits.

With death comes a new consciousness of the nature of reality. Tuan, the Buddhist seminarian, notes that every day of his life he had recited the *Prajnaparamita Sutra*. When the armed man aimed his gun at Tuan's head, the seminarian finally understood what transcendent wisdom really was. When pressed to explain his realization, Tuan demurs: "It is not something to be understood, but to be *seen*. We can easily explain what we understand, but not what we see or perceive" (23). Tuan suddenly realized that the man could not shoot *him*, for he had no idea who Tuan really was. The man could aim at an object of hatred and fear, but that object had nothing to do with who Tuan really was. The murderers did not see their victims at all; all they saw were projections of their own frustrations and fears. Blinded by hatred, they saw the faces of monsters, and strove in vain to destroy them. They themselves were victims of their own superiors, who were in turn also victims of illusions and misperceptions.

Mai draws out the conclusion that each of us creates our own reality and fashions for ourself a world of terror or of freedom: "We create our own worlds with our own visions, our own conceptions, our own thoughts. We may create for ourselves a tightly shut world of suffering and sorrow. We may also create one that is immense and free, a world that is truly beautiful" (25). We are all like painters who call into being a world of our own making which we then inhabit. Hatred and fear can be our prison wardens if we choose, or we can open out in a spirit of freedom and love and tolerance.

The dead express the hope that their lives and deaths have sown seeds of tolerance and love that may yet bear fruit in the future. No matter how powerless their actions and witness may have seemed, they contribute to awakening people to wisdom and compassion. As the play concludes, dawn approaches, and they see Lien awaiting them on the riverbank.

THE STONE BOY

In the short story "The Stone Boy," from the collection *The Moon Bamboo*, a young Vietnamese girl named Hoang Thi Tô, the daughter of woodcutters, grows up in a land torn apart by war and suffering. When she was seven, her father had been killed in battle. To cope with the sadness, Tô takes her bamboo flute with her into the forest and plays, expressing both grief and joy together. One day as she is playing, a plane drops chemical defoliants which leave her blinded and gasping for air.

The next time she visits the forest, she becomes aware of the world in a way she had never known. Now totally blind, she plays her flute for the birds that come, and she hears the sounds of all the creatures of the forest. She meets a golden bird that comes and sings to her for nine days in a row. As time goes by and she continues to listen and to play, she becomes more and more part of the world of the forest:

> Little by little Tô forgot that she was a young girl playing an instrument, and she became a tiny creature living in the forest with thousands of friends. The sounds of the flute resonated with the cries of the other creatures. She was at one with the forest. Trees, moss, grass, and roots began to dance, and her pain dissolved. Tô was no longer only Tô.[11]

The sense of interconnectedness with all beings gives her a new sense of identity. After this transforming experience of oneness, Tô meets Stone Boy, who mysteriously appears in the forest one day without parents or home. Stone Boy is silent at first, but then asks her to play. As she does, she has another joyful experience, forgetting the suffering of the past, feeling reunited with her father and with all the world. Since he has no home of his own, she takes him home and he stays with her. They converse at length amid nature, and become close friends.

One day when they are in the market, the war returns abruptly, with bullets flying, explosions destroying buildings, and people wounded. Though Tô and Stone Boy are unharmed, the girl's mother is nowhere to be found. Since the mother is neither dead nor wounded, they can only conclude that the attackers led her away. Tô is overcome with sorrow and can barely breathe. Stone Boy begins to sing a song that rises like a strand of smoke and envelopes the earth and sky. Tô feels a great release, hears the songs of the birds, and begins to play her own flute as well. After the songs subside, they sit in silence, and Stone Boy explains: "I only sing when the sky and the earth are ill at ease, sad, and angry, when black clouds come down towards earth and the sky is about to explode" (21).

Tô and Stone Boy go off in search of her mother, but she is nowhere to be found. After they lie down for the night near a marketplace, the war once again intervenes, with bombs exploding in the middle of the night. Amid the confusion of the battle, Stone Boy goes to the marketplace and begins to sing. The sounds of battle come to an end, and Tô's flute begins a song of mourning for the many victims of war, for the children dead, the soldiers forced to fight and die, for the old women and babies struck by stray bullets and left to bleed to death. The song of the flute attracts the attention of children and soldiers alike. As the flute fades away, Stone Boy begins to sing again: "In his voice there was a deep faith in the interconnectedness and love among all beings which soothed all pains like a spring breeze. It was autumn dew cooling the fire of hatred, the miraculous water that brought forth young buds on dying trees" (27).

Soldiers arrest Stone Boy and Tô as suspected spies because they are strangers to the area, unknown to the villagers. They are taken to a Center for Juvenile Reform. Both excel in classes, but Stone Boy is constantly bullied by other boys because he refuses to fight back and thus earns the nickname, "the dumb one." After a year they are separated, and Tô is sent to a school for the blind, and Stone Boy to a school for wards of the state. A year later Tô has a strange dream about Stone Boy and the horrors of war. When she awakes, she plays her flute and then hears the golden bird tell her that Stone Boy has come to find her.

They start off again in search of Tô's mother, and Stone Boy recounts his experiences. He had sung songs of peace at the school for wards of the state, and so he had been sent to a strict Cadet School to be trained for war. Instead, Stone Boy and a number of other students requested that they be trained as social workers to help repair the damage of war. For this Stone Boy was accused of being a propagandist for the enemy and thrown in prison. In prison he met a number of Buddhist monks, imprisoned because they had asked both sides to stop the fighting. When the monks began a hunger strike, Stone Boy was accused of inciting it through his singing, and he was taken to another prison for political prisoners.

In the new prison Stone Boy had met a strange Taoist monk with long hair and penetrating eyes. The monk had a cage with a cat and two mice, and the animals never harmed one another. For the monk, the message was clear: "I'm here to tell the government that if a cat can live in peace with two mice, why can't we human beings and compatriots live in peace together? We ought to stop killing one another this very day and start rebuilding our homeland" (38).

Many people told the old monk how foolish and naive his image was, and so they put him in prison. The monk and Stone Boy went on a hunger strike, and then were taken to the border of North Vietnam and released. In the north they find still more suffering. On hearing the explanations of

North Vietnamese, Stone Boy was not persuaded. He pondered the tragedy of northern soldiers invading the south, with millions of people homeless and countless wounded and dead. He had thought: "The real pain was shared by people of the same race and same history who were unable to sit down and resolve their differences. This was the real cause of the suffering, not this or that exploitative foreign power" (40).

Stone Boy was taken to different re-education camps, where he sings his songs, tells of events in the south, and touches people's hearts. He had discovered, however, that lies and harsh discipline dominated the north at least as much as the south, and he had been forced to make a very difficult march to a harsh camp where prisoners were deprived of basic necessities and health care until they became seriously ill or incapacitated. While working in the forest near this camp, Stone Boy had heard the cries of the golden bird together with a multitude of birds from all directions. The golden bird had led Stone Boy on a two-week journey back to the south to find Tô.

Having recounted his adventures, Stone Boy accompanies Tô back to her home, and they arrive at her old house. After they fix it up and spend the night, Tô asks Stone Boy to take her to see his parents and home. Stone Boy reluctantly realizes that it is time for him to tell Tô his true identity. He does not know his parents or his age: "I was born here a long time ago. It is possible that since I was born, the full moon has gone over the summit of this mountain one thousand times, or perhaps ten thousand times" (45). When Tô presses further, Stone Boy admits he may have been born by Heaven and Earth, or by the stones, but he insists: "But look, Tô, I do have a mother! My mother is Mrs. Ba Ty, your mother, your loving, wonderful Ma. You and I, we are Ma's children" (46).

Through Stone Boy, Tô comes to see the interconnectedness of all reality. In giving birth to her, Tô realizes that her mother had also given birth to all things: "Were there no Mother, how could there be forests, fields, grasses, and flowers?" (46). Stone Boy notes that if Tô's mother really did give birth to Heaven and Earth and the forests, then she will never die. He recalls how he used to hear the sound of suffering in Tô's music as he listened from atop the mountain. Because he had heard her suffering, he had come down to guide her: "We were two persons, yet we walked together and became one person. In truth, you and I are one, because I am within you and you are within me. You may not see this now, but one day you will" (47).

As day turns into night, Stone Boy leads Tô up high on the mountain to the very summit. They arrive at midnight, with the moon overhead, and Stone Boy points out the miraculous dew that can heal Tô's eyes and allow her to see. Tô drinks the miraculous waters from Stone Boy's hands, and feels a sense of peace transform her as her fears and worries dissolve. Stone Boy washes her eyes in the water, and then invites her to lie down and sleep, covering her with his jacket. Tô lies awake a long time, listening to the sound of Stone Boy's breathing become one with the wind.

As she awakes, she discovers that she can see in the morning sunlight. As she looks on the mountains and forest below her, she feels "she had escaped an existence full of suffering and sorrow" (50). When she calls Stone Boy, there is no answer. She searches frantically until she sees the face of Stone Boy in the very highest peak of the mountain. Though she had never seen him before, she recognizes him immediately in the rock. Her mind races back over the enigmatic things he had told her about his birth and his lack of normal parents. The golden bird returns and sings the words of Stone Boy himself:

> But one day, when you no longer see me,
>   smile, and quietly look for me
>   in all the things that come and go.
> You will find that I am
>   that which never comes
>   and never goes.
> I am that reality beyond time,
>   beyond perception (52).

Tô asks the golden bird to sing the song again, and the bird repeats the same words: this is the only message. As she ponders the meaning of the song, she begins to understand the Stone Boy is indeed the mountain top and also all other things: the sky, the rocks, the trees, the clouds. Wherever she goes, he will be with her, allowing her to see. She and he are one. She realizes too that her mother is indeed alive and that when she finds her all wars will cease. She knows that she will return to the world with her new awareness, but for the moment she lingers atop the mountain and plays her flute again, and all the world is at peace: "Sky and clouds, mountain and trees, settled down in peace and listened to her song" (54).

Dharmakaya, the reality beyond time that is the mountain and forest and birds, appears in the forms of the Stone Boy and the golden bird to awaken Tô to the meaning of life, to the interpenetration of all realities. In a world marked by unbearable sufferings and lies, the first step is to awaken to the sounds of heaven and earth, to see the wonder of existence right before us. Empowered by this awakening, Stone Boy and the monks in the tale have the courage to say the truth as they see it, no matter what the consequences. With eyes transformed by this awareness, Tô can return to the world with compassion for all suffering beings. Peace begins with the transformation of one's own consciousness.

A LONE PINK FISH

The pattern of transforming one's consciousness to see the marvels in the world in spite of the sufferings runs through the tale of "A Lone Pink

Fish" as well. This tale tells of a nineteen-year-old woman named Dao who escapes from Vietnam on a small boat. The boat is attacked by pirates, and Dao is repeatedly raped. When she fights back, her third attacker throws her into the sea. Although she loses consciousness, she is rescued by a lone pink fish who brings her safely to a small island. Dao falls asleep naked on the beach.

That night a young girl wakes her up with a gentle stroking of her forehead. The girl, Hong, who appears to be ten or eleven years old, brings Dao clothing and food. As they converse, the young girl strikes Dao as remarkably calm and well-informed. Dao recounts how difficult life had been for her family in Vietnam. In 1976 her father had been put in a reeducation camp in northern Vietnam, where he wasted away. He had urged his family to escape the country, but his wife had refused. Dao and her fiancé had decided to flee on a boat, but the boat's engine had failed in the middle of the sea. They became easy prey to the sea pirates' attacks. Dao is on the verge of killing herself on the rocks, but Hong holds her hand so strongly that Dao falls on her knees.

Hong encourages Dao, reassuring her that the pirates' attack has not taken away her innocence, and warns her: "Wounds can poison your spirit as well as your body. In ten days or so, you will make it to shore, and there you can find a doctor who can prevent the poison from infecting your body. But no doctor can heal the wounds of your spirit. That is up to you" (65). Hong encourages her to continue living out of responsibility and love: "Living for responsibility and love can be a source of great happiness, elder sister" (64). Hong continues to encourage Dao, chanting the *Heart of Perfect Understanding Sutra*.

Hong mysteriously vanishes periodically, only to return with new information and encouragement. She finally explains to Dao that she is not only a refugee from Vietnam, the ten-year-old Hong, but also a fish. As her refugee boat was floundering in international waters with a stalled engine, her younger brother had died of fever and had to be buried at sea. That evening the boat was attacked by pirates. Hong had thrown herself on one of the pirates as he attacked her mother, but he kicked her over the side of the boat into the sea. Suddenly Hong found herself swimming as a pink fish about the size of a young girl. She discovered that she could rescue people, especially children, from refugee boats when they sank. One night, after rescuing a young boy, she tried to push him up on the beach, and discovered that as she left the water, she became a young girl again.

Hong had witnessed the attack on Dao's boat and carried her to the island. On hearing the marvelous tale, Dao reflects on her own life and thinks what a miracle it would be to see her fiancé, Dat, again. She had seen him and her family so many times and had taken them for granted. "Now for the first time she realized how truly wondrous all these things were. Everything was infinitely precious, just like the child Hong sitting before her" (88). Hong goes on to tell stories of horrendous suffering: some refugee boats sink, others approach the shore only to be towed out to sea again by the marine police, where the boats are attacked by pirates. During the brutal attacks, men are killed and thrown into the sea, women are raped, and terrified children jump into the sea. The sheer enormity of the suffering is shattering to Dao.

Then Hong tells of a different type of boat that she had discovered, a boat that presented itself as a fishing boat, but actually carried a mission of assistance to the refugee boats at sea. On the boat were followers of a Thai spiritual leader who lived in northern Thailand. The group brought refugees dried foods, water, gasoline, and directions on how to reach the refugee camps safely.

One day, after Hong has gone out to sea, Dao sits cross-legged to meditate for the first time. After breathing deeply and relaxing, she recites the Heart Sutra. Even though she does not understand its mysterious words, she is strangely attracted to them. The sutra proclaims that all things are empty: "neither produced nor destroyed, neither defiled nor immaculate, neither increasing nor decreasing" (101).

When Hong returns, she advises Dao to prepare to leave the island. A refugee boat is coming close enough to the island to see her. Hong warns her of how difficult life in the refugee camps will be and asks her to use her energy to help those suffering in the camp. In the camp Dao can write to her uncle in France and request permission to settle there. As the story ends, Hong swims toward the boat, Dao waves a signal back and forth, and a boat sees the signal and heads for the island.

PATTERNS OF TRANSFORMATION

In the play and in each of these stories the consciousness of the central character is transformed through an awareness of both the depth of suffering and also the deep interconnectedness of all beings. In each case the change in awareness is accompanied by an encounter with a guide who plays the role of a miraculous bodhisattva and offers a new vision of reality.

Insight into the "interbeing" of all things transforms a world of senseless violence and cruelty into the world of the bodhisattva's wisdom and compassion. As the slain young men look back on the world of the living with new eyes, as Tô learns that she is in a deep way one with the mountains and forest and Stone Boy, as Dao learns how precious are the everyday persons and realities of her life, their worlds are radically changed. They are freed from preoccupation with their own losses and are able to be compassionate to others. Their own individual suffering becomes bearable as it is placed in a broader context where life, however painful, is filled with miracles and bodhisattvas.

The cryptic words of Buddhist texts about dependent co-arising suddenly become translucent descriptions of the way the world is: nothing can be destroyed, and nothing can be born. An angry, frightened soldier cannot really kill a person. In giving birth to a baby girl, a mother gives birth to the mountains and the forest, and heaven and earth. The healing music of Tô's flute, evoking a sense of the interconnectedness of all that is, can soothe the pain of all beings like autumn dew descending on the fires of hatred.

In a strange way the secret had been there all the time, obvious as can be, but the characters had somehow never seen it. Nhat Hanh recalls that the central problem in ancient Buddhist monasteries was the problem of life and death. "And it was often reported that the monk who was enlightened most of the time just smiled, as if he were someone who had been searching for something and had suddenly found that he had not lost that something—it was in his pocket all the time."[12]

Infinite compassion is around us all the time, even in a world of cruelty, suffering, and loss, but we often need bodhisattvas like Mai and Stone Boy and Hong to make this compassion present to us in ways we can understand. For Nhat Hanh, a bodhisattva can be any being who has compassion on us and calls us to awaken to reality. Once we have been touched by a bodhisattva, we, like the slain social workers and Tô and Dao, are then called to be bodhisattvas to one another.

MEDITATION: BREATHING AND SEEING CLEARLY

For Thich Nhat Hanh, the path to wisdom and compassion begins above all with meditation. If we want to change the world, the first step is to change our awareness of ourselves and our world. In becoming truly aware, we also become one with ourselves and our world and thereby enter a wondrous new world. "When we illuminate something with our awareness, it changes, it blends and merges with the awareness."[13] Commenting on the tradition of Soto Zen meditation, Nhat Hanh endorses the practice of looking at something without reasoning, interpreting, or evaluating: "through the activity of looking, reality gently reveals itself. In meditation, the subject and object of pure observation are inseparable."[14] For Nhat Hanh, any efforts for peace and justice in the political realm must be based upon clear awareness rooted in meditation. Without such awareness, efforts for peace risk being one-sided.

Nhat Hanh insists that if we wish to relieve suffering, we must be in touch not only with the suffering of the world, but also its beauties: "To suffer is not enough. We must also be in touch with the wonders of life. They are within us and all around us, everywhere, any time."[15] Meditation puts us in touch with what is, with both the wonder of life and the pain. Genuine meditation reveals itself in the smile of the meditator: "Smiling means that we are ourselves, that we have sovereignty over ourselves, that we are not drowned in forgetfulness."[16] The ability of all humans to wake up to who we are is what is meant by the Buddha-nature. Each of us is a potential Buddha, but we need to wake up and return to ourselves.

The Buddha needs this, too, in order to become manifest. Nhat Hanh interprets taking refuge in the Buddha to be a mutual relationship: "The Buddha needs us for awakening, understanding, and love to be real things and not just concepts. They must be real things that have real effects on life."[17]

The heart of meditation is awareness of ourselves, our bodies, our feelings, our perceptions, our mental formations, our consciousness in all its aspects, and the storehouse from which our consciousness emerges. Meditation calls us out of the past or the future into the present: "The essential teaching of Buddhism is to be free of all desire for the future in order to come back with all our heart and mind into the present. To realize awakening means to arrive at a deep and full insight into reality, which is in the present moment."[18]

Living deeply in the present is the real meaning of the Buddhist practice of living alone. Nhat Hanh notes the Buddha's teaching that one can live in the forest physically isolated but not genuinely alone if one has not let go of past regrets or future anxieties. Moreover, one can live in the midst of society and be alone.[19] Indeed, according to the Buddha, "living alone means living in the present moment deeply observing what is happening."[20]

The quickest and surest way to return to the present is through attention to our breathing. For Nhat Hanh, all the later major ideas of Mahayana Buddhism are implicit in the early sutras on the Full Awareness of Breathing (*Anapanasatti Sutta*) and on the Four Establishments of Mindfulness (*Satipatthana Sutta*).[21] The Sutra on the Full Awareness of Breathing promises that full awareness of breathing will bring great rewards, leading to mindfulness, wisdom, and freedom. "Without full awareness of breathing," the Buddha warns, "there can be no development of meditative stability and understanding."[22]

According to the Sutra on the Full Awareness of Breathing, there are sixteen methods of breathing meditation, grouped in four series of four methods, each focusing on different objects. The Sutra tells us that attention to breathing leads to awareness of the present condition of (1) the body, (2) the feelings, (3) the mind, and (4) the objects of the mind. By attending carefully to the state of each of these without judgment or conceptualization, the practitioner attains insight into the interdependence of all things and finds freedom.[23]

The first four methods focus on the breath and the body. By breathing consciously and deliberately, the mind and the breath and the body become one. By continuing to breathe in the second set of methods, we become aware of our feelings, whether pleasant or unpleasant or neutral. Negative feelings that have been repressed may come forward, but continued attention to them without judgment will dissolve their power to disturb. Continued breathing meditation will transform seemingly neutral feelings into pleasurable ones and allow us truly to enjoy the simple act of breathing as a wondrous gift. For Nhat Hanh, observation meditation does not mean fighting against negative feelings, but accepting them, seeing the roots of our affliction, and coming to peace and understanding with them.[24] Attention to feelings in breathing makes breath, body, mind, and feelings one.

In the third set of methods, attention to mind (*citta*) includes all the states of consciousness: perceptions, psychological states, mental functions. Again, continued breathing makes the mind joyful and banishes all anxieties. Breathing develops freedom to concentrate deeply and dissolve the knots that often bind up our perception of realities. Finally, the last set of methods focuses on the objects of mind, which can never be separated from the mind as consciousness. As Nhat Hanh explains: "The mind is, at one and the same time, the subject of consciousness and the object of consciousness."[25] Objects of mind include all the things of which we are aware, from feelings and thoughts to physical objects around us. Breathing meditation opens our eyes to the impermanence of all objects and also to their interconnectedness. Indeed, these two insights are one: "The fact of impermanence is very important, because it opens the way for us to see the inter-related, inter-conditioned nature as well as the selfless nature (nothing has a separate, independent self) of all that exists."[26]

When we see that every object of mind passes, we are freed from the temptation of grasping at them as independent objects. The acceptance of the radical transience of all objects of mind brings tremendous joy, culminating in the very last method, which is "to let go of ourselves, to give up all the burdens of our ignorance and our grasping. To be able to let go is to already have arrived at liberation."[27]

The final set of four methods leads to awareness of nonduality: "The key to 'observation meditation' is that the subject of the observation and the object of the observation not be regarded as two separate things."[28] We do not remain outside as external observers of ourselves, our feelings, or other realities. We enter into whatever we are observing and become one with that reality.

THE WISDOM OF INTERBEING: THE HEART SUTRA

The Heart Sutra, which Mahayana Buddhists have chanted daily for centuries, expresses the core vision of the universe of Thich Nhat Hanh: All things "inter-are."[29] The Heart Sutra is one of the early *Prajnaparamita* Sutras, and has long been taken as expressing the heart of early Mahayana Buddhism's wisdom.

The language of the brief sutra is puzzling to the uninitiated, for it relentlessly negates anything that one could grasp at, even the teaching of the Buddha, but the awakened consciousness understands its view of the world.

To introduce us to the sutra's vision, Nhat Hanh begins by pointing to "a cloud floating in this sheet of paper. Without a cloud, there will be no rain; without rain, the trees cannot grow; and without trees, we cannot make paper. The cloud is essential for the paper to exist. . . . So we can say that the cloud and the paper *inter-are*."[30] Look further, he advises, and note the sunshine in the paper, for without sunshine the forest cannot grow, either. Pursuing this line of meditation, we can see all things in the sheet of paper: the logger who cut the tree, the food that nourishes the logger, the parents of the logger, the mind of the author, and the mind of the reader: "So we can say that everything is in here with this sheet of paper. . . . 'To be' is to inter-be. You cannot just *be* by yourself alone. You have to inter-be with every other thing. This sheet of paper is, because everything else is."[31]

This radical sense of interdependence and interpenetration, rooted in the earliest Mahayana sutras and the later Hua-Yen School of Chinese Buddhism, is the foundation for Nhat Hanh's whole vision and practice. It is his appropriation of the ancient Buddhist theme of dependent co-arising: Because this is, that is.[32] This is the essential message of the sutra and of Buddhism.

The sutra presents the wisdom of the Bodhisattva Avalokita, also known as Avalokiteshvara or Kwan Yin (Chinese) or Kannon (Japanese) or Quan Am (Vietnamese), the bodhisattva of compassion who hears the cries of suffering of all beings. Avalokiteshvara, the most popular of all bodhisattvas in East Asia, was originally a male figure in Indian Buddhism, but is often portrayed as a woman in East Asian representations.

According to the Heart Sutra, Avalokita finds all the aggregates or elements that comprise a human being empty. In Buddhism the five elements (*skandhas*) are form (body), feelings, perceptions, mental formations, and consciousness. In finding all these empty, the sutra proclaims they are empty of a separate self: "That means none of these five rivers can exist by itself. . . . They have to co-exist; they have to inter-be with all the others."[33] No aspect of ourselves can exist as an entity unto itself. To be real is to be interdependent.

This insight allows Avalokita to overcome all pain. True wisdom is identification with the reality being understood, the realization of nonduality. If we do not penetrate the reality, we do not truly understand it. Avalokita then proclaims the basic principle that "form is emptiness, emptiness is form, form does not differ from emptiness, emptiness does not differ from form."[34] Nhat Hanh comments: "Emptiness is the ground of everything. Thanks to emptiness, everything is possible."[35] But emptiness is not an eternal creative ground independent of form; emptiness *is* the ever-changing world: "Emptiness is impermanence, it is change."[36] Being empty of a separate self means that all things have the possibility of being full.

Nhat Hanh explains that emptiness means that nothing comes into existence or goes out of existence: "[N]othing can be born, nothing can die."[37] Each of us preexisted in our parents, indeed in all reality: "As I look more deeply, I can see that in a former life I was a cloud. . . . Without the cloud, I cannot be here. . . . This is not a question of belief in reincarnation. This is the history of life on earth."[38] For Nhat Hanh, as for the Heart Sutra, nothing can come from nothing. Every reality arises from every other reality in a process that is beginningless and endless: "We cannot conceive the birth of anything. There is only continuation."[39]

Nor can anything go out of existence. The destruction of any form in this world only transforms its existence into a different mode. Paper burnt becomes heat and ashes which affect all other things in the future. Thus even human beings are not born and do not die in the ultimate sense. We existed in all the elements of the universe before our birth, we are one with all the elements of the universe during our life, and we will be one with all the elements of the universe after our death. The interconnection of all things with all other things is indestructible.

Just as a leaf *is* the tree it nourishes and a cloud *is* the river it fills and a wave *is* the ocean, so all things are empty of a separate, independent self and inter-are with all other things: "Each wave is born and is going to die, but the water is free from birth and death."[40] Seeing this is the basis for optimism and the overcoming of all pain, all fear of birth and death: "Birth and death are only ideas we have in our mind, and these ideas cannot be applied to reality."[41] If we see with the eyes of wisdom, we see that we have always been and always will be.

Insight into emptiness leads to the overcoming of all discrimination between pure and impure, increasing or decreasing. Nhat Hanh uses the example of roses and garbage: "Roses and garbage inter-are. Without a rose, we cannot have garbage; and without garbage, we cannot have a rose. They need each other very much. The rose and the garbage are equal."[42] Applying this perspective to questions of social justice, Nhat Hanh insists that we see the young prostitute in Manila as who she is because of the way nonprostitutes are. The social system of a society works as a unity. A poor girl is pressured to become a prostitute because of the entire structure of the society that supports wealthy families on the poverty of the poor: "Wealth is made of non-wealth elements, and poverty is made by non-poverty elements."[43] Nhat Hanh challenges us to see the prostitute in the non-prostitute people and the non-prostitute people in the prostitute.

This is true, Nhat Hanh insists, even of Buddha and the tempter, Mara: Each needs the other. Even the Buddha is empty of a self, and so even the Buddha is composed of non-Buddha elements: "As soon as the idea of good is there, the idea of evil is there. Buddha needs Mara in order to reveal himself, and vice versa. . . . Do not take sides. If you take sides, you are trying to eliminate half of reality, which is impossible."[44] To eliminate one side or the other is an act of violence which leads to further suffering. Genuine breakthroughs in politics or social justice demand a more inclusive, nondualistic framework which can do justice to both sides.

To illustrate the rather shocking application of this principle to the Buddha, Nhat Hanh tells the story about Mara coming to visit the Buddha. The Buddha's assistant, Ananda, did not want to welcome Mara at all, but the

Buddha was delighted to see such an old friend and welcomed Mara warmly to his cave. Mara confessed his discomfort with his role of always tempting people. He was tired of having to be deceitful and clever. Mara was especially annoyed with his disciples who had begun using the language of social justice and equality and nonduality and peace. Mara wanted to resign his position and become someone else. The Buddha listened very carefully to Mara's frustrations and noted how difficult it was to be a Buddha: "You don't know what my disciples have done to me! They put words into my mouth that I never said. They build garish temples and put statues of me on altars in order to attract bananas and oranges and sweet rice, just for themselves."[45]

In the more paradoxical language of the sutra, in emptiness there is "no suffering, no origination of suffering, no extinction of suffering, no path; no understanding, no attainment."[46] In these words the Four Noble Truths of the Buddha are negated one by one (no suffering, no origination, no extinction of suffering, no path) and the goal of the entire quest, understanding and attainment, is denied. The negation is the negation of independent existence apart from all other realities. Even Buddhist understanding does not exist apart from its opposite. Nhat Hanh explains that the negation means "understanding has no separate existence. Understanding is made of non-understanding elements, just as Buddha is made of non-Buddha elements."[47]

The overcoming of discriminating consciousness is the advent of perfect freedom, and so the apparent nihilism of negating any possible object of wisdom or attainment becomes the delight in all things. Having negated any attainment, the Heart Sutra proclaims: "Having no obstacles [the bodhisattvas] overcome fear, liberating themselves forever from illusion and realizing perfect Nirvana."[48] This is the overcoming of desire and fear.

The sutra concludes with a mantra, a chant to be used as a tool for the transformation and liberation of all beings. The mantra challenges us with the vision of the entire community of beings gone to the other shore, from the world of suffering to perfect liberation. As Nhat Hanh translates: "Gone, gone, gone all the way over, everyone gone to the other shore, enlightenment, svaha ["Welcome" or "Hallelujah"].[49] In chanting the mantra with full concentration of mind and body, one makes the passage to liberation and brings about liberation for all beings.

For Nhat Hanh, this transformation of our consciousness and of ourselves is the indispensable basis for all work for peace and justice in the world. Sitting meditation allows one to be in touch with oneself and one's world and find peace. "Meditation brings happiness. This happiness comes, first of all, from the fact that you are master of yourself, no longer caught up in forgetfulness."[50] Nhat Hanh asks: "If you do not begin your peace work with yourself, where will you go to begin it? To sit, to smile, to look at things and really see them, these are the basis of peace work."[51]

ENGAGEMENT IN THE WORLD

In Buddhist tradition, wisdom and compassion are inseparable. The wisdom of insight into interbeing inevitably expresses itself in compassionate action in the world. Thich Nhat Hanh himself has been deeply involved in the quest for peace and in efforts to help the victims of war and refugees from Vietnam. His insistence on the necessity and power of meditation for effective peace work is born of his own experience. In working with the School of Youth for Social Service, he knew the suffering of students injured and killed by fighting. Precisely because he refused to choose sides in the Vietnam war, he and his fellow workers were attacked by both sides. As he later recalled: "The Communists killed us because they suspected that we were working with the Americans, and the anti-Communists killed us because they thought that we were with the Communists. But we did not want to give up and take one side."[52]

One of his friends was later put into a reeducation camp in Vietnam. By meditating every day, he lived in peace, and did not count the four years in the camp a loss: "On the contrary, he knew he had 'reeducated' himself in meditation."[53]

After the war was over and the boat people were fleeing Vietnam, Nhat Hanh helped organize relief operations, renting two small ships to communicate and bring food and supplies to the boat people and two large ships to rescue refugees at sea and bring them to Australia or Guam. When the mission was discovered by the governments in the area, the Singapore police descended on the house where Nhat Hanh was staying at 2:00 in the morning, confiscated his travel documents, and ordered him to leave the country in twenty-four hours. Overwhelmed by a multitude of problems and unable to find a way out at first, Nhat Hanh began to practice a meditation topic he had earlier written down: "If you want peace, peace is with you immediately."[54] He resolved that he must be peaceful in this moment of crisis, or any other peace would be an illusion: "If I could not be peaceful in the midst of danger, then the kind of peace I might have in simpler times would not mean anything."[55] Meditating on the theme of immediate peace, he was able to remain calm and resolve the problems one by one.

The first step in working for peace, for Nhat Hanh, is to organize one's daily life to resist the colonization of our minds by modern society. Amid the countless messages assaulting our consciousness, Nhat Hanh challenges us to organize communities of resistance, places where people can take time to breathe, to see, to return to themselves.[56] He notes that the boat people had told him that when a storm threatened to sink their ship, if one person could remain calm and not panic, that was a great help.

Our earth is like a small boat in danger of capsizing, and each of us is challenged to be the person who remains calm. The first step is to see the interrelations among all things, the connections between our lives and the lives of people dying and nature threatened with pollution and pesticides. The life of each individual is intimately linked to every other life. Everything in a community of resistance should call us back to ourselves and to communion with reality. To do this at least one person is necessary who can radiate an atmosphere of peace and freshness. Even when the person is absent, his or her influence will be felt.[57]

Nhat Hanh laments that many peace organizations claim to work for peace without living a spirit of peace themselves. He considers two alternative strategies in peace work: "[T]o use words, or to be peaceful ourselves and to speak with our lives and our bodies. I think the second way is more effective."[58] He also notes the frustration of many young people who have worked for peace groups and have not had results. Anger and frustration build up and prevent communication: "The peace movement can write very good protest letters, but they are not yet able to write a love letter."[59]

The individual is the starting place for social change. "Among the three — individual, society and nature — it is the individual who begins to effect change. But in order to effect change he or she must have personally recovered, must be whole."[60] Such healing requires a healthy environment, and so transformation of the individual and of society must go hand in hand, but Nhat Hanh stresses the priority of individuals recovering their humanness. If we change our own life, then the world is a different world.

Nhat Hanh notes that the ideas of the Buddha himself radically challenged the ideas of Hindu society, but the Vietnamese Buddhist tradition has often been reticent in relation to political powers.[61] He himself sees religion as a form of permanent opposition to the government, but to carry out this role of opposition, he thinks it better that monks not be directly involved in politics.[62] The role of the monastery is not to rule the social and political order but to serve as a laboratory where people can make discoveries and then go elsewhere to aid other people.[63] He opposes violence in any situation: "If you think that violence is sometimes needed, then I think you need more awareness and more love. Then I am sure you will go in the other direction."[64]

To change the world, we need to breathe and open our eyes to see who we are and what must be done: "Each time we feel ourselves about to leave our Buddha, we can sit and breathe until we return to our true self. Doing these kinds of things can change our civilization."[65]

STRUCTURING THE LIFE OF COMPASSION: FOURTEEN PRECEPTS

Thich Nhat Hanh has established fourteen precepts as the guiding principles of the Tiep Hien Order. They are so many calls to awaken to reality: "Perhaps the most appropriate definition of *sila* (precepts) is being awake, mindful during each bodily, verbal and mental activity."[66] They are ways to structure the life of a bodhisattva, to realize the vow of saving every living being.

According to the charter of the order, the precepts are founded on four fundamental principles: nonattachment, direct practice-realization, appropriateness, and skillful means. Nonattachment to views challenges us to be free from rigid attachment to any set views, including Buddhist teachings. It is, for Nhat Hanh, "the most important teaching of Buddhism."[67] Direct practice-realization stresses that Buddhism aims at direct experience of reality, not at a merely intellectual interpretation. Appropriateness measures the worth of any teaching in terms of the needs and condition and reality of a particular people and society. Skillful means are the myriad ways of teaching the wisdom of the Buddha's path.

The basic principles are closely related to one another:

> The spirit of non-attachment to views and the spirit of direct practice-realization bring about tolerance and compassion in our way of looking at and interacting with living beings. The spirit of appropriateness and the spirit of skillful means bring about the power of creativity and the ability to reconcile. Both are necessary in order to realize the vow of helping in the world.[68]

The Tiep Hien Order embraces a core community, whose members have accepted all fourteen vows, and a broader extended community, which pledges to live in the spirit of the order. The fourteen precepts themselves are a development and application of the traditional eightfold path.

The first three precepts express the foundational principles of nonattachment to views and skillful means. The First Precept warns not to "be idolatrous about or bound to any doctrine, theory, or ideology, even Buddhist ones. All systems of thought are guiding means; they are not absolute truth."[69] Absolutizing any given position, including Buddhist positions, leads to narrowness, prejudice, and in extreme cases, fanatical violence born of hatred. Nhat Hanh notes that the Tiep Hien Order was founded in Vietnam in the 1960s, in the specific context of suffering caused by the bitter rivalry of competing ideologies. Both sides of the Vietnam war were blinded by clinging to one-sided views as if they were complete and absolute. The result was untold misery for all the victims of the war, including the combatants.

Another problem with clinging to present views is that it can block development of our understanding. The Buddha had warned that accepting some position as if it were absolute means that one has ended the process of seeking and enlightenment. Whatever our present level of attainment is, Nhat Hanh insists, it is not absolute. Thus the Second Precept advises us: "Do not think the knowledge you presently possess is changeless, absolute truth. . . . Truth is found in life and not merely in conceptual knowledge. Be ready to learn throughout your entire life and to observe reality in yourself and in the world at all times."[70] To *see* the world of dependent co-arising is not another theory about the universe; it is to experience the world directly, apart from conceptual distinctions.

The Third Precept expresses the implications of the first two for our relations with others. No one, including children, should be forced or unfairly pressured to adopt another person's views. Compassionate dialogue, which includes both speech and nonviolent action, is to replace the imposition of views through whatever means of pressure. This principle appeals to the memory of the Buddha challenging his followers to test every teaching for themselves, to take nothing on faith, but to experience the truth for themselves.

The Fourth Precept challenges us to open our eyes to suffering and to be in touch with those suffering. The purpose of meditation is to help us in this process of becoming ever more aware of the forms of suffering in ourselves and others. Nhat Hanh notes that while an excess of suffering may damage one's capacity to love, nonetheless, "suffering can help to open our eyes and has a therapeutic power."[71] This precept also challenges the Buddhist to practice Buddhism actively by helping others. Wisdom and compassion are inseparable: "When a village is being bombed and children and adults are suffering from wounds and death, can a Buddhist sit still in his unbombed temple? Truly, if he has wisdom and compassion, he will be able to practice Buddhism while helping other people."[72]

The Fifth Precept instructs us to live simply and avoid greed, the pursuit of fame, and sensual pleasure. The accumulation of wealth in a world of hunger leads to an endless and destructive cycle of desiring more and more. The quest for wealth is endless. To live simply allows us to share time and energy with others. The Sixth Precept challenges us to let go of anger and hatred through meditation and to practice compassion toward others, especially those who have wronged us. Nhat Hanh stresses that meditation is the proper medicine for anger and hatred, but meditation presupposes awareness of dependent co-arising, the ability to see the interconnectedness of all lives and circumstances and how each of us shares responsibility for the condition of the world. The challenge is simple but profound: "Looking at living beings with compassionate eyes."[73]

The Seventh Precept expresses the very heart of the Tiep Hien path: "Do not lose yourself in dispersion and in your surroundings. Learn to practice breathing in order to regain composure of body and mind, to practice mindfulness and to develop concentration and understanding."[74] Mindfulness is the practice of all of life. It is not restricted to formal times of meditation but challenges us to break through our ignorance and prejudices and emotions to see.

The Eighth Precept concerns proper speech and challenges us to avoid language that divides and to seek reconciliation. "The reconciler is able to transcend the conflict by understanding the suffering of both sides. . . . The conflict's resolution should be offered on the basis of an ideal common to both sides."[75] The Ninth Precept addresses itself to truthful speech. Our words can contribute to shaping a world of trust or a hell of division and hatred. One of the most powerful ways to become more aware of our speech is through the practice of silence. Retreats done in silence can help to purify and enrich our speech.

The Tenth Precept forbids the abuse of the Buddhist community for personal gain and also the transformation of the community into a political party. For Nhat Hanh, "to transform a religious community into a political party is to divert its true aim."[76] Nonetheless, while avoiding partisan conflicts, religious communities have the right and duty to oppose injustice and oppression and to transform the situation. The basis for this action is found in the Four Noble Truths, which first expose the reality of suffering (first truth) and then analyze the causes of the suffering (second truth). The third truth expresses the hope and goal of an end to injustice, oppression, and suffering; an intelligent application of the eightfold path (fourth truth) can propose measures to achieve this goal. Thus, while the religious community as such should not seek to exercise political power, it must express its analysis of an unjust situation and support those actions which promise to heal it.

The Eleventh Precept involves one's vocation or right livelihood. Our employment should not harm life in whatever form, human or other, and should contribute to building up compassion. The Twelfth Precept forbids killing or allowing others to kill. Nhat Hanh notes that this is an ideal which no one can perfectly follow, for even in boiling water for a cup of tea, tiny organisms are killed. Nonetheless, the challenge of this precept is most urgent in a world of starvation and poverty and massive defense budgets.

The Thirteenth Precept advises us: "Possess nothing that should belong to others."[77] While we should respect others' property, we should also oppose efforts of others to grow rich at the expense of the suffering of humans and other living beings. The Fourteenth Precept concerns our treatment of our body. We are to respect it and not regard it merely as an instrument to be used or abused in any way. This means preserving "vital energies (sexual, breath, spirit) for the realization of the Way."[78] Sexual relations must be based on love and long-term commitment and respect the commitments of others. They must also be based on awareness of the future suffering that sexual relations can cause and of the responsibility of bringing new lives into this world. This precept expresses the Middle Way of Shakyamuni Buddha, who realized that both excessive asceticism and hedonism were wrong.

The three energies are part of the common heritage of South and East Asia. In addition to sexual energy, these traditions distinguish the energy of breath and of spirit: "Vital breath is the energy expended when we speak more and breathe less. Spirit is the energy used when we are overly worried and anxious."[79] Meditation and concentration build up reserves of energy of breath and spirit so that it may used wisely.

The goal of all the precepts is to enable us to understand the very nature of reality as interbeing: "We cannot just be; we can only inter-be."[80]

8

Gustavo Gutiérrez and Thich Nhat Hanh

The Theology of Liberation in Relation to Engaged Buddhism

In recent decades Christians have wrestled with the question of how to respond to a world of massive unjust suffering and death. One of the most influential movements to take up this challenge has been the liberation theology of Latin America, particularly as represented by one of its founding figures, Gustavo Gutiérrez. Like Thich Nhat Hanh, Gutiérrez has sought to reinterpret and apply his own religious tradition in response to the enormous strains of contemporary existence. For Gutiérrez, the central paradox and deepest challenge of liberation theology is how to proclaim a God of life in the midst of a world of poverty and death. The unjust sufferings of millions of people has meant, for Gutiérrez, that a rupture had to be made with the approach of European and North American theology, and a new starting point found in the experience of the poor.

LIFE OF GUSTAVO GUTIÉRREZ

Gustavo Gutiérrez was born in 1928, two years after Thich Nhat Hanh, in the Monserrat barrio of Lima, Peru. He was born into a mestizo family with both Hispanic and Quechuan roots. From the age of twelve until eighteen, he was confined to bed and then to a wheelchair by osteomyelitis. After considering a career in medicine, he decided to enter the Catholic priesthood. He studied philosophy and theology in Santiago, Chile, and then was sent to study psychology and philosophy at the University of Louvain, Belgium, and theology at the University of Lyons, France.

Returning to Peru, he discovered that his European education had not

adequately prepared him for the realities of poverty and social and economic oppression in his homeland. During the 1960s, the same years that
Nhat Hanh was developing his ideas on engaged Buddhism and founding
the Tien Hiep Order, Gutiérrez was rethinking the role of Christian theology in relation to the history and political and social situation of Latin
America. From the efforts of Gutiérrez and others would emerge the theology of liberation, which received official endorsement from the Conference of Bishops of Latin America (CELAM) at their meeting in Medellín,
Colombia, in 1968. In 1971 he published *A Theology of Liberation*, which
became one of the crucial texts of the movement.

Gutiérrez has worked primarily as a parish priest in Rimac, one of the
poorer areas in Lima. He founded the Centro Bartolomé de Las Casas in
Rimac to study the role of religion in society and to effect constructive
change in the social, political, and economic context of Latin America. He
has participated in countless theological and ecclesiastical conferences, has
taught at a number of universities in Lima and abroad, and is the author
of numerous books and articles. In 1985 he received a doctorate in theology
from the theological faculty of the Catholic Institute of Lyons, France,
based upon the body of his published work.[1]

TRANSFORMATION OF CONSCIOUSNESS

Like Nhat Hanh, Gutiérrez insists that the awareness of most people is
distorted and that a change of consciousness is necessary. In particular,
Gutiérrez warns that for the most part, modern Western consciousness
denies the reality of massive suffering and assumes that the dominant economic and political system is adequate to human needs. For Gutiérrez, as
for Nhat Hanh, our false understanding of ourselves and our world must
first be destroyed so that we can see clearly and truly the situation of the
world.

OVERCOMING THE DENIAL OF SUFFERING

For both Gutiérrez and Nhat Hanh, coming to an awareness of suffering
is the first step on the path to liberation. Both figures recognize, however,
that we usually avoid such painful awareness as much as possible, and thus
both have a profound suspicion of our ordinary consciousness of the world.
Both thinkers warn us that we systematically block out awareness of certain
aspects of our world, especially of suffering, and thereby imprison ourselves
and others in categories that divide and oppress. For both, the refusal to
face and identify with the reality of suffering is the first barrier to be
overcome on the path to liberation.

For Gutiérrez, the denial of suffering in the contemporary world takes
the particular form of denying and ignoring the suffering of the poor. The
dominant powers and sectors of society systematically avoid giving attention

to the perspectives, needs, and rights of the poor. It is "unpleasant" to focus on their suffering and inconvenient to attend to their claims to justice, and so the poor are often treated as "non-persons," unheard and invisible. For centuries, the poor have been systematically ignored by the dominant classes and powers. This has affected both the distribution of resources in the present and the way the memory of the past has been handed on.

Too often historians have written their narratives from the perspective of the conquerors, the rich, the powerful. The poor have been silent, invisible, and thus apparently absent; the poor have effectively been dismissed from the stage of history. The absence of the poor from history deprives them of the consciousness of their own position and thus of the power to change it.

> History has been written from the viewpoint of the dominating sectors. . . . But history's winners have sought to wipe out their victims' memory of the struggles, so as to be able to snatch from them one of their sources of energy and will in history: a source of rebellion.[2]

By being systematically ignored, the poor have been reduced to the status of "non-persons." The powerful have not taken their interests into account, and the poor themselves have not had the awareness necessary to mobilize resources for change.

Gutiérrez adopts and adapts the category of ideology to name the problem and to begin to outline a response.[3] Ideology in Marxist theory is the corruption of reason by interest.[4] The powerful conceal oppressive relations of domination by presenting a theory that makes the status quo appear to be reasonable and just and therefore acceptable. Ideology presents a justification of an oppressive present by disguising unjust power relations and making them appear "natural" and inevitable. Ideology justifies the ignoring of the poor by blaming them for their poverty and covering up systemic causes of poverty. The first step on the road to liberation is a thoroughgoing critique of ideology, an unmasking of the human suffering caused by social, economic, and political systems, and an exposing of the deceptions of dominant rationalizations of the system. This project demands a concrete interpretation of the relations of power in a given social, economic, and political context.

Awareness of the widespread suffering of the innocent sets up the central dilemma of theology for Gutiérrez. The experience of Latin America is marked by massive starvation, systematic degradation of despised races, mistreatment of women, and violent repression of efforts to assist the poor. Gutiérrez notes that where European theologians have struggled with how to do Christian theology after Auschwitz, Latin American theologians find themselves in the midst of an ongoing historical process that massively violates human life and dignity and must ask: "How are we to do theology while Ayacucho lasts? How are we to speak of the God of life when cruel murder on a massive scale goes on in 'the corner of the dead'?"[5]

While he does not focus as specifically on the situation of the poor, Nhat Hanh also recognizes the power of ideologies to distort perceptions, block out awareness of the suffering of victims, and thus perpetuate cycles of violence. He witnessed this process firsthand in the violence unleashed by ideologies in Vietnam in the 1960s. He noted the paradox of American soldiers filled with ideological ideas coming to Vietnam to fight the Viet Cong, when they had no real idea who the Viet Cong were or what the history and culture of Vietnam had been.[6] Because of the combined power of ignorance and ideologies, American soldiers were able to kill people they did not know or understand. Competing ideologies, which dominated the Cold War and saw all struggles in light of the struggle between the Soviet Union and the United States, systematically distorted the major powers' interpretations of Vietnamese experience. Nhat Hanh's journey to the United States was an attempt to inform the American people and government of the Vietnamese experience and help end the fighting.

The even deeper tragedy, however, was that the Vietnamese themselves allowed themselves to be blinded by rivalries and used by competing powers to kill each other so brutally. Nhat Hanh decried the distortions and deceptions of both the Communist government of North Vietnam and also the government of South Vietnam. As the fictional character Stone Boy speaks with people in North Vietnam, he learns that they have been deceived by their government. People of North Vietnam had little awareness of the suffering caused by North Vietnamese troups in the South. As Stone Boy reflected on his experience of both North and South Vietnam, he saw the real cause of the people's suffering in their inability to resolve their differences on their own without appealing to outside powers.[7]

For Nhat Hanh, the principles of becoming aware of suffering and of critique of ideology are deeply rooted in Buddhist tradition, for they flow directly from the First Noble Truth of the Buddha and the Buddhist principle of not clinging to any doctrine. Nhat Hanh notes that we often deaden our consciousness to avoid pain. We flee negative feelings and experiences by running to distractions or by using drugs or alcohol to dull our sensibilities. The First Noble Truth challenges us to open our eyes to suffering, and meditation breaks through barriers to perception and allows us to experience ourselves and our world without distortion. Meditation opens us to a courageous confrontation with suffering, a realization of the First Noble Truth.

The Fourth Tiep Hien Precept directly poses this challenge: "Find ways to be with those who are suffering by all means, including personal contact and visits, images, sounds. By such means, awaken yourself and others to the reality of suffering in the world."[8] The First and Second Tiep Hien Precepts set forth the Buddhist principles for a critique of ideologies: no doctrine or perspective is to be absolutized, including Buddhist ones. Every perspective is to be tested in experience according to the principle of appropriateness.

Gutiérrez's principles of becoming aware of suffering and of ideology critique are also deeply rooted in his religious tradition. Hebrew prophets warned that religious ceremonies, even worship in the Temple of the Lord, would not save people who oppressed the poor. Prophets such as Amos and Micah and Jeremiah were acutely aware of how religion could function to distort the consciousness of a people, to make the status quo appear to be blessed by God, while unjust practices ravaged the lives of the poor.[9] The Bible repeatedly witnesses to God's special concern for the poor, the widow, and the orphan, and challenges us to make God's concern our own by becoming especially aware of the suffering of the most vulnerable in society. As we shall see, Gutiérrez also finds precedent for suspecting any merely conceptual theory in the example of Job's rejection of the theology of his friends. Any theology that accepts the challenge of the Book of Job will have to be willing to enter into the concrete experience of innocent suffering to test its claims.

For both Gutiérrez and Nhat Hanh, the awareness of suffering is a crucial first step which leads to a search for the causes of suffering and to imagining how different the world could be.

IMAGINING ANOTHER WORLD

Gutiérrez finds one of the most significant events of recent world history to be the irruption of the poor, the "breaking-in" of the poor into history. This means that the poor, especially in impoverished countries, are coming to a new awareness of their condition and its causes, and are taking new initiatives to transform their lives. This process has radically changed the situation of Latin America since the 1960s, leading to the emergence of a new historical subject, the poor, and a new awareness of the implications of the Gospel. A new awareness of the human causes of poverty leads to a changed perception of the social and political situation and of the role and responsibility of religion in this situation. For Gutiérrez, the new consciousness is already beginning to transform the Church and the world, especially in communities of the poor.

As the poor become more aware of their condition and its causes, they begin to imagine a world of justice in which they would be able to live in accord with their dignity as children of God. As they see how profoundly contrary to the will of God the present structures are, they begin to imagine another world of justice and freedom. The dream of a different world, a world that does not yet exist but can be imagined, is called utopia.[10] Utopia creatively imagines a new order of relations among persons in society, and thereby undermines the claim of ideology to be "natural" and inevitable. Even if utopias are not concretely realizable immediately, as imaginative presentations of an ideal they can be powerful driving forces in history, critiquing present structures and mobilizing energies for change.

Nhat Hanh does not focus so specifically on the recent change in consciousness of the poor but rather on the threat that Western civilization poses to the entire planet and the importance of dialogue between Eastern and Western spiritual traditions as a response. The materialist consumerism of modern Western culture, whether capitalist or socialist, threatens to reduce humans to cogs in a giant machine, devoid of a spiritual center. Nhat Hanh notes that young people of the East and West are discovering a fundamental need which modern civilization is unable to meet: *"the need to be a human being. In reality, this need is not truly new, it is one of the fundamental needs of man, stifled by arbitrary needs. This need can be considered as our greatest hope."*[11]

The awareness of this danger and this need has led many Westerners to explore the resources of Eastern religious traditions, especially Zen. Nhat Hanh notes the irony that many Westerners have turned to Zen at a time when Zen itself in East Asia is in decline. While Zen monasteries still exist, he comments that "young Westerners seem more interested in Zen than are the young people in the East, who are more preoccupied with revolution and industrialization."[12]

Nonetheless, Nhat Hanh hopes that spiritual traditions of both East and West will be able to work together to address the vacuum created by modern Western culture. Though he does not use the term *utopia*, Nhat Hanh imagines his own form of utopia, modeled on the experience of Zen monasteries:

> "Awakened" people are certainly going to form small communities where material life will become simple and healthy. Time and energy will be devoted to the enrichment of spirituality. These communities will be Zen monasteries of a modern style where there will be no dogma. In them the sickness of the times will be cured and spiritual health will be acquired.[13]

Such small communities can be a harbinger of the future, pathfinders for a new civilization. Nhat Hanh notes that Zen has not yet really established itself in the West, for it still has too much of an Asian appearance. To take root and flourish, Zen must take on a new Western form, transforming and being transformed by Western culture. Both East and West will be changed in this process of learning. The creation of ceaseless desires by modern consumer capitalism is a dangerous threat to human existence on the planet. Nhat Hanh hopes that the perspective of interbeing lived out by small communities can model a more human way of life and offer hope for the future.

Nhat Hanh's hope flows from the basic link between the First Noble Truth and the Third: life is suffering, but there is a cessation of suffering. Genuine awareness of present suffering and its causes inevitably leads to awareness of different ways of living in the world. The principle of inter-being shows the profound interdependence of the human community:

> The only alternative to co-existence is co-non-existence. A civilization in which we must kill and exploit others in order to live is not a civilization of mental health. . . . Awareness of what is happening to the human family is necessary to repair the damage already done.[14]

Nhat Hanh imagines a world in which all persons are truly equal, "with the right to education, work, food, and shelter, to world citizenship, to freely circulate and settle on any part of the earth."[15] This vision of another way of living can be a powerful impetus to change.

For both figures, visions of the future have to be related to the daily practice of a religious path. For Gutiérrez, the first step in theology is discipleship, the following of Jesus. Given the repeated biblical demands for justice and respect for the poor, the challenge of discipleship includes solidarity with the poor. For the poor themselves, this means a new sense of their own dignity and their just claims on society. For the nonpoor, solidarity means a serious effort to listen to the experience of the poor, to penetrate their world and identify with their concerns. For Nhat Hanh, the heart of Buddhism is not a theory about the world or a vision of the future, but a way of living in the present. As we have seen, Nhat Hanh proposes a concrete guide to the contemporary Buddhist life in the Tiep Hien Precepts, which focus attention on the present and call for understanding of those who suffer and compassionate action. By attending to ourselves and our world at this moment, we prepare the future.

PRINCIPLES OF INTERPRETATION

For both figures, the process of transforming consciousness profoundly influences the way they read their tradition's founding scriptures. Each is wary of dangers in interpreting their tradition's scriptures, and each insists on a creative dialogue between present experience and traditional wisdom. The concrete ways that this dialogue proceeds, however, are rather different.

Gutiérrez begins with a suspicion of many past interpretations of the Bible. He fears that the dominant classes' interpretation of the Bible has been all too often dominated by ideology. To remedy this situation, he calls for a rereading of history and the Bible from the perspective of the poor. A new consciousness of history and the Bible will lead to new forms of action: "But *rereading* history means *remaking* history. It means repairing it from the bottom up. And so it will be a subversive history. History must be turned upside-down from the bottom, not from the top."[16]

One of the basic principles of Gutiérrez's reading of the Bible is that God's revelation comes gratuitously to humans, and in a special way to the poor, the simple, the despised: "The scorned of this world are those whom the God of love prefers."[17] The gratuitous love of God for all humans, and especially for those who suffer unjustly, is the basis of all Christian life and reflection on it. God's preference for the poor comes from God's own goodness, and is revealed repeatedly in the history of Israel and the life of Jesus. It is not based on any analysis of society.

Theology and the interpretation of the scriptures always presuppose the acceptance of the Christian life, which includes both contemplation and practice. Contemplation and practice together form the "first act," which Gutiérrez describes as the stage of silence:

> Contemplation and practice feed each other; the two together make up the stage of silence before God. In prayer we remain speechless, we simply place ourselves before the Lord. To a degree, we remain silent in our practice as well, for in our involvements, in our daily work, we do not talk about God all the time; we do indeed live in God, but not by discoursing on God.[18]

Where Nhat Hanh insists on meditation and silence in order to see clearly the meaning of the Buddhist scriptures, Gutiérrez bases his own practice of silence on meditation upon the mystery of God's gratuitous love and on the practice of discipleship. Only as a "second act" can one do Christian theology. Once one has made the passage through silence, contemplation, and practice, one can reflect upon this experience in theology: "Theology will then be speech that has been enriched by silence. This reflective discourse will in turn feed the silence of contemplation and practice and give it new dimensions."[19] In this context, reading the Bible becomes a profoundly transformative experience. As we interpret the Bible, the Bible interprets us.

For Nhat Hanh, the great danger in interpreting Buddhist scriptures is that we are tempted to take them as conceptual theories about reality and cling to them as absolute and final expressions of truth. The key to understanding the meaning of Buddhist texts is deep, aware experience of the present. Nhat Hanh embraces the Zen tradition of direct mind-to-mind transmission. This is not opposed to studying the Buddhist scriptures, but it does mean that direct experience is necessary to understand the teaching of the sutras.[20] This sets up the basic method for interpreting all Buddhist texts: "As reality can only be lived and experienced, Buddhist doctrine would never have as an aim the description of reality; the doctrine serves only as a method, as a guide, to the practitioner in his experience of this reality."[21]

If the terms of Buddhism are taken as concepts describing reality, they lead us astray. If they are accepted as adequate and final knowledge, they deceive us. If, however, they are used as skillful means integrated into religious practice, they can lead us to wisdom.

ON JOB

Where Nhat Hanh dramatically expressed the process transformation of consciousness in his short stories and play, Gutiérrez finds a classic expression of the process of transformation of consciousness in the Book of Job. Because of the acuteness with which it poses the question of language about God in a world of innocent suffering, the Book of Job is especially important for Latin America today. In the experience of Job, Latin Americans can find an archetype for understanding their own experience. The characters in Nhat Hanh's writings and Job all go through bitter experiences of separation and suffering and come to a new awareness of the meaning of suffering, of their relations to other people and to the entire universe, and to a new vision of reality.

RELIGION AND REWARD

As the Book of Job opens, all seems well among Job and God and the world. Job is pious, successful, and happy, and God delights in his fidelity. The prologue, however, quickly introduces the question of language about God in more difficult circumstances: granted that Job is pious when contented; will Job speak ill of God if he loses his comfortable life-style and his own family? The satan appears as a cynic who suspects that Job's uprightness is simply a prudent gratitude for favors received: his loyalty and piety to God are tied to his prosperity. For Job, the satan suggests, religion is intimately linked to reward.

Thus the satan, for Gutiérrez, poses the central question of the entire book: "the role that reward or disinterestedness plays in faith in God and in its consistent implementation."[22] The close link between religion and reward will have to be cut. A self-seeking religion which looks for rewards for fidelity is a form of self-deception, an obstacle which must be destroyed before a genuine relation to God can develop. As Gutiérrez notes, for the author of Job, "disinterested religion is true religion."[23]

The question of a relation to God never arises in Nhat Hanh's writings, but it is clear that for him, Buddhism cannot be a means of self-advancement. In Buddhist terms, the notion of linking religion and reward presupposes a discriminating consciousness which grasps at pleasures and thus still clings to the ego-self. The path of the bodhisattva renounces any expectation of personal reward, for the notion of an independent ego-self has lost its power to deceive. Thus Nhat Hanh insists on the aimlessness and wishlessness of Buddhist practice. To practice Buddhism for the sake of reward is to cling to illusion and deepen one's self-deception.

ACCEPTANCE AND QUESTIONING

Job passes the initial phase of his trial. After the catastrophic losses of his family and property recounted in the prose introduction, Job does indeed prove faithful and utters nothing sinful against God, despite his wife's urging him to curse God and die (Job 2:9).

Job's early acceptance of his suffering as coming from God, the source of all things (Job 1:21) foreshadows the ultimate resolution of his dilemma at the end of the book. Since God is the absolute source of all reality, everything comes as sheer gift, and humans have no autonomous standpoint for pressing their demands. Gutiérrez notes that Job's initial simple acceptance is often echoed by the poor who mourn the dead by saying, "God gave them to me, God has taken them away from me."[24]

Gutiérrez defends this simple faith as not simply naive, but as expressing a deep truth which must be probed. He also warns, however, that this naive level of faith is powerless to defend itself against ideological language, and thus is vulnerable to being abused and manipulated. The powerful can take advantage of the long-suffering attitude of the poor and allow unconscionable conditions to continue endlessly. Then the simple faith of the poor becomes an uncritical acceptance of their unjust lot, as if God directly willed the conditions of their lives. To prevent this danger, further exploration is necessary. Despite the innocence of Job's initial response, his understanding of his situation is incomplete and will have to be probed and deepened through the discussions with his friends and his encounter with God.

Where the Buddhist tradition stressed that learning wisdom required a series of separations and the proper acceptance of separation, Gutiérrez finds separation at the heart of the process of deepening the faith of the poor.[25] There is an initial painful separation in the loss of his children and possessions, but a series of separations will take place throughout the book. Another separation will take place in Job's rejection of the theology of his friends; but as the book continues, Job will pass through "complaint, bewilderment, and confrontation," in effect, a painful separation from his earlier notions of God and his earlier too-easy acceptance of suffering as God's will.[26]

In the writings of Nhat Hanh, the characters also move through separation to an acceptance of suffering, though their path does not proceed through a struggle with God but rather through encounters with bodhisattvas that guide them to an awakening to the vision of interbeing. Their initial reactions to suffering vary: Tô is deeply saddened by the loss of her father and later of her sight, Dao is depressed to the point of suicide by the memory of her violent rape, the slain young men are calm as they continue their journey. In each case, their initial understanding is limited and will have to be deepened and challenged by a process of reflection and questioning.

CONCEPTS AND EXPERIENCE

The friends of Job come to console him and interpret his misfortune for him. They are well-meaning, learned men who have accepted all too uncritically the theology of reward and punishment expressed in many biblical texts. Through their heated debates with Job, the author will explore the meaning of suffering and the way in which God is experienced.

After sitting in silence with his friends for seven days and nights, Job gives voice to his grief and pain. Job's experience is so painful, so chaotic, so devoid of justice or any trace of God's presence, that he wishes he had never been born. Gutiérrez suggests that this passionate expression of grief is, however paradoxical it may sound, "a profound act of self-surrender and hope in God. It springs from a situation of suffering that has no intelligible cause."[27]

This poses the fundamental question: What sense does it make to speak of God in light of the suffering of the innocent? The fundamental choice at issue in the debate between Job and his friends is the choice "between a religion based on the rights and obligations of human beings as moral agents, and a disinterested belief based on the gratuitousness of God's love."[28] One can either calculate the basis of reward and punishment that humans deserve and measure God's actions accordingly, or one can abandon all attempts at calculation and place one's trust in the gratuitous love of an incomprehensible God.

The speeches of Job and his friends begin with the friends proposing and Job rejecting the theology of reward and punishment. This theology, rooted in the earlier Deuteronomic and sapiential traditions of Israel, presents God as rewarding the just and punishing the guilty. From this clear principle, the friends logically conclude that Job must have done something to deserve his sufferings, and urge him to confess his sin, be reconciled to God, and thus be restored to favor and prosperity. The thoughts of the friends move in a world of concepts cut off from experience. The logic of reward and punishment appears adequate to explain whatever happens, and thus no experience is allowed to challenge it. God, they reason, could not be unjust.

Where the friends are confident of the validity and adequacy of the theology of retribution, Job's own experience has shattered the credibility of this perspective for him. He may not be completely innocent, but nothing he has done deserves this much suffering. From beginning to end, Job rejects the theology of retribution in the name of his own painful experience. The concepts of reward and punishment simply do not fit his experience, and thus must be changed.

Where the friends typify the attitude of clinging to a merely conceptual perspective and making it absolute, Job himself is much closer to the First Precept of the Tiep Hien Order, which forbids absolutizing any given doctrine or teaching.[29] Rather than falsify his experience, Job now openly questions the validity of the theory of retribution, which he too had formerly accepted. Even though he has no new theory to replace it, he refuses to accept the traditional theology of reward and punishment as changeless, absolute truth. Because of his honesty in questioning, he is open to further learning. In this openness he lives the Second Tiep Hien Precept by being ready to learn throughout an entire lifetime and not regarding his present knowledge as absolute. However different the religious contexts may be, Job's rejection of a merely conceptual approach to religion exemplifies the honesty to experience and openness to learning commended by Nhat Hanh.

Gutiérrez also notes the social and political implications of the theory of retribution. It has served as a classic example of ideology, reassuring the rich that their prosperity is a reward for virtue and advising the poor that they really deserve their suffering. Capitalism in particular has turned this theory to its own advantage and claimed religious justification from it.[30]

BROADENING THE HORIZON

Gutiérrez notes two stages in Job's ongoing process of discovery: (1) Job leaves behind the narrow focus on his own personal situation and expands his range of concern to include the poor who also suffer unjustly, and (2) Job encounters God directly and discovers an even broader horizon in the sheer gratuitousness of the love of God in creation. Two different forms of language express these new insights: prophetic language gives voice to the concern for all who suffer injustice, and contemplative language gives voice to the experience of God in creation.[31]

There is a twofold development of the awareness of the Buddhist characters, as well. In each case they become more aware of the suffering of other people. As Dao recounts the sufferings she and her fellow passengers had endured, she is changed: "But now she was aware of the tragic plight of all her people."[32] For all the characters, reflection on their own situation leads to a greater sensitivity to others' pain. The Buddhist characters also move toward a direct experience of the truth of interbeing, a mystery they had heard spoken of before but had not genuinely *seen*.

While the friends repeat their arguments over and over in ever-angrier tones, Job continues to reflect and finds his own perspective being transformed. As Job ponders, he realizes more and more that his own suffering is not unique. He learns that his own bitter frustrations are also those of other innocent sufferers, especially the poor: "The poor of this world are in the same boat as he: instead of living, they die by the roadside, deprived of the land that was meant to support them."[33] Job sees that the suffering of the poor is caused by the greed and power of the rich and powerful (Job 24:2–14), and he begins to denounce injustice in prophetic terms. The poor die every day, and the rich who exploit them are guilty of murder. Job's cries to God for justice now embrace the sufferings of the poor as well as his own situation.

While the characters of Nhat Hanh never cry to God for justice, they do come to see the depth of human suffering in a new light. Like Job, they also leave behind the focus on their own sufferings, reflect on other persons' experiences, and thus gain deeper insight into how others suffer. Where

Job and Gutiérrez focus mainly on the suffering of the oppressed, the narratives of Nhat Hanh focus on the suffering of the oppressors, as well. The murderers of the young social workers and even their superiors become objects of compassion. In the vision of interbeing, all dualisms are overcome.

At this point in the book, Job's perspective is broader and deeper than it was, and Job has seen more clearly that even his own suffering is no reason to neglect the needs of the poor. What Gutiérrez terms the prophetic language of Job allows him to speak of God more profoundly and truthfully, but this language is still ultimately inadequate, for Job's questions remain all the more poignant. To move further requires a new level of awareness and still another type of language to express it, the language of contemplation and mysticism.

SEEING

For Gutiérrez, the basis of the language of contemplation and mysticism is the awareness of the origin of all things in God. For Job, this comes from a direct experience of God, but his encounter itself comes only after a crisis in Job's relation to God.

Job is all too aware of the paradoxical character of any struggle with God. He knows that no one can claim to be upright before God (Job 9:2). He also knows that he needs an arbiter, a witness, and a liberator to press his case before God, but only God can fulfill these roles. To bring a lawsuit against God seems necessary but impossible. How can he accuse God of injustice when God is the only possible judge? (Job 9:32–35.) Nonetheless, Job presses his case, convinced that God will acknowledge his innocence in the end. In continuing his struggle even when it seems impossible, Job "splits God in two and produces a God who is judge and a God who will defend him at that supreme moment; a God whom he experiences as almost an enemy but whom he knows at the same time to be truly a friend."[34] This paradoxical dialectic places all Job's hope in a liberator who will ransom and redeem him from his accusers. Only God can redeem Job from his misery, but this very God is also the source of his suffering. In this paradox Gutiérrez finds "one of the most profound messages of the Book of Job."[35] God is both adversary and redeemer, both accuser and vindicator, both enemy and friend. This marks the final collapse of conceptual consistency: the neat, rational categories of Job's friends are completely inadequate to express this painful experience.

Gutiérrez notes a similar "splitting of God" in the Latin American author César Vallejo, who expressed his own faith in God in terms very close to Job's: "Whatever be the cause I must defend before God after death, I myself have a defender: God."[36] The contradiction seems complete, and Gutiérrez notes that the only way to accept the seeming contradiction of all logic is to learn "that God's justice is to be understood only in the context of prior and gratuitous love."[37] The full meaning of this lesson, however, Job must learn from God's own speeches.

In Buddhism there is no God to bear the brunt of this paradox, and the relation to ultimate reality is not set in the image of a juridical relationship. There is no question of an anguished personal relationship to absolute reality. The experience of a similar paradox does, nonetheless, appear in the suffering and joy of existence: "Life is filled with suffering, but it is also filled with many wonders, like the blue sky, the sunshine, the eyes of a baby. To suffer is not enough. We must be in touch with the wonders of life."[38] For Nhat Hanh, life is both suffering and miraculous, and awareness of suffering deepens our capacity for joy.

When God does speak directly to Job at the end of the book, Gutiérrez insists that the divine speeches do not simply overpower Job with a sheer display of might, but reveal the creative freedom of God and God's own respect for human freedom. Where Job had earlier feared that God would simply crush him, God refrains from doing so, preferring to reveal the greatness of God in freedom and gratuitous love.[39]

God never accuses Job of any guilt, and thus implicitly confirms his innocence. Later God will explicitly state that Job, not his friends, has spoken rightly of God (Job 42:8). God does accuse Job of obscuring God's "intentions" or "plans" (38:2), but this is not necessarily sinful. Gutiérrez takes "intentions" in this context as referring to God's plan for action in history, a plan which arises from the gratuitousness of God's creative love.[40]

In the first speech (Job 38–39), God completely rejects any anthropocentric reading of creation. Where both Job and his friends had assumed that the world should be related to human needs, God insists that the world was not created to be of benefit for human beings. Many things come into being, live, and die far from human habitation. Rain falls in areas where no humans live. Thus God's action need not follow the wishes or needs of humans. Creation did not take place to reward or punish human beings, and so the premises of Job and his friends alike are mistaken. God enjoys creating from sheer gratuitous love. This gratuitous love, not retribution, "is the hinge on which the world turns."[41]

Nhat Hanh's interpretation of interbeing also assumes that all things do not exist for the sake of humans. Humans are an important part of the play of the universe, but no form of existence is central. Nhat Hanh, however, never finds a divine intentionality behind the interrelationships of things. The universe is as it is without ultimate origin in or guidance from a creating God.

One implication of God's first speech to Job is that humans can foresee what the divine freedom will do. If God's love is really gratuitous, then it is cause and not effect, and thus not open to human rational penetration, prediction, or control. Gutiérrez stresses that Job must learn "that nothing, not even the world of justice, can shackle God; this is the very heart of the answer."[42] Gutiérrez draws the further implication: "what holds for the world of nature, holds with all the greater reason for the world of history."[43] In response to the first speech of God, Job admits his own smallness, acknowledging that humans are not indeed the center of the universe. As Gutiérrez notes, this is an expression of humility, but not of repentance or resignation.

God presses further in a second speech (Job 40:7–41) which focuses more directly on God's just government of the world. In the second speech God notes that human freedom itself demands respect. Even though God wills that justice be done, "God cannot impose it, for the nature of created beings must be respected. God's power is limited by human freedom; for without freedom God's justice would not be present within history."[44] Paradoxically, the all-powerful, free God is limited by creation itself. If God wills to have free human beings who can freely convert, then God cannot destroy the wicked. Thus, "the all-powerful God is also a 'weak' God."[45] God respects the freedom of humans even when they abuse it and chooses to work in human history by appealing to human freedom rather than by abolishing it. God's nondiscriminating love embraces all, just and wicked alike.

Nhat Hanh could agree with the principle behind God's restraint and nondiscriminating compassion, but in a rather different context. While there is no creator to make any such decision on government of the cosmos, the universe of interbeing is itself marked by a nondiscriminating acceptance of good and evil alike; for in the perspective of dependent co-arising, roses and garbage are interdependent, as are wealthy and poor, oppressors and oppressed. Each side of a seeming opposition "inter-is" with its polar opposite. To abolish one side of an apparent opposition would be to do violence to both sides. Nhat Hanh repeatedly calls for understanding to see that there is nothing pure or defiled. This is the central Buddhist resolution of what Christians name the problem of evil. As Nhat Hanh explains:

> But in the light of non-duality, there is no problem: As soon as the idea of good is there, the idea of evil is there. Buddha needs Mara in order to reveal himself, and vice versa. . . . Do not take sides. If you take sides, you are trying to eliminate half of reality, which is impossible.[46]

After the second speech, Job acknowledges that the marvels revealed are beyond his grasp. By the end of the book, Job's understanding of God and of himself has been profoundly transformed. For Gutiérrez, the heart of this transformation is a new understanding of the relationship between justice and gratuitousness. Gutiérrez distinguishes three steps in Job's second response to God: "an acknowledgment that God has plans and that these are being carried out; a discovery of previously unrecognized aspects of reality; a joyous encounter with the Lord."[47] The first moment recognizes the reality and effectiveness of divine plans, even when humans cannot comprehend them. The inability of humans to grasp the divine intentions is no argument against their reality and power.

The second moment of awareness is not the communication of new concrete items of information, but rather a new discernment that allows Job to accept God's plan of gratuitous love as freely guiding all reality. Divine freedom and love are the source of all that is. The third moment in Job's awareness is what he describes as seeing God face-to-face, as opposed to hearing about God by hearsay. This direct encounter with God exacts a price, for Job, like Jacob, leaves the meeting limping, but "the revelation given to him has opened up a new world to him."[48]

These three steps establish a new relationship to God in which Job accepts his creaturely status. Job expresses this in the language of retracting and repenting, but Gutiérrez points out that the verb translated as "retract" has no object, and understands the line as saying: "I repudiate and abandon (change my mind about) dust and ashes."[49] "Dust and ashes" is an imaginative way of expressing the groaning and lamentation that Job had endured at the beginning of the dialogue with his friends. According to Gutiérrez, Job now sees that his initial attitude of lamentation and dejection was unjustified. Even though Job nowhere retracts his insistence on his innocence, Job does experience a change in his horizon of awareness. "Job realizes that he has been speaking of God in a way that implied that God was prisoner of a particular way of understanding justice. It is this whole outlook that Job says he is now abandoning."[50] This new awareness is the basis for contemplative and mystical language about God.

Nhat Hanh could strongly concur that wisdom is not found through new information but in a new way of seeing and in the letting go of any attitude of lamentation and dejection. He could also agree that wisdom involves a new relation between gratuitousness and justice, and that the latter must be grounded in the former. There is, however, no God with whom to dialogue and no inscrutable divine intentions or agency to accept. Things are as they are, impermanent and conditioned, but in a process which is itself everlasting and unconditioned. Things are not separate from the process, nor is the process separate from the things that comprise it. Illusions cause much unnecessary suffering, but there is no cause for anger or revenge. Once we see the process of interbeing, we realize that there is nothing to lament, nothing to mourn, nothing to be angry over.

Job's newfound wisdom turns on the distinction and relation between justice and the gratuitous love of God. Justice is grounded in the love of God, not the other way around. The rules of cause and effect do not govern the way of love, for love of its very nature is a free gift. God's love does not simply follow human merits, but freely dispenses its favors, especially to the poor. Gutiérrez summarizes his interpretation of the central point of the book:

> The world of retribution—and not of temporal retribution only—is not where God dwells; at most God visits it. The Lord is not prisoner

of the "give to me and I will give to you" mentality. Nothing, no human work however valuable, merits grace, for if it did, grace would cease to be grace. This is the heart of the message of the Book of Job.[51]

This insight gives Gutiérrez the resolution of the problem posed at the beginning of the book. To speak of God in a world of innocent suffering, we must use both the language of prophecy, which stresses the requirements of justice in this world, and the language of contemplation, which exults in the gratuitous love of God. Without the prophetic challenge to practice justice, contemplative or mystical language could be a flight from responsibility. Without the contemplative emphasis on gratuitous love, the prophetic insistence on justice could imprison God in a framework of retribution. These two forms of speech are fundamental for all Christian theology. As Gutiérrez puts it elsewhere: "To sing and to set free; thanksgiving and demand for justice. Christian existence unfolds between the freely given gift and the demand."[52]

This perspective offers a fundamental warning that action for justice must never be absolutized, but must always be set in the broader horizon of God's love: "[E]mphasis on the practice of justice and on solidarity with the poor must never become an obsession and prevent our seeing that this commitment reveals its value and ultimate meaning only within the vast and mysterious horizon of God's gratuitous love."[53]

The final resolution for the characters of Nhat Hanh takes place in a radically different understanding of the universe. Nonetheless, there is a twofold rhythm of seeing and acting common to both traditions. Where the contemplative language of Gutiérrez celebrates the gratuitous love of God manifest in creation, the wisdom of the Buddhist tradition displays the mystery of dependent co-arising. For both Gutiérrez and Nhat Hanh, the sheer fact of existence is a marvel to be grateful for. Both visions also lead to new forms of action. Gutiérrez's contemplative vision of the gratuitous love of God leads to prophetic condemnations of injustice and work for establishing justice. Nhat Hanh's vision of the wisdom of interbeing leads to the compassion of the path of the bodhisattva. For both figures, the realization of the mystery of existence gives a basis for creative action and also relativizes any concrete program of action. Where Gutiérrez maintains the primacy of love over justice, Nhat Hanh relativizes any concrete political program that claims to implement the path of engaged Buddhism.

Where Job accepts his status as a creature with a new depth after encountering God face-to-face, the characters of Nhat Hanh experience their relation to all else in a new way, realize that they are indestructible, without beginning or end, and are filled with compassion for all beings.

CREATION AND INTERBEING

Both Gutiérrez and Nhat Hanh insist on breaking through any merely conceptual understanding to direct, honest experience of reality itself. It is the experience of God in creation or of the mystery of interbeing that is crucial for resolving the different struggles. Where Gutiérrez embraces the honest questioning of Job against the conceptual categories of his friends, Nhat Hanh warns that all the language of Buddhism serves as a skillful means to allow us to see. Words such as *interbeing, no-self,* and *emptiness* lead us astray if we grasp them as concepts. For both figures, seeing reality involves direct and not merely conceptual experience and acceptance of the origin of all things. For Gutiérrez, this means an experience of God.

ORIGIN

The center of Gutiérrez's understanding of God is that God is love, the source of all that is, the giver and defender of all life. We experience God as the absolute origin and nurturer of life, as both Father and Mother.[54] God gives life and wills life for all beings. Gutiérrez notes that the Wisdom of Solomon assures us that God did not make death.[55] Life means justice, and so God is the defender of all life, but especially of the lives of the poor who are threatened by injustice. God sets before us the path of life and death and bids us choose life. Life means communion with God and with God's people; death means isolation and subjection to idols. We face a clear choice: either the God of life or the idols of death.[56]

For Nhat Hanh, the question of absolute origin does not arise in the way that it does for Gutiérrez's creation-based theology. Nhat Hanh claims that the "Buddhist Genesis" is the basic principle of dependent co-arising from the early sutras: "This is because that is; this is not because that is not; this is born because that is born; this dies because that dies."[57] For this vision, all things in the universe are our mother, and we ourselves are mother to them, for all things give birth to each other, and we give birth to them. Everything is what it is because of the way everything else is, and there is no absolute origin or destruction of any reality: "[T]his sheet of paper has never been born, and it will never die. It can take on other forms of being, but we are not capable of transforming a sheet of paper into nothingness. Everything is like that, even you and I. We are not subject to birth and death."[58]

Looking into the palm of his hand, Nhat Hanh sees generations of ancestors of both the past and the present and sees himself as the continuation of a process without beginning or end. Nothing comes into being, and nothing goes out of being: "One form of energy can only become another form of energy."[59] Thus the leaf on the tree that is not afraid to die can teach us not to fear, for the leaf is both the daughter and the mother of the tree. When the leaf has lost its present form, its life will pulse not only in the tree, but in all the universe.

REVERENCE

Gutiérrez's experience of creation sets up a profound reverence for the natural world, and he stresses the importance of the contemplation of God's presence in all of nature. Belief in the God of creation sets up not only the ethical demands to work for justice but also the esthetic call to delight in God's glory revealed in the natural world. Gutiérrez challenges Christians to recover the vision of Francis of Assisi and see all creatures as our brothers and sisters joining together to praise God: "This vision of things is extremely important, and we need to recover it through contemplation and the celebration of the liturgy. It represents the phase of silence to which I referred in the introduction."[60]

Where Nhat Hanh sees the mystery of interbeing in everything that is, Gutiérrez discovers the beauty and power of God in all things. For each, the mystery of who we are and who the cosmos is can be seen all around us, and our blindness to our true origin is the source of unnecessary suffering for ourselves and others. For both, a moment of silence is necessary to appreciate what is right before our eyes. The experiences of silence that Nhat Hanh deepens in meditation and that Gutiérrez cultivates in contemplation are in no way flights from political engagement, but are ways to penetrate into the meaning of what is, methods of transforming our awareness so that we may act with freedom, unhindered by illusions.

For both thinkers, the experience of meditation or contemplation can free us from a narrowly anthropocentric view of the universe. Nhat Hanh, faithful to the Buddhist tradition, stresses the value of all beings and the necessity to respect all living beings. Humans are an important part of the universe of interbeing, but everything does not exist for human convenience. Gutiérrez, faithful to the message of the Book of Job, rejects the notion that creation exists for the sake of human beings. The plan of God's gratuitous love is not measured by human convenience or need.

IGNORANCE AND IDOLS

For both Gutiérrez and Nhat Hanh, the unjust sufferings of human existence arise from ignorance of the origin of all reality. Gutiérrez finds the origin of sin in idolatry, the worship of powers that masquerade as God. Idols pretend to offer the gifts of life, but in reality they are constructions of our own minds and hands, fabrications that imprison us in a web of deceit and lead us to our destruction.[61] Idols deny our status as creatures of the God of life and love and give us a false self-understanding based upon other, illusory sources of self-esteem. Power and money can be especially dangerous idols, dominating entire societies, distorting consciousness, and dealing death. Their power comes from the denial of creation and creation's God.

The choice of idols on a massive scale sets up situations in which God appears to be absent, which Gutiérrez describes as the dialectic of the visible and invisible God or the obvious and the hidden God. Even though God is the source of all creation, concretely God is absent where justice is not done. Even in supposedly sacred places such as the Temple of Jerusalem, the prophet Jeremiah warns that the presence of God depends on people dealing justly with their neighbors (Jer. 1:1–7). The dialectic of the obvious and hidden God runs throughout the Bible and human history. The God who is the source of all is not found in settings where justice is denied.[62]

For Nhat Hanh, the origin of suffering is ignorance of our true identity as interbeing:

> If you look at anything carefully, deeply enough, you discover the mystery of interbeing, and once you have seen it you will no longer be subject to fear — fear of birth, or fear of death. Birth and death are only ideas we have in our mind, and these ideas cannot be applied to reality. . . . So please continue to look back and you will see that you have always been here.[63]

When we ignore our true identity, we imprison ourselves in fears and hatreds and prejudices that set us at odds with other beings. Nhat Hanh laments: "If only the United States had had the vision of non-duality concerning Vietnam, we would not have had so much destruction in both countries. The war continues to hurt both Americans and Vietnamese."[64]

STRATEGIES OF RESISTANCE

Both Gutiérrez and Nhat Hanh protest the colonization of human consciousness by the powers that dominate contemporary society. Both thinkers root their strategies of transforming society in a process of transforming consciousness. For Gutiérrez, this transformation is rooted in the vision of Christ in the poor, as presented in the Parable of the Last Judgment in Matthew 25. For Nhat Hanh, this transformation is rooted in the vision of oneself in all beings and of all beings in oneself.

For Nhat Hanh, this takes the simple but powerful form of attending to one's breathing and experiencing the world around us and within us as if for the first time. This can be as simple as turning off the windows of our selves to the bombardment of stimuli from television and movies and noise, in order to come in contact with ourselves.[65] Even for those seriously wounded in spirit, meditation can be profoundly healing. Nhat Hanh tells of a retreat he conducted for veterans of the Vietnam War in the United States. Participants recounted horrors of war: one man had lost 417 men killed in a single engagement, and another man had killed children in a village. Veterans recounted the painful aftereffects of isolation from others, fear, distrust, the inability to be alone with children or to eat normally. Nhat Hanh's response was basic meditation: "You have to offer a lot of loving kindness in order to help such a person touch things again. During the retreat, we practiced mindful breathing and smiling, encouraging each other to come back to the flower in us, and to the trees and the blue sky that shelter us."[66]

Silent meals, mindful walking, tea ceremonies, as well as listening to one another, brought healing. One man who had cut himself off from others for fifteen years began to open up after several days of practice. Nhat Hanh stresses the necessity to learn from experiences of suffering without judging:

> We need the vision of interbeing—we belong to each other; we cannot cut reality into pieces. The well-being of "this" is the well-being of "that," so we have to do things together. Every side is "our side"; there is no evil side. Veterans have experience that makes them the light at the tip of the candle, illuminating the roots of war and the way to peace.[67]

For Gutiérrez, the process of resistance begins with a realization of the dignity of every person as a child of God and the value of all creation. Contemplation on the mystery of creation itself helps us become aware of a God beyond all calculation or control, a God who cannot be predicted or manipulated, a God who acts from sheer gratuitous love.

The process of resistance for Gutiérrez continues in a harsh rejection of all forms of oppression. For Christians in Latin America, Gutiérrez insists, the demands of Christian love lead to conflict with oppressive structures: "The universality of Christian love is only an abstraction unless it becomes concrete history, process, conflict."[68] In a situation of institutionalized violence, Gutiérrez argues: "Neutrality is impossible. It is not a question of admitting or denying a fact which confronts us; rather it is a question of which side we are on."[69] To feign neutrality is to support the status quo, which is killing the poor. Gutiérrez notes the relevance of the biblical command to love one's enemies and applies it to the contemporary situation:

> In the context of class struggle today, to love one's enemies presupposes recognizing and accepting that one has class enemies and that it is necessary to combat them. It is not a question of having no enemies, but rather of not excluding them from our love. But love does not mean that the oppressors are no longer enemies, nor does it eliminate the radicalness of the combat against them.[70]

Gutiérrez also repeats both the harsh biblical warnings of divine judgment on oppressors and also the more recent application of these warnings by Pope John Paul II:

> Nevertheless, in the light of Christ's words, this poor South will judge the rich North. And the poor peoples and poor nations—poor in different ways, not only lacking food, but also deprived of freedom and other human rights—will judge those people who take goods away from them, amassing to themselves the imperialistic monopoly of economic and political supremacy at the expense of others.[71]

Those who profit from the hunger of the poor will find that God was hidden in the lives of the poor, and what they have done to the poor they have done to God. This is the full meaning of the dialectic of the presence and absence of God in history. It is not a speculative paradox, but the harsh reality of human suffering and oppression. Gutiérrez comments:

> The Lord hides his presence in history, and at the same time reveals it, in the life and suffering, the struggles, the death, and the hopes of the condemned of the earth. But we must also bear in mind that this condemnation, this rejection of the kingdom of life, is what motivates God's absence.[72]

The movement of Gutiérrez's thought follows the classical biblical and Christian pattern of creation–sin–judgment–grace. What God has created as good and beautiful, humans mar through sin. God's judgment vindicates the oppressed, but always in the context of the overarching victory of divine grace. While each of these themes is interpreted anew from the perspective of solidarity with the poor, the fundamental structure of Christian experience and thought remains.[73] For Nhat Hanh, solidarity with the oppressed is also of critical importance, but the reliance on God as origin and goal of all creation and the harsh prophetic tones of judgment found in Gutiérrez nowhere appear.

For Nhat Hanh, the context for understanding any situation of violence and oppression is interbeing. In this perspective, understanding the perspective and the suffering of both the oppressed and also the oppressor is central. The movement of resistance to oppression proceeds first by way of understanding the illusions that give rise to oppression and secondly by way of compassion for both the oppressed and the oppressor. The tone of Nhat Hanh's language of resistance is gentler than Gutiérrez's, though no less insistent and firm. For Nhat Hanh, it is not a question of taking part on one side or the other of a class struggle, but rather of overcoming the opposition by understanding the situation of each side.

Nhat Hanh notes the interdependence of poor and wealthy: just as the poor are composed of nonpoor elements, so the wealthy are composed of nonwealthy elements. Each side goes into the composition of the other. The poor girl in Manila who becomes a prostitute from desperation is intimately related to the girls from wealthy families who would never even consider such an option. The life-style of the wealthy families contributes to the poor girl's desperation and choice of life-style: "Because the 'good family's' way of life is the way it is, the prostitute has to live as a prostitute. No one among us has clean hands. No one of us can claim that it is not our responsibility."[74] Similarly, in meditating on a sea pirate who robs and rapes, Nhat Hanh sees himself, and refrains from condemnation: "In my meditation I saw that if I had been born in the village of the pirate and raised in the same conditions as he was, I am now the pirate. There is a great likelihood that I would become a pirate. I cannot condemn myself so easily."[75]

Nhat Hanh's meditation leads not to excusing the actions of the sea pirate, but (1) to understanding the type of world which makes such actions thinkable and even "routine," and then (2) to an urgent call to change the conditions which make piracy so forceful an option for so many young men. Like Gutiérrez, Nhat Hanh stresses that the key is to see the situation in a new light, thereby making possible new forms of action. Where Gutiérrez turns to the biblical witness to condemn oppression and to enlighten the poor to their true identity and dignity, Nhat Hanh refrains from any condemnation and applies the perspective of interbeing to the situation of the young prostitute in Manila: "Only by seeing with the eyes of interbeing can that young girl be freed from her suffering. Only then will she understand that she is bearing the burden of the whole world."[76]

Where Gutiérrez urges us to love our enemies in the context of class struggle, Nhat Hanh insists that no person or group, even in the brutal violence of the war in Vietnam, is our enemy. Only hatred, prejudice, and anger are our enemies.[77] Thus in *The Path of Return Continues the Journey*, the young men from the School of Youth for Social Service who were murdered feel no anger for their killers, but only compassion. Now that they are enlightened to the truth of interbeing, there is no reason for them to be imprisoned by anger toward the unenlightened. Mai explains: "Men kill because on the one hand, they do not know their real enemy and on the other hand, they have been pushed into a position where they cannot *not* kill."[78] Even the most furious violence is impotent to kill, and an angry judgment would only perpetuate the cycle of illusion and suffering. Nhat Hanh sees no role for violence whatsoever in the struggle for peace.

A FLOWER SMILES — ALL IS GRACE

The people of Peru and of Vietnam have suffered tremendously in recent decades, and conditions for both nations continue to be extremely difficult. Nonetheless, despite their profound concern for those who suffer, both Gutiérrez and Nhat Hanh can write with a serene confidence. For Gutiérrez, this confidence is grounded not in any human calculation but in the ultimate power of God's gratuitous love, the origin and the end of all history. The basis for all contemplation and mysticism, the ground of all rejoicing amid the suffering of history, is the fundamental assurance: "Everything is grace."[79] Gutiérrez even dares to assert: "In the final analysis, to believe in God means to live our life as a gift from God and to look upon everything that happens in it as a manifestation of this gift."[80] For Nhat Hanh, peace is offered to us at every moment, even by the smile of a flower by the road:

> Peace is every step.
> The shining red sun is my heart.

Each flower smiles with me.
How green, how fresh all that grows.[81]

Both Gutiérrez and Nhat Hanh offer reasons to hope and even rejoice even in the midst of unjust suffering, but the ways in which they explicate this hope are very different. For Gutiérrez, the ground for hope in a world of suffering is that all reality comes from God and is absolutely dependent upon God, and God is love. Because the gratuitous love of God is the ultimate power in the universe, we can sing even when our efforts at liberation meet opposition and failure. For Nhat Hanh, the ground for hope is the experience of awakening to dependent co-arising, the realization that nothing comes into being and nothing goes out of being, that no one can ultimately kill anyone, that the dead still live. Meditation opens our eyes to both the suffering and the joy of all being around us and allows us to become one with them.

For Gutiérrez, the reason for hope is the reign of God, the power of God becoming present and effective in this world, overturning idols, calling humans to true love and life. We experience the reign of God as both gift and demand. Precisely because it comes as a gratuitous gift, it changes our lives, sets us free, and makes new demands upon us. For Gutiérrez, the beatitudes of Matthew's Gospel are the Magna Carta of the Christian community.[82] Because God has made us daughters and sons, we are to live as sisters and brothers. The promises of the beatitudes offer a vision of the meaning of life as God intends it: an existence assured of land, comforted in sorrow, with hunger and thirst for justice satisfied, a life filled with mercy and culminating in the vision of God. By accepting the beatitudes, we pledge ourselves to perform the twofold task of discipleship: to sing and set free, praising God for the wonders God has done and working concretely for justice in this world.

For Nhat Hanh, the reason for joy is the sheer miracle of existence itself. Life is also gift and demand, even though there is no transcendent creating and redeeming Giver. Life comes to us as a gift of all the things in the universe and as a call to play our part in realizing the harmony of the universe. Interbeing is the way the universe is, without need of absolute origin or goal. Everything that we receive and are comes to us as gift, for all the things in the universe converge to make us who we are. In accepting this gift, we also accept responsibility for all the things in the universe, for our actions will make all other things what they are. In wisdom we discover ourselves as if for the first time; in compassion we express our new understanding in concrete actions to relieve suffering and promote life.

AIMLESS MEDITATION AND GRATUITOUS PRAYER

While both Gutiérrez and Nhat Hanh insist on the importance of compassionate, informed action in the world to resist injustice, they both also

acknowledge the importance of the seemingly "goal-less" activities of meditation or prayer in nurturing and sustaining a religious life. Buddhists and
Christians deepen their experience of joy and their participation in their
respective traditions in experiences of meditation and prayer.

Nhat Hanh notes the contrast between traditional Buddhist attitudes
and many Western goal-oriented approaches. He explains what Buddhists
mean in speaking of wishlessness or aimlessness: "The idea is that you do
not put something in front of you and run after it, because everything is
already here, in yourself. . . . If we keep thinking of the future, of what we
want to realize, we will lose our steps."[83]

Hurrying toward a goal can cause us to miss the present moment. The
rush to produce more in order to be more secure, Nhat Hanh warns, has
led to the restless, ceaseless strivings of a consumer society and the modern
arms race: "Humankind's survival depends on our ability to stop rushing.
We have more than 50,000 nuclear bombs, and yet we cannot stop making
more."[84] Buddhist meditation calls us back to who we already are.

Gutiérrez balances his insistence on informed action with a recognition
of the importance of gratuitous prayer. His emphasis on the experience of
gratuitousness gives rise to an analogous insistence that prayer need not
be "useful" in any ordinary sense:

Like every dialogue of love, prayer runs the risk of being interpreted
as a "useless activity," whereas in point of fact it is precisely an experience of a gratuitousness that creates new forms of communication.
It is expressed, for example, in the silence proper to prayer.[85]

Buddhist aimlessness is the proper response to and the inevitable fruit
of seeing the mystery of interbeing. Nhat Hanh notes the traditional three
gates of liberation are emptiness, no-trace, and non-pursuit:

Emptiness is the absence of permanent identity of things. No-trace is
the nature of non-conceptualization of things. Non-pursuit is the attitude of someone who does not feel the need to run after an object,
the need to realize it or obtain it. It is, for example, not pursuing
enlightenment as an object of knowledge.[86]

For Nhat Hanh, as for the Mahayana tradition in general, these three
are different aspects of one experience: "Absence of an absolute identity
in each thing (emptiness) is manifested by the non-conceptual (no-trace)
knowledge in which a subject in quest of its object does not exist (non-
pursuit)."[87]

While the gratuitousness of Christian prayer in some ways resembles the
aimlessness of Buddhist meditation, Gutiérrez's and the biblical tradition's
orientation to history finds no full parallel in the Buddhist tradition. At the
core of Christianity is what Gutiérrez calls "an irruption smelling of the

stable."[88] God "irrupts," breaks into human history, in the birth of Jesus: "an incarnation into littleness and service in the midst of the overbearing power exercised by the mighty of this world."[89] In the Incarnation, something new happens in human history that humans could never have attained on our own. The Incarnation is the ultimate expression of God's gratuitous love, the final reason for hope and rejoicing amid the sufferings of this world.

While Buddhists are grateful for the appearance of the Buddha in our world to teach us wisdom and compassion, the Buddha is not an incarnation of God, but one who calls us to awaken to our true identity. Nhat Hanh explains what happens in Zen Buddhist awakening: "The Master does not transmit his Awakening to the disciple; he does not even create Awakening in the disciple. He only helps him to realize this Awakening already latent within him."[90]

For Gutiérrez, the powers of life and death are opposed to each other throughout human history, and we are called to take sides in the struggle. The God of life is at war with the powers of death that murder the poor, and enters fully into the human condition to set all humans free, especially the poor. For Nhat Hanh, life and death are not in conflict but imply each other; oppressors and oppressed are interdependent. The distinctions we make arise from concepts that falsify reality:

> The world built of concepts is different from living reality. The world in which birth and death, good and bad, being and non-being are opposed, exists only for those who do not live as Awakened. But the vicissitudes of this world no longer affect the "awakened" man because he has already come to the world of reality in which there is no discrimination between birth and death, between good and bad, between being and non-being.[91]

For Nhat Hanh, reality is itself, beyond all concepts and discriminations, without beginning or end. No attack on us can destroy us, and so we can live serene and free from fear. For Gutiérrez, the absolute source of all reality was born in a stable to intervene in the battle between life and death. Because of God's victory, life has the final word, and we can rejoice.

Epilogue

In the autumn of 1957, Shin'ichi Hisamatsu, a leading Japanese Zen Buddhist philosopher, and Paul Tillich, a leading Christian theologian, had a series of conversations, while both were teaching at Harvard University. In the last conversation Tillich was struggling to understand the meaning of Zen language concerning each particular reality and the ultimate. At the heart of the difficulty in understanding was the difference between creation and dependent co-arising. Faithful to the Zen tradition, Hisamatsu affirmed the traditional Hua-Yen Buddhist principles that there is no impediment between particular and particular or between particular and universal. Each reality is itself and each is the other. Thus, Hisamatsu's interpreter, Richard DeMartino, explained: "Zen would regard each as a *Self*-expression of ultimacy. You are the 'ultimate'—or Selfless Self; I am the 'ultimate'—or Selfless Self; hence, I am you and I am the flower."[1]

Tillich, faithful to his Christian understanding of God immanent in creation and of creation participating in God but distinct from God, refrained from accepting this affirmation: "I never would suggest that I am the ultimate. 'I am you' because I participate as you do in the ultimate."[2]

In reply, Hisamatsu reaffirmed that Zen nonduality is not participation, and he wondered if Tillich's reluctance to pronounce himself or any other thing ultimate might come from the judgment of the distinction between good and evil. Tillich agreed that for him the ultimate is good as opposed to evil. DeMartino then explained Hisamatsu's perspective: "In Zen, as every duality—including the axiological polarity of good-and-evil—is broken through, there is no uneasiness to be felt in professing, 'I am the ultimate.'"[3]

After further discussion, Tillich expressed his own perspective: "Nevertheless, the flower cannot be, for me, more than a particular. I would not refer to it *as* the ultimate—or Formless Self. Experientially—in my emotions—I could not countenance that."[4] As the conversation continued, the frustration in communication grew deeper, and DeMartino suggested to Hisamatsu that he deal with Tillich in Zen fashion, through a direct nonverbal expression, such as a push in the stomach. Hisamatsu, however, refrained, and the discussion continued on the conceptual plane, ending on a note of incompletion.

The conversation reveals what is in some ways a tragic situation for communication. Two of the most profound thinkers of their respective traditions throw themselves into the effort to communicate without fully succeeding. The difficulties in communication between two of the deepest thinkers of the Buddhist and Christian traditions in our century is a sign and warning of the difficulties of dialogue.

Throughout the comparisons of Buddhist and Christian perspectives, creation and dependent co-arising appear as important structuring principles for the two traditions, creation being constantly presupposed by Christian authors and dependent co-arising by Buddhist authors. These fundamental assumptions shape the teachings of Jesus Christ and of Shakyamuni Buddha, the analyses of the problems of human existence, and the interpretation of the proper religious response. The inexorable differences between the perspectives of creation and dependent co-arising play back and forth across the two traditions throughout the centuries, raising to prominence the underlying question of the relation of language and reality.

Conceptual clarification of religious perspectives is important for both traditions, and is one major concern of interreligious dialogue. But on the terms of both Buddhism and Christianity, the process of conceptual clarification is utterly subordinate to religious practice. Both traditions challenge their followers in different ways to abandon the effort to control their religious practice, and so it would be strange for either tradition to attempt to predict or control the course of interreligious dialogue. The clinging, grasping self must die. Where the intellectual process of reflection raises the question of the limits of understanding, the experience of grace may appear.

For both traditions, language comes to the point of collapse when it seeks to describe ultimate reality literally, only to be sustained by the power of reality itself manifesting itself in the world of time. For both traditions, words are to transcend themselves and lead us into the experience of reality itself; but both traditions know that words can all too quickly congeal, harden, and function like names for things out there, objective descriptions of external realities. Whether *dharma* or *logos*, *shunyata* or *God*, words begin to masquerade as the reality itself, and our limited conceptual understanding of the word pretends to substitute for the reality itself. Before we know it, we are imprisoned in the walls of our own concepts, and we need to be liberated by firm negations. Even to name the differences between the two traditions too univocally or objectively risks mistaking our concepts for the realities they seek to name. Augustine's warning bears pondering by Christians and Buddhists alike: "If you have comprehended, what you have comprehended is not God."[5]

The problem of communication would not have come as a surprise to either Shakyamuni Buddha or Jesus Christ. After his enlightenment, Shakyamuni reflected somberly on the prospect of his insight being understood. Gadjin Nagao summarizes Shakyamuni's reflections after awakening, as expressed in the biographies of the Buddha:

Now if I endeavor to preach the Dharma, people will surely fall into confusion. That is, they would be unable to believe what I would be saying and instead respond with slander. As a result, they would fall into hell and undergo a variety of pain and suffering. For this reason, I will remain silent.[6]

Jesus, for his part, knew that his own teaching was likely to be misunderstood, with dire consequences for his hearers. The Gospel of Mark presents him quoting Isaiah 6:9–10 and telling his disciples:

To you is granted the secret of the kingdom of God, but to those who are outside everything comes in parables, so that they may look and look, but never perceive; listen and listen, but never understand; to avoid changing their ways and being healed (Mk. 4:11–12).

Neither Shakyamuni Buddha nor Jesus Christ expected to be understood, and both knew that their preaching might actually cause confusion. Yet in both traditions there is also a confidence that at the very point that language breaks down, the power of ultimate reality itself manifests itself as grace, allowing words to break open and transcend themselves, making present the power of infinite wisdom and compassion. The skillful means of the Mahayana bodhisattvas are capable of cutting through the bonds of ignorance. The words of Christian proclamation are capable of bearing the power of God and becoming themselves sacraments of saving grace.

Apart from the path of religious practice and spiritual discipleship, creation and dependent co-arising become all too quickly reduced to the status of objective theories about the universe, and the teachings of Jesus Christ and Shakyamuni Buddha become reduced to mere speculations. The meaning of each perspective reveals itself only to a consciousness that has undergone a path of transformation. The true meaning of Christian belief in creation expresses itself in the refigured consciousness of the Sermon on the Mount, in Dionysius's movement of procession and return and of affirming and negating, in Augustine's experience at Ostia, and in Gustavo Gutiérrez's astonishing affirmation that *everything* in this life is a gift of God. In each case the meaning of Christian language about creation is only clear in light of the experience of Jesus Christ, the Word made flesh. Because the one through whom all things were made has entered our world as a human being, we can understand the meaning of the absolute origin and future of the cosmos as infinite, overwhelming love.

The meaning of dependent co-arising expresses itself in the Four Noble Truths of the Buddha, in the following of the eightfold path, in the paradoxical zigzagging logic of Mahayana Buddhism, in the koans and just-sitting of Zen masters, in the faith of Pure Land Buddhists in Amida Buddha, and in Thich Nhat Hanh's affirmation that a flower smiles and that existence itself is miraculous.

For each tradition, the message is very simple, but so profound as to be inexhaustible. For each, the message presents a new way of being in the world, a message which must be lived to be truly understood. The Buddha's teaching is lived and understood in the path of wisdom and compassion, a path which is itself the realization of absolute reality. Jesus' teaching is lived and understood in the practice of love of God and love of neighbor, a path which leads to union with absolute reality itself, sheer love.

The lives of both Jesus Christ and Shakyamuni Buddha are parables which challenge us more than we ever comprehend or measure them. It is of the nature of a parable to be an open-ended invitation to ponder, to reflect, to be converted. Often the invitations of the Gospels remain open: Did the elder brother of the prodigal son go in to join the feast? (Lk. 15:31–32.) Did the rich young man sell all he had to follow Jesus? (Mk. 10:21–22.)

Is true understanding possible between two traditions as profoundly different as Christianity and Buddhism? Is union in the nameless silence beyond all words even thinkable? From the perspective of human conceptual thought alone, the prospects do not seem hopeful, and yet each tradition in its own way calls for a surrender of human thinking in the movement into ultimate reality. For a Christian, it may be that in the end the situation of dialogue is not unlike the question of who can be saved. When asked by his disciples, "Jesus gazed at them and said, 'By human resources it is impossible, but not for God, because for God everything is possible' " (Mk. 10:27).

Glossary

Amida Buddha: Buddha of limitless light and life, who rules over the Land of Bliss; for Pure Land Buddhists, the manifestation of absolute reality as grace.

Amitabha Buddha: Buddha of limitless light (wisdom).

Amitaya Buddha: Buddha of limitless life (compassion).

anatta/anatman: no-self; the Buddhist denial of any substantial, independently existing, perduring self.

apophatic theology: the term of Dionysius the Areopagite for theology that negates all symbols and concepts applied to God.

Ashvaghosha: author of the Buddhacarita; an Indian Buddhist, probably of the first or second century C.E.

Avalokita/Avalokiteshvara: the bodhisattva of compassion.

bodhisattva: a future Buddha; in Mahayana Buddhism a person who vows to attain enlightenment for the sake of all living beings.

Buddha-nature: ultimate reality; our capacity to awaken.

caritas: Augustine's term for the self-giving, salvific love which worships God and loves all other realities in light of God.

cataphatic theology: term of Dionysius for affirming theology that applies symbols and concepts to God nonliterally.

Ch'an: Chinese word for meditation, Zen in Japanese; the tradition of Buddhism that stresses direct mind-to-mind transmission of Buddhist awakening.

cupiditas: Augustine's term for the self-destructive love that places some finite object or concern in the place of God.

dependent co-arising: the Buddhist view of the universe as interdependent; everything arises out of every other thing of the universe and passes into every other thing.

Dhammapada: the Path of Dharma; an early collection of sayings of the Buddha.

dharma: duty, law, teaching, especially the teaching of the Buddha.

dharma-dhatu: the source of dharma, the source of all existence and all Buddhist teachings.

Dharmakara: an individual who practiced for endless ages, became a Buddha, and now shares his merit with all living beings as Amida Buddha.

dharmakaya: the body of the Buddha, the eternal aspect or essence of the Buddha, absolute reality; the basis for the enjoyment body and the transformation body of the Buddha.

dharmata: dharma-nature; absolute reality.

dhyana: meditation; the Sanskrit word which is translated as *Ch'an* in Chinese, *Zen* in Japanese, and *Thien* in Vietnamese.

dukkha: suffering, impermanence.

essence-body: dharmakaya, absolute reality.

exitus: the Christian neo-Platonic term for the flowing forth or procession of all things from God.

Hinayana: the Lesser Vehicle; the name used, especially by Mahayana Buddhists, for the Buddhist traditions of Burma, Thailand, and Sri Lanka.

Hozo: another name for Dharmakara, who became Amida Buddha.

Interbeing: the term of Thich Nhat Hanh for dependent co-arising.

Jataka tales: accounts of the previous lives of Shakyamuni Buddha.

karuna: compassion.

Land of Bliss: the land of Amida Buddha where people can hear the Buddhist teaching proclaimed without obstacle and become enlightened.

Lin-chi: a Chinese Ch'an master (d. 866 C.E.; Rinzai in Japanese); the tradition of Ch'an Buddhism in China which is named for him and which emphasizes the use of koans.

Manjushri: the bodhisattva of wisdom.

mystical theology: term of Dionysius the Areopagite for the final stage of the journey into God, beyond affirming and negating.

Namu Amida Buddha: adoration to Amida Buddha; a chant recited by Pure Land Buddhists.

Nembutsu: the Namu Amida Buddha.

nirmana-kaya: the transformation-body of a Buddha, such as the physical Buddha of Shakyamuni Buddha which is visible to all.

nirvana: the extinguishing of the illusory self; absolute reality beyond all duality.

nonduality: the Buddhist perspective that all things are not other than each other or than ultimate reality.

no-self: the Buddhist denial of any enduring substance or soul of humans or other beings.

prajna: wisdom.

prajnaparamita: transcendent wisdom; the early Mahayana scriptures which present transcendent wisdom.

Pure Land: the Land of Bliss of Amida Buddha; the Buddhist tradition which focuses on the Other-power of Amida Buddha.

reditus: the Christian neo-Platonic term for the return of all things into God.

reward-body: the enjoyment body; the body in which the Buddha enjoys the reward of his awakening and preaches to those in the process of becoming enlightened.

Rinzai: Japanese name for Lin-chi; the Japanese Zen tradition which continues the Chinese Lin-chi tradition and uses koans.

samadhi: state of concentration or oneness of mind.

sambhoga-kaya: enjoyment body or reward body of the Buddha; the body of the Buddha in which he enjoys the reward of his awakening and in which which he appears to those gathered to hear the Buddha's preaching, as in the Pure Land.

samsara: the world of impermanence and suffering.

sangha: the Buddhist community.

Shakyamuni: the sage of the Shakya clan; a title for Siddhartha Gautama after his enlightenment.

shila: Buddhist ethical conduct; Buddhist precept.

shinjin: Shinran's term for the experience of conversion.

shramana: a homeless, wandering ascetic in India.

shunyata: emptiness, emptying; absolute reality beyond all duality.

skandha: the elements of the person in Buddhist analysis.

skillful means: the Buddhist view of all teachings and practices as tools to lead one to awakening and not as absolute truth.

Soto: the Japanese Zen tradition which continues the Chinese Ts'ao-tung tradition and emphasizes just-sitting.

storehouse consciousness: in Buddhist thought, the primordial subjectivity in which the past and future seeds are stored.

suchness: a Buddhist term for absolute reality just as it is, free from distortions.

Sukhavati: the Land of Bliss of Amida Buddha.

sutra: a Buddhist scripture which presents the teaching of the Buddha.

tathata: a Buddhist term for suchness, reality just as it is, free from distortion.

tetralamma: the fourfold negation of Buddhist logic which negates any view or theory about reality.

Theravada: the way of the elders; the name for the Buddhist traditions of Thailand, Burma, and Sri Lanka.

Thien: Vietnamese term for Zen; the major Vietnamese Buddhist tradition which combines elements of Zen and Pure Land Buddhism.

Tiep Hien: Interbeing; the Buddhist order founded by Thich Nhat Hanh.

transformation body: the physical, visible body of a Buddha as a human being.

trikaya: the three bodies of the Buddha: dharmakaya (dharma-body or essence body), sambhoghakaya (enjoyment body or reward body), and nirmanakaya (transformation body).

Ts'ao-tung: the Chinese Ch'an tradition which emphasized just-sitting as the path to enlightenment.

Vimalakirti: a wealthy Buddhist householder who is enlightened.

Vinaya: collection of Buddhist monastic rules.

Zen: meditation; translation of Chinese *Ch'an* and Sanskrit *dhyana*; a Buddhist tradition which emphasizes meditation and direct mind-to-mind transmission.

Notes

PROLOGUE

1. Aloysius Pieris, *Love Meets Wisdom: A Christian Experience of Buddhism* (Maryknoll, NY: Orbis Books, 1988), 3.

2. *The Holy Teaching of Vimalakirti: A Mahayana Scripture*, trans. Robert A. F. Thurman (University Park, PA: Pennsylvania State University Press, 1976), 77.

3. Gadjin Nagao notes that the silence of the Buddha appears in a variety of different forms in the early scriptures: the silence after his enlightenment caused by his fear that no one would understand, the silence of approval or acknowledgment, and the silence of disagreement which refuses to take sides on an argument because both sides err. Gadjin Nagao, *Madhyamika and Yogacara: A Study of Mahayana Philosophies*, ed. and trans. L. S. Kawamura in collaboration with G. M. Nagao (Albany, NY: State University of New York Press, 1991), 36. On the silence of the Buddha, see also T. R. V. Murti, *The Central Philosophy of Buddhism: A Study of the Madhyamika System* (2nd ed., London: George Allen & Unwin, 1960; reprint, London: Unwin Paperbacks, 1980), 36–54.

4. Walpola Rahula, *What the Buddha Taught* (New York: Grove Press, Inc., 1959; reprint, Evergreen Edition, 1962), 35.

5. Ibid., 11–12.

6. Nagarjuna, *Mulamadhyamakakarikas: Fundamentals of the Middle Way*, 24, in Frederick J. Streng, *Emptiness: A Study in Religious Meaning* (Nashville and New York: Abingdon, 1967); see also Gadjin Nagao, *The Foundational Standpoint of Madhyamika Philosophy*, trans. John P. Keenan (Albany, NY: State University of New York Press, 1989), 21–32.

7. Michael Pye, *Skilful Means: A Concept in Mahayana Buddhism* (London: Duckworth, 1978).

8. On the relation of Buddhism to the forms of thought of major Asian cultures, see Hajime Nakamura, *Ways of Thinking of Eastern Peoples: India-China-Tibet-Japan*, revised translation, ed. Philip P. Wiener (Honolulu: University of Hawaii Press, 1964); and Joseph M. Kitagawa and Mark D. Cummings, eds., *Buddhism and Asian History: Religion, History, and Culture: Readings from The Encyclopedia of Religion*, ed. Mircea Eliade (New York: Macmillan, 1989).

9. J. C. Cleary, *Zen Dawn: Early Zen Texts from Tun Huang*, trans. J. C. Cleary (Boston: Shambhala, 1986), 6.

10. Augustine, *Soliloquies*, 1, 2, 7; trans. John J. O'Meara, *An Augustine Reader* (Garden City, NY: Image Books, 1973), 42.

11. Helmuth von Glasenapp, *Buddhism: A Non-Theistic Religion*, trans. Irmgard Schloegl (New York: George Braziller, 1966), 35–47.

12. Frithjof Schuon, *The Transcendent Unity of Religions* (Wheaton, IL: Theosophical Publishing House, 1984).

13. Thomas Aquinas, *Summa Theologiae* 1.3. Introduction.

1. THE LIFE AND TEACHING OF SHAKYAMUNI BUDDHA

1. Mircea Eliade, *A History of Religious Ideas*, vol. 2, *From Gautama Buddha to the Triumph of Christianity*, trans. Willard R. Trask (Chicago: University of Chicago Press, 1982), 72.

2. Frank E. Reynolds and Charles Hallisey, "Buddha," *The Encyclopedia of Religion*, 16 vols., ed. Mircea Eliade et al. (New York: Macmillan, 1987), 2:321.

3. Gadjin Nagao, "The Life of the Buddha: An Interpretation," *Eastern Buddhist*, New Series 20/2(1987):1–31. See also Gadjin Nagao, "The Buddha's Life as Parable for Later Buddhist Thought," *Eastern Buddhist*, New Series 24/2(1991):1–32.

4. Nagao, "Life of the Buddha," 2. On Shakyamuni Buddha in relation to India's social and political context, see Trevor Ling, *The Buddha: Buddhist Civilization in India and Ceylon* (New York: Charles Scribner's Sons, 1973; reprint, Harmondsworth, England: Penguin Books, 1976), 43–129. There are various retellings of narratives from the early Pali scriptures which omit the mythological additions; see David J. and Indrani Kalupahana, *The Way of Siddhartha: A Life of the Buddha* (Boulder: Shambhala, 1982); Thich Nhat Hanh, *Old Path White Clouds: Walking in the Footsteps of the Buddha*, trans. Mobi Ho (Berkeley, CA: Parallax Press, 1991); and Richard H. Drummond, *Gautama the Buddha: An Essay in Religious Understanding* (Grand Rapids, MI: William B. Eerdmans, 1974).

5. For a summary of the teaching of the Buddha in these writings, see Walpola Rahula, *What the Buddha Taught* (New York: Grove Press, 1959; reprint, Evergreen Edition, 1962).

6. It is, nonetheless, the teaching of the Buddha rather than the events of his life that is central for Buddhism. Because of this, some scholars, such as Edward Conze, have minimized the importance of Shakyamuni's life for the Buddhist tradition. Edward Conze, *Buddhism: Its Essence and Development* (Oxford: Bruno Cassirer, Ltd.; reprint, New York: Harper Torchbooks, 1959), 34. Murti distinguishes Hinayana Buddhism, for whom the historicity of Shakyamuni Buddha is "indispensable," from Mahayana Buddhism, which "escapes the predicament of having to depend on any particular historical person as the founder of its religion" (287).

7. Ashvaghosha, *The Buddhacarita or, The Acts of the Buddha*, Part I: Sanskrit Text, ed. and trans. E. H. Johnston (Lahore: University of the Punjab, 1936; reprint, New Delhi, India: Oriental Books Reprint Corp., 1972). Part I includes cantos 1–14 and recounts the life of the Buddha up to his enlightenment. Cantos 15–28 are not extant in Sanskrit and are found only in Tibetan and Chinese translations. See "The Buddha's Mission and Last Journey: *Buddhacarita*, xv to xxviii," trans. E. H. Johnston, *Acta Orientalia* 15(1937):85–111, 231–51, and 253–92. All references will be to this translation unless otherwise noted. Some scholars think that only the first thirteen cantos are authentic (Lucien Stryk, ed., *World of the Buddha: An Introduction to Buddhist Literature* [Garden City, NY: Doubleday, 1968; reprint, New York: Grove Press, 1982], 11).

8. Roma Chaudhuri, *Ashvaghosha: Makers of Indian Literature* (New Delhi, India: Sahitya Akademi, 1988), 14.

9. Nagao, "Life of the Buddha," 5. Siddhartha's mother is often referred to as "Mahamaya," or "great Maya." Maya was also the name of a number of female deities in India.

10. Ibid., 8. On the association between giving birth near a tree and the power of the earth and its plant life as the inexhaustible source of all life, see Mircea Eliade, *Patterns in Comparative Religion*, trans. Rosemary Sheed (New York: Sheed & Ward, 1958; reprint, New York: New American Library, 1963), 306–7.

11. Nagao, "Life of the Buddha," 9.

12. Roger J. Corless, *The Vision of Buddhism: The Space under the Tree* (New York: Paragon House, 1989), 49.

13. Some commentators speculate that the webbed fingers may have been originally a device of "mechanical expediency" for statues that later became part of the story. See Corless, 48.

14. Nagao, "Life of the Buddha," 11. The name may also come from a mythological demon, Rahu, who periodically swallowed up the sun and the moon, causing eclipses and confusion on earth. Ashvaghosha comments that Rahula had "the face of Rahu's adversary" (2.46; p. 29), i.e., a face like the sun or the moon who fight against Rahu. See Kalupahana, ix–x.

15. Heinrich Dumoulin, *Christianity Meets Buddhism*, trans. John C. Maraldo (LaSalle, IL: Open Court Publishing Co., 1974), 146.

16. E. B. Cowell translates "dharma" in the Buddhacarita sometimes as "religion" and sometimes as "duty." The *Buddha-karita of Asvaghosha*, trans. E. B. Cowell, in *Buddhist Mahayana Texts, The Sacred Books of the East*, ed. F. Max Müller, 49 (Oxford: Clarendon Press, 1894; reprint, New York: Dover Publications, Inc., 1969).

17. *Majjhima Nikaya* (Pali Text Society) i, 190-91; *Itivuttaka* (Pali Text Society), 91; *Samyutta Nikaya* (Pali Text Society), iii, 120; cited by Kenneth K. Tanaka, *The Dawn of Chinese Pure Land Buddhist Doctrine: Ching-ying Hui-yüan's Commentary on the Visualization Sutra* (Albany, NY.: State University of New York Press, 1990), 5.

18. Eliade, *History of Religious Ideas*, 2:75.

19. Nagao, "Life of the Buddha," 17.

20. Ibid., 18.

21. Ibid., 19-20.

22. Ibnid., 20.

23. Ibid., 21.

24. Not all modern scholars agree with the older Buddhist tradition that the Four Noble Truths actually represent the content of the Buddha's first sermon, but the Noble Truths do most probably express the fundamental experience of his conversion and enlightenment. Yoshinori Takeuchi and John P. Keenan, "Buddhist Philosophy," *Encyclopedia of Religion*, 2:540-41.

25. Ibid., 2:542.

26. *The Dhammapada: The Path of Perfection* 11:146, trans. Juan Mascaro (London: Penguin Books, 1973), 56. All references will be to this translation unless otherwise noted.

27. Yoshinori Takeuchi, *The Heart of Buddhism: In Search of the Timeless Spirit of Primitive Buddhism*, ed. and trans. James W. Heisig (New York: Crossroad, 1983), 110.

28. Ibid., 119.

29. Rahula, 29-31.

30. Daisetz Suzuki, "Transmigration," *Eastern Buddhist*, New Series 17/2 (1984): 3. Suzuki went on to give a positive interpretation of *trishna* (craving) as a very good thing which allows one to experience all kinds of beings (6).

31. *Vinaya-pitaka* 2:154-59, trans. I. B. Horner, in *Buddhist Texts through the Ages*, trans. and ed. Edward Conze et al. (New York: Philosophical Library, 1954; reprint, Boston: Shambhala, 1990), 18.

32. Rahula, 37.

33. Eliade, *History of Religious Ideas*, 2:99; Theodore Stcherbatsky, *The Conception of Buddhist Nirvana* (2nd ed., enlarged; Delhi: Motilal Banarsidass, 1977; reprint, 1989), 193–222.

34. Rahula, 45–50. For a somewhat different division of the components into the three stages, see Pieris, 58–59; and also Taitetsu Unno, "Eightfold Path," *Encyclopedia of Religion*, 5:70.

35. Eliade, *History of Religious Ideas*, 2:100; Mircea Eliade, *Yoga: Immortality and Freedom*, trans. Willard R. Trask, Bollingen Series 56 (2nd ed.; Princeton, NJ: Princeton University Press, 1969), 162–67.

36. Thich Nhat Hanh, *Breathe! You Are Alive: Sutra on the Full Awareness of Breathing* (Berkeley, CA: Parallax Press, 1988), 22.

37. Ibid., 19.

38. Gadjin Nagao, "On the Theory of the Buddha-Body (*Buddha-kaya*)," *Eastern Buddhist*, New Series 6/1 (1973): 40.

39. Corless, 26.

40. Daisetsu Teitaro Suzuki, *Mysticism Christian and Buddhist* (London: George Allen & Unwin, 1957; reprint, London: Unwin Paperbacks, 1979), 27.

41. Eliade claims that the process of "mythologization" of the Buddha began during his own lifetime and was the source of creativity in later Buddhist thought, art, and literature (*History of Religious Ideas*, 2:72–73). Trevor Ling, however, holds that the development only came later, after the earliest generation of his followers had passed (142).

42. Tanaka, 7.

43. Daisetz Teitaro Suzuki, *A Miscellany on the Shin Teaching of Buddhism* (Kyoto: Shinshu Otaniha Shumusho, 1949), 61.

44. Nagao, "Buddha's Life as Parable," 16.

45. *Dighanikaya*, xvi (*Mahaparinibbana-sutta*), 2, 26; quoted by Nagao, *Madhyamika and Yogacara*, 104.

46. *Majjhima Nikaya* (Pali Text Society), 1, 190-91; quoted by Tanaka, 5.

47. Nagao, "Buddha's Life as Parable," 16–17.

48. Nagao, *Madhyamika and Yogacara*, 108.

49. Ibid., 109.

50. Ibid., 110–11.

51. Tanaka, 6.

52. *The Flower Ornament Scripture: A Translation of the Avatamsaka Sutra*, Vol. I, trans. Thomas Cleary (Boulder: Shambhala, 1984), Book 20, p. 445.

53. Ibid., Bk. 114; p. 372.

2. JESUS THE CHRIST AND SHAKYAMUNI BUDDHA

1. See two recent accounts: John P. Meier, *A Marginal Jew: Rethinking the Historical Jesus*, Vol. I, *The Roots of the Problem and the Person*, Anchor Bible

Reference Library (New York: Doubleday, 1991); and John Dominic Crossan, *The Historical Jesus: The Life of a Mediterranean Jewish Peasant* (San Francisco: Harper SanFrancisco, 1991). On the earlier research, see Norman Perrin, *Rediscovering the Teaching of Jesus* (New York: Harper & Row, 1967); Norman Perrin, *Jesus and the Language of the Kingdom: Symbol and Metaphor in New Testament Interpretation* (Philadelphia: Fortress, 1976); and also Marcus J. Borg, *Jesus, A New Vision: Spirit, Culture, and the Life of Discipleship* (San Francisco: Harper & Row, 1988). For a very different reconstruction of the origins of early Christianity, see Burton L. Mack, *A Myth of Innocence: Mark and Christian Origins* (Philadelphia: Fortress, 1988).

2. E. P. Sanders, *Jesus and Judaism* (Philadelphia: Fortress, 1985), 11.

3. John Dominic Crossan, *In Parables: The Challenge of the Historical Jesus* (New York: Harper & Row, 1973), xiv.

4. Gadjin Nagao, "The Buddha's Life as Parable for Later Buddhist Thought," *Eastern Buddhist*, New Series 24/2(1991):1–32.

5. Mircea Eliade, *The Myth of the Eternal Return* or, *Cosmos and History*, trans. Willard R. Trask, Bollingen Series 46 (Princeton, NJ: Princeton University Press, 1971), 104–11, 115–17.

6. Mircea Eliade, *Patterns in Comparative Religion*, trans. Rosemary Sheed (New York: Sheed & Ward, 1958; reprint, New York: New American Library, 1963), 1–30, 378.

7. Athanasius, *Orations against the Arians*, 1, 38–39; idem, *On the Incarnation*, 54.

8. Raymond E. Brown, *The Birth of the Messiah: A Commentary on the Infancy Narratives in Matthew and Luke* (New York: Doubleday & Co., 1977; reprint, Garden City, NY: Image Books, 1979), 8. Joseph A. Fitzmyer, *Luke the Theologian: Aspects of His Teaching* (New York: Paulist, 1989), 29–30. I use the traditional designations of the canonical Gospels without implying any specific theory of authorship. Each of the Gospels is anonymous in the oldest texts, and the designations of the authors come from later Church tradition.

9. Krister Stendahl, "Quis et Unde? An Analysis of Mt 1–2," in *Judentum, Urchristentum, Kirche*, ed. W. Eltester (Berlin: Töpelmann, 1960), 94–105; Brown, 52–54, 133–35; John P. Meier, *The Vision of Matthew: Christ, Church, and Morality in the First Gospel* (New York: Paulist, 1979), 52.

10. On the similarity between the roles of traditional Indian gods in Buddhism and angels in Christianity, see Helmuth von Glasenapp, *Buddhism: A Non-Theistic Religion*, trans. Irmgard Schloegl (New York: George Braziller, 1966), 23.

11. Brown, 49, n. 14. The only trace of remembrance of the infancy narrative in Luke is the reference to John the Baptist as "the son of Zechariah" (Lk. 3:2).

12. Brown, 97–98.

13. Fitzmyer, 35, 45.

14. For a representative sample of the tales of the Buddha's previous lives, see Edward Conze, *Buddhist Scriptures* (Harmondsworth: Penguin, 1959), 19–33.

15. Ibid., 20.

16. Meier, *Vision of Matthew*, 52–53.

17. Edward Conze, *Buddhist Thought in India: Three Phases of Buddhist Philosophy* (London: George Allen & Unwin, 1962; reprint, Ann Arbor, MI: University of Michigan Press, 1967), 232.

18. See John P. Meier, *The Mission of Christ and His Church: Studies in Christology and Ecclesiology* (Wilmington, DE: Michael Glazier, 1990), 21.

19. In Mark the voice speaks to Jesus alone; in Matthew the voice is a public manifestation of the identity of Jesus; in Luke the voice serves to identify Jesus as Son and servant of God, and the descent of the Spirit prepares him for his ministry. See Joseph A. Fitzmyer, *The Gospel According to Luke*, The Anchor Bible, vols. 28, 28a (Garden City, NY: Doubleday & Co., 1981), 1:480–81.

20. All biblical quotations will be from *The New Jerusalem Bible* (New York: Doubleday, 1985) unless otherwise indicated. Some manuscripts of Luke quote Ps. 2:7 as what the voice said. While some commentators and translations accept this as the original text, it is problematic. See Fitzmyer, *Gospel According to Luke*, 1:485. On the relation of Ps. 2:7 to Matthew's scene, see Meier, *Vision of Matthew*, 58–59.

21. Meier, *Vision of Matthew*, 59.

22. Fitzmyer, *Gospel According to Luke*, 1:510–11; Fitzmyer, *Luke the Theologian*, 157.

23. Walpola Rahula, *What the Buddha Taught* (New York: Grove Press, 1959; reprint, Evergreen Edition, 1962), 3.

24. Walter Brueggemann, "Scripture and an Ecumenical Life-Style," *Interpretation* 24(1970):11; James L. Crenshaw, *Old Testament Wisdom: An Introduction* (Atlanta: John Knox Press, 1981), 19, 54–55, 66.

25. Rahula, 17.

26. Charles E. Carlston, "Proverbs, Maxims, and the Historical Jesus," *Journal of Biblical Literature* 99(1980):87–105; Raymond E. Brown, *The Gospel according to John*, Anchor Bible, vols. 29–29A (Garden City, NY: Doubleday & Co., 1966, 1970), 1:cxxii–cxxv; C. H. Dodd, *The Interpretation of the Fourth Gospel* (Cambridge: Cambridge University Press, 1965), 274–77.

27. On the meaning of the reign of God in the preaching of Jesus, see Perrin, *Rediscovering the Teaching of Jesus*; and Perrin, *Jesus and the Language of the Kingdom*. On the meaning of the reign of God in Mark, see Werner Kelber, *The Kingdom in Mark: A New Place and a New Time* (Philadelphia: Fortress, 1974).

28. On the role of the Spirit of God in the experience of Jesus himself, see Borg, 39–71.

29. Juan Mascaro, "Introduction," to *The Dhammapada: The Path of Perfection*, trans. Juan Mascaro (Harmondsworth: Penguin Books, 1973), 9. Unless otherwise noted, all references will be to this translation.

30. Hans Dieter Betz, *Essays on the Sermon on the Mount* (Philadelphia: Fortress, 1985), 17.

31. Gary A. Tuttle, "The Sermon on the Mount: Its Wisdom Affinities and their Relation to its Structure," *Journal of the Evangelical Society* 20(1977):213–30; Rudolf Bultmann, *The History of the Synoptic Tradition*, trans. John Marsh, revised ed. (New York: Harper & Row, 1976), 73–108; Richard A. Edwards, *A Theology of Q: Eschatology, Prophecy, and Wisdom* (Philadelphia: Fortress, 1976), 61–62.

32. George Strecker, *The Sermon on the Mount: An Exegetical Commentary*, trans. O. C. Dean (Nashville: Abingdon, 1988), 174; Hans Dieter Betz, "Cosmogony and Ethics in the Sermon on the Mount," in *Cosmogony and Ethical Order: New Studies in Comparative Ethics*, eds. Robin W. Lovin and Frank E. Reynolds (Chicago: University of Chicago Press, 1985), 159.

33. Herman Hendrickx, *The Sermon on the Mount*, revised ed. (London: Geoffrey Chapman, 1984), 10.

34. Fitzmyer, *Gospel According to Luke*, 1:632–33.

35. Hendrickx, 10–13; Luise Schottroff and Wolfgang Stegemann, *Jesus and the Hope of the Poor*, trans. Matthew J. O'Connell (Maryknoll, NY: Orbis Books, 1986), 17–21.

36. Strecker, 31; on the relation of the Lukan beatitudes to the earliest tradition of Jesus, see Schottroff and Stegemann, 19–20.

37. Hendrickx, 15.

38. Ibid., 21.

39. Strecker, 32.

40. Ibid., 35–36; see also Hendrickx, 25.

41. Walter Wink, *Violence and Nonviolence in South Africa: Jesus' Third Way* (Philadelphia and Santa Cruz, CA: New Society Publishers, 1987), 12–16.

42. Ibid., 16–21.

43. Keiji Nishitani, *Religion and Nothingness*, trans. Jan Van Bragt (Berkeley, CA: University of California Press, 1982), 58.

44. Ibid.

45. Ibid.

46. Rahula, 1.

47. Thich Nhat Hanh, *Breathe! You Are Alive: Sutra on the Full Awareness of Breathing*, trans. Annabel Laity (Berkeley, CA: Parallax Press, 1988), 6–12.

48. Betz, "Cosmogony and Ethics," 161, 169.

49. Thich Nhat Hanh, *Our Appointment with Life: The Buddha's Teaching on Living in the Present*, trans. Annabel Laity (Berkeley, CA: Parallax Press, 1990), 5.

50. W. D. Davies, *The Setting of the Sermon on the Mount* (Cambridge: Cambridge University Press, 1966), 429–30; see also Hans Dieter Betz, "Cosmogony and Ethics in the Sermon on the Mount," 160, 174.

51. Francis H. Cook, *Hua-yen Buddhism: The Jewel Net of Indra* (University Park, PA: Pennsylvania State University Press, 1977), 6.

52. *Questions of Milinda*, in *World of the Buddha: An Introduction to Buddhist Literature*, ed. Lucien Stryk (Garden City, NY: Doubleday, 1968; reprint, New York: Grove Press, 1982), 102.

53. Raimundo Panikkar, *The Silence of God: The Answer of the Buddha*, trans. Robert R. Barr (Maryknoll, NY: Orbis Books, 1989), 55.

54. Herman Hendrickx, *The Passion Narratives of the Synoptic Gospels*, revised ed. (London: Geoffrey Chapman, 1984), 96; Don Senior, *The Passion of Jesus in the Gospel of Matthew* (Wilmington, DE: Michael Glazier, 1985), 136–41.

55. Daisetsu Teitaro Suzuki, *Mysticism Christian and Buddhist* (London: George Allen & Unwin, 1957; reprint, London: Unwin Paperbacks, 1979), 99.

56. Ibid., 94.

57. Yoshinori Takeuchi and John P. Keenan, "Buddhist Philosophy," *Encyclopedia of Religion*, 16 vols., ed. Mircea Eliade (New York: Macmillan, 1987), 2:541.

58. Suzuki, 100.

59. Robert Grant, *Augustus to Constantine: The Rise and Triumph of Christianity in the Roman World* (San Francisco: Harper & Row, 1970; reprint, Harper & Row Paperback, 1990), 42–44; Richard A. Horsley, *Jesus and the Spiral of Violence: Popular Jewish Resistance in Roman Palestine* (San Francisco: Harper & Row, 1987), 318–26.

60. Sanders, 61–76; Borg, 172–85.

61. Senior, *Passion of Jesus in the Gospel of Matthew*, 30–33; Don Senior, *The*

Passion of Jesus in the Gospel of Mark (Wilmington, DE: Michael Glazier, 1984), 28–36.

62. Karl Rahner, *Foundations of Christian Faith: An Introduction to the Idea of Christianity*, trans. William V. Dych (New York: Crossroad, 1978), 282–85.

63. Leonardo Boff, *Passion of Christ, Passion of the World: Their Facts, Their Interpretation, and Their Meaning Yesterday and Today*, trans. Robert R. Barr (Maryknoll, NY: Orbis Books, 1987), 3.

64. Edward Schillebeeckx, *Jesus: An Experiment in Christology*, trans. Hubert Hoskins (New York: Seabury Press, 1979), 319.

65. On the resurrection in the New Testament, see Pheme Perkins, *Resurrection: New Testament Witness and Contemporary Reflection* (Garden City, NY: Doubleday, 1984); and Norman Perrin, *The Resurrection According To Matthew, Mark, and Luke* (Philadelphia: Fortress, 1977).

66. Senior, *Passion of Jesus in the Gospel of Matthew*, 40, 43.

67. Rahula, 8; Nagao, "Life of Buddha as Parable," 22.

68. W. D. Davies, *Paul and Rabbinic Judaism: Some Rabbinic Elements in Pauline Theology* (London: SPCK, 1962), 150–52; Jack Sanders, *The New Testament Christological Hymns: Their Historical Religious Background* (Cambridge: Cambridge University Press, 1971), 75–87.

69. *The Flower Ornament Sutra: A Translation of the Avatamsaka Sutra*, Vol. I, trans. Thomas Cleary (Boulder, CO: Shambhala, 1984), Book 6, 264.

70. Daisetz Teitaro Suzuki, *Outline of Mahayana Buddhism* (London: Luzac and Co., 1907; reprint, New York: Schocken Books, 1963), 238.

71. *Suvarna Prabha Sutra*, ch. 3, quoted by Suzuki, *Outlines of Mahayana Buddhism*, 267–68. The parenthetical remarks are by Suzuki.

72. Suzuki, *Outlines of Mahayana Buddhism*, 268.

73. Ibid., 259.

74. Karl Rahner, "Christianity and the Non-Christian Religions," *Theological Investigations*, Vol. V: *Later Writings*, trans. Karl-H. Kruger (New York: Seabury Press, 1966), 129.

3. ASCENDING AND DESCENDING

1. Masao Abe, *Zen and Western Thought*, ed. William R. LaFleur (Honolulu: University of Hawaii Press, 1985), 3.

2. Zenkei Shibayama, *Zen Comments on the Mumonkan*, trans. Sumiko Kudo (San Francisco: Harper & Row, 1974), 53.

3. Edward Conze, *The Prajnaparamita Literature*, Indo-Iranian Monographs 6 (The Hague: Mouton & Co., 1960). See also Edward Conze, *Buddhist Wisdom Books, Containing The Diamond Sutra and The Heart Sutra*, 2nd ed. (London: George Allen Unwin, 1975; reprint, London: Unwin Paperbacks, 1988); and D. T. Suzuki, *Essays in Zen Buddhism, Third Series*, ed. Christmas Humphreys (London: Rider & Co., 1970), 222–331.

4. *Saptasatika Sutra* 223–224; Edward Conze, ed. and trans., *Selected Sayings from the Perfection of Wisdom* (1955, reprint, Boulder, CO: Prajna Press, 1978), 115.

5. *Ashtasahasrika Sutra* I, 20–21; trans. Edward Conze, *Selected Sayings*, 99.

6. *The Perfection of Wisdom in Eight Thousand Lines & Its Verse Summary* 1:5, trans. Edward Conze (San Francisco: Four Seasons Foundation, 1973), 9.

7. Gadjin Nagao, *Madhyamika and Yogacara: A Study of Mahayana Philosophies*,

ed. and trans. L. S. Kawamura (Albany, NY: State University of New York Press, 1991), 201.

8. Ibid., 204.

9. Masao Abe, "Kenotic God and Dynamic Sunyata," in *The Emptying God: A Buddhist-Jewish-Christian Conversation*, ed. John B. Cobb, Jr., and Christopher Ives (Maryknoll, NY: Orbis Books, 1990), 27–28.

10. Edward Conze, *Buddhism: Its Essence and Development* (Oxford: Bruno Cassirer, 1951; reprint, New York: Harper Torchbook, 1959), 130.

11. Edward Conze, *Buddhist Thought in India: Three Phases of Buddhist Philosophy* (London: George Allen & Unwin, 1962; reprint, Ann Arbor, MI: University of Michigan Press, 1967), 17–21, 242–49.

12. Nagao, *Madhyamika and Yogacara*, 198; Conze, *Buddhist Thought in India*, 249.

13. Nagao, 199.

14. Ibid., 206.

15. Ibid.

16. *The Buddha-karita of Asvaghosha* 15.11, trans. E. B. Cowell, in *Buddhist Mahayana Texts*, The Sacred Books of the East, vol. 49 (Oxford: Clarendon Press, 1894; reprint, New York: Dover Publications, 1969), 160.

17. *Buddhacarita* 15.12; trans. E. B. Cowell, p. 160.

18. Nagao, "The Life of the Buddha: An Interpretation," *Eastern Buddhist*, New Series 20/2(1987):6.

19. Nagao, *Madhyamika and Yogacara*, 203.

20. D. T. Suzuki, *Essays in Zen Buddhism, First Series* (London: Rider & Co., 1949; reprint, New York: Grove Press, 1961); *Essays in Zen Buddhism, Second Series*, ed. Christmas Humphreys (1953; reprint, New York: Samuel Weiser, 1971); *Essays in Zen Buddhism, Third Series*, ed. Christmas Humphreys (London: Rider & Co., 1970); *Studies in Zen*, ed. Christmas Humphreys (New York: Philosophical Library, 1955; reprint, New York: Delta Publishing Co., 1978).

21. Carl Bielefeldt, *Dogen's Manuals of Zen Meditation* (Berkeley, CA: University of California Press, 1988), 11.

22. *The T'ien-sheng Record of the Widely Extending Lamp*, Book 2, quoted by Heinrich Dumoulin, *Zen Buddhism: A History*, 2 vols., trans. James W. Heisig and Paul Knitter (New York: Macmillan Publishing Co., 1988, 1990), 1:8.

23. Ibid., 1:85. Parenthetical remarks by Dumoulin.

24. Bielefeldt, 92.

25. Dumoulin, 1:93.

26. Zenkei Shibayama, *A Flower Does Not Talk: Zen Essays*, trans. Sumiko Kudo (Rutland, VT, and Tokyo: Charles E. Tuttle, 1970), 28.

27. Abe, *Zen and Western Thought*, 27. On the background of this notion, see Sallie B. King, *Buddha Nature* (Albany, NY: State University of New York Press, 1991).

28. Shibayama, *A Flower Does Not Talk*, 117.

29. Abe, *Zen and Western Thought*, 4.

30. Ibid., 5.

31. Ibid., 7.

32. Ibid.

33. Ibid., 10.

34. Ibid., 4.

35. Ibid., 15.

36. Shibayama, *Zen Comments*, 259.

37. D. T. Suzuki's writings on Zen focus predominantly on the Rinzai tradition and have made this form of Zen the most commonly known in the West. See Suzuki, *Essays in Zen Buddhism, First, Second, and Third Series*.

38. Suzuki, *Essays, Second Series*, 40. Dumoulin claims that the first master known to have used koans is Nan-yüan Hui-hung, who died in 930 (Dumoulin, 1:246). Hee-Jin Kim claims that Mu-chou Tao-tsung (780?–877?) was the first to do so (Hee-Jin Kim, *Dogen Kigen: Mystical Realist* [rev. ed.; Tuscon, AZ: University of Arizona Press, 1987], 76).

39. Shibayama, *Zen Comments*, 92.

40. Suzuki, *Essays, Second Series*, 18.

41. Shibayama, *Zen Comments*, 253.

42. Ibid.

43. Ibid., 173–74.

44. Suzuki, *Essays, Second Series*, 36.

45. Ibid.

46. Dumoulin, 1:253.

47. Ibid., 1:255.

48. Hee-Jin Kim, " 'The Reason of Words and Letters': Dogen and Koan Language," in *Dogen Studies, Studies in East Asian Buddhism*, no. 2, ed. William R. LaFleur (Honolulu: University of Hawaii Press, 1985) 80, n. 12.

49. See Dumoulin, 1:222–30.

50. Hung-chih Cheng-chüeh, *Cultivating the Empty Field: The Silent Illumination of Zen Master Hongzhi*, trans. Taigen Daniel Leighton with Yi Wu (San Francisco: North Point Press, 1991), 4.

51. Hung-chih did collect old koans, and one of his collections became the foundation for a famous collection of koans: *Book of Serenity* (Taigen Daniel Leighton, "Introduction," *Cultivating the Empty Field*, xx). See *Book of Serenity*, trans. Thomas Cleary (Hudson, NY: Lindisfarne Press, 1990).

52. Cheng-chüeh, 4.

53. Ibid., 8–9.

54. Ibid., 6.

55. Masao Abe, "Dogen on Buddha Nature," *Eastern Buddhist*, New Series 4(1971):28–71. See also the revised version of this essay in Masao Abe, *A Study of Dogen*, ed. Steven Heine (Albany, NY: State University of New York Press, 1992), 35–76.

56. Bielefeldt, 131–32.

57. Dogen, *A Primer of Soto Zen: Dogen's Shobogenzo Zuimonki*, trans. Reiho Masunaga (Honolulu: University of Hawaii Press, 1971), 4.

58. Dogen, *Tenzo-kyokun*; quoted by Kim, 26. See also Kim, " 'The Reason of Words and Letters,' " 54–82.

59. Dogen, *Gakudo Yojin-Shu*, trans. Ed Brown and Kazuaki Tanahashi, in *Moon in a Dewdrop: Writings of Zen Master Dogen*, ed. Kazuaki Tanahashi (San Francisco: North Point Press, 1985), 43.

60. Kim, *Dogen Kigen*, 17. For a critique of the traditional account, see Carl Bielefeldt, "Recarving the Dragon: History and Dogma in the Study of Dogen," in *Dogen Studies*, 21–53.

61. Kim, *Dogen Kigen*, 20.

62. Masao Abe, "Dogen's View of Time and Space," *Eastern Buddhist*, New Series 21/2(1988):4. See also Masao Abe, *Study of Dogen*, 77–105.

63. Abe, "Dogen's View of Time and Space," 3–4.

64. On this period of his life, see Takashi James Kodera, *Dogen's Formative Years in China: An Historical Study and Annotated Translation of the Hokyo-ki* (London and Henley: Routledge & Kegan Paul, 1980).

65. Kim, *Dogen Kigen*, 25.

66. Ibid.

67. Ibid., 34.

68. Ibid., 35.

69. Bielefeldt, *Dogen's Manuals*, 162.

70. Abe, "Dogen's View of Time and Space," 6.

71. Dogen, *Shobogenzo Bendowa*, trans. Norman Waddell and Masao Abe, *Eastern Buddhist* 4/1(1971):129.

72. Abe, "Dogen's View of Time and Space," 9.

73. Dogen, *Shobogenzo Buddha-nature (Bussho)*, trans. Norman Waddell and Masao Abe, *Eastern Buddhist*, New Series 8/2(1975):96–102. See also Masao Abe, *Zen and Western Thought*, 27; Kim, *Dogen Kigen*, 120–21.

74. Dogen, *Shobogenzo Bussho*, quoted by Kim, *Dogen Kigen*, 122.

75. Masao Abe, "The Oneness of Practice and Attainment: Implications for the Relation between Means and Ends," in *Dogen Studies*, 105–8.

76. Ibid., 108–9.

77. Ibid., 109–10.

4. DIONYSIUS THE AREOPAGITE AND MAHAYANA PERSPECTIVES

1. Dionysius, *The Mystical Theology* 1.3 (1001A). In Pseudo-Dionysius, *The Complete Works*, The Classics of Western Spirituality, trans. Colm Luibheid, et al. (New York: Paulist Press, 1987), p. 137. Unless otherwise noted, all references will be to this translation. The titles of his works are *The Divine Names* (DN), *The Mystical Theology* (MT), *The Celestial Hierarchy* (CH), *The Ecclesiastical Hierarchy* (EH), and nine letters. References will include the abbreviated title, the chapter and section number, the column number of the Migne edition, and the page number of the Luibheid translation.

2. Andrew Louth, *Denys the Areopagite* (Wilton, CT: Morehouse-Barlow, 1989), 1–14.

3. See Denys Rutledge, *Cosmic Theology: The Ecclesiastical Hierarchy of Pseudo-Denys: An Introduction* (Staten Island, NY: Alba House, 1965); and Denys l'Aréopagite, *La hiérarchie céleste*, introduction by René Roques, trans. Maurice de Gandillac (Paris: Editions du Cerf, 1958).

4. René Roques, *L'univers dionysien: structure hiérarchique du monde selon le pseudo-Denys* (Aubier: Editions Montaigne, 1954), 92–116; Ronald F. Hathaway, *Hierarchy and the Definition of Order in the Letters of Pseudo-Dionysius* (The Hague: Martinus Nijhoff, 1969), 37–60.

5. Roques, *L'univers dionysien*, 196, 198.

6. The terms *cataphatic* and *apophatic* theology were used by Proclus (ca. 410–85). Dionysius appears to have been the first Christian to use them, but he transformed the meaning of the terms by applying them to the Christian God. For Proclus, apophatic theology applied only to the One, the source of all, and cata-

phatic theology applied to all the manifestations of the One on lower levels of reality. For Dionysius, both apophatic and cataphatic theology apply to God.

7. Bernard McGinn, *The Foundations of Mysticism*, Vol. I of *The Presence of God: A History of Western Christian Mysticism* (New York: Crossroad, 1991), 177.

8. Edward Conze, *Buddhist Thought in India: Three Phases of Buddhist Philosophy* (London: George Allen & Unwin, 1962; reprint, Ann Arbor, MI: University of Michigan Press, 1967), 219.

9. Ibid.

10. Ibid., 220.

11. This was also a principle of the mystery religions. Aristotle had commented that in the Eleusinian mysteries the initiates did not learn anything but rather experienced something. See Aristotle, *De Philosophia*, Fragment 15, in *The Complete Works of Aristotle*, 2 vols., ed. Jonathan Barnes (Princeton, NJ: Princeton University Press, 1984), 2:2392.

12. McGinn, 178.

13. Zenkei Shibayama, *Zen Comments on the Mumonkan*, trans. Sumiko Kudo (San Francisco: Harper & Row, 1974), 97.

14. In his debate with the Donatists in North Africa, Augustine offered a different perspective: Since the real minister in the sacraments is Christ, the human minister can validly adminster a sacrament even if he is in a state of heresy or sin. For Augustine and the tradition following him, it is not the consciousness of the minister that is critical, but the power of Christ at work in the sacrament. See Augustine, *On Baptism against the Donatists, Answer to Letters of Petilian, Bishop of Cirta*, and *The Correction of the Donatists*, in *St. Augustin: The Writings against the Manichaeans and against the Donatists*, A Select Library of the Nicene and Post-Nicene Fathers, vol. IV, ed. Philip Schaff (1887; reprint, Grand Rapids, MI: Wm. B. Eerdmans Publishing Co., 1983).

15. See Caroline Canfield Putnam, *Beauty in the Pseudo-Denis. Philosophical Studies*, 190 (Washington, DC: Catholic University of America Press, 1960); and Hans Urs von Balthasar, *The Glory of the Lord: A Theological Aesthetics, Vol. II: Studies in Theological Style: Clerical Styles*, trans. Andrew Louth, et al. (San Francisco: Ignatius Press, 1984), 144–210.

16. Louth, 94.

17. Hung-chih Cheng-chüeh, *Cultivating the Empty Field: The Silent Illumination of Zen Master Hongshi*, trans. Taigen Daniel Leighton with Yi Wu (San Francisco: North Point Press, 1991), 4.

18. Shibayama, 110.

19. The neo-Platonists sometimes called this approach "ontological prayer," prayer in which we come to awareness of our ontological condition. See Louth, 92.

20. Louth, 17–31.

21. Lin-chi, "Discourses," section 10; quoted by Dumoulin, 1:191.

22. Bielefeldt, *Dogen's Manuals*, 170.

23. Ibid.

24. Shibayama, 127.

25. The word *synaxis* comes from the Greek word *sunagein*, to gather together, or assemble. It was commonly used by many of the Greek Fathers to designate the Eucharist. See Dionysius the Pseudo-Areopagite, *The Ecclesiastical Hierarchy*, translated and annotated by Thomas L. Campbell (Washington, D.C.: University Press of America, 1981), 136–37, n. 87. See also Roques, *L'univers dionysien*, 256–70.

5. PURE LAND BUDDHISM

1. *The Larger Sukhavati-vyuha*, trans. F. Max Müller, in *Buddhist Mahayana Texts*, Sacred Books of the East, vol. 49 (Oxford: Clarendon Press; reprint, New York: Dover Publications, 1969), Part II, 1–72. The two other major early Pure Land Sutras, *The Smaller Sukhavati-vyuha*, translated by F. Max Müller (Part II, 89–103), and the *Amitayur-Dhyana Sutra*, translated by J. Takakusu (Part II, 162–201), are also in this volume. Unless otherwise noted, all references to these three texts will be to these translations. On the date, see Kenneth K. Tanaka, *The Dawn of Chinese Pure Land Buddhist Doctrine: Ching-ying Hui yüan's Commentary on the Visualization Sutra* (Albany, NY: State University of New York Press, 1990), 3.

2. The Sanskrit text has only forty-six vows, but the Chinese translation of this text has forty-eight, and it is usually to this version that the later Pure Land tradition has referred. See *Buddhist Mahayana Texts*, Part II, 73–75.

3. Tanaka, 2.

4. Tanaka finds the earliest witness to recitation practice in the *Kuan-ching*, a text of the late fourth century which describes practices which would have been common before that time (10).

5. *Buddhist Mahayana Texts*, Part II, v.

6. Tanaka, 10–11.

7. D. T. Suzuki, *Shin Buddhism* (New York: Harper & Row, 1970), 20.

8. Ibid., 22.

9. Alfred Bloom, *Shinran's Gospel of Pure Grace*, Association for Asian Studies Monographs, 20 (Tucson, AZ: University of Arizona Press, 1965), 11.

10. Carl Bielefeldt, *Dogen's Manuals of Zen Meditation* (Berkeley, CA: University of California Press, 1988), 66–68, 165–68.

11. D. T. Suzuki, *A Miscellany on the Shin Teaching of Buddhism* (Kyoto: Shinshu Otaniha Shumusho, 1949), 131.

12. Kenneth S. Ch'en, *Buddhism in China: A Historical Survey* (Princeton, NJ: Princeton University Press, 1964; paperback reprint, 1972), 344.

13. Tanaka, 18.

14. Suzuki, *Shin Buddhism*, 17.

15. Gadjin Nagao, *Madhyamika and Yogacara: A Study of Mahayana Philosophies*, ed. and trans. L.S. Kawamura (Albany, NY: State University of New York Press, 1991), 206.

16. Ibid., 207.

17. Ryojin Soga, "Dharmakara Bodhisattva," in *The Buddha Eye: An Anthology of the Kyoto School*, ed. Frederick Franck (New York: Crossroad, 1982), 223.

18. Ibid., 225, 228.

19. Ibid., 231.

20. Bloom, x, xii.

21. On his life, see Alfred Bloom, *The Life of Shinran Shonin: The Journey to Self Acceptance* (Leiden: E.J. Brill, 1968).

22. Bloom, *Shinran's Gospel*, 29.

23. Shinran, *Tannisho: A Shin Buddhist Classic*, trans. Taitetsu Unno (Honolulu, HI: Buddhist Study Center Press, 1984), 14.

24. Bloom, *Shinran's Gospel*, 50–51.

25. On the meaning of *eshin*, "turning the mind" or "conversion" in Shinran,

see Dennis Gira, *Le sens de la conversion dans l'enseignement de Shinran* (Paris: Edition Maisonneuve et Larose, 1985).

26. Nobuo Haneda, "Translator's Introduction," in Shuichi Maida, *The Evil Person: Essays on Shin Buddhism*, trans. Nobuo Haneda (Los Angeles: Higashi Honganji North American Translation Center, 1989), 7.

27. Shinran, *Notes on Once-calling and Many-calling* (Kyoto: Hongwanji International Center, 1980), 32; cited by Yoshifumi Ueda, "The Mahayana Structure of Shinran's Thought," Part I, *Eastern Buddhist*, New Series 17/1(1984):72.

28. Shinran, *Notes on the Inscriptions on Sacred Scrolls* (Kyoto: Hongwanji International Center, 1981), 53–54; cited by Yoshifumi Ueda, "The Mahayana Structure of Shinran's Thought," Part II, *Eastern Buddhist*, New Series 17/2(1984):35.

29. Ueda, I, 75.

30. Shinran, *Shinshu shogyo zensho* II (Kyoto: Oyagi Kobundo, 1941); cited by Ueda, I, 77.

31. Ibid.

32. Sallie B. King notes that while the Pure Land tradition generally neglected the notion of the Buddha-nature, Shinran "stated that the actualization of faith (the faith upon which all else hinges in his Jodo Shinshu sect) is accomplished in the individual by the action of the Buddha nature." *Buddha Nature* (Albany, NY: State University of New York Press, 1991), 3. See also Bloom, *Shinran's Gospel*, 37–44.

33. Shinran, *Notes on "Essentials of Faith Alone"* (Kyoto: Hongwanji International Center, 1979); cited by Ueda, II, 37.

34. Ueda, II, 38–39.

35. Shinran, *Koso wasan* 39, 40; cited by Ueda, II, 45–46.

36. Ueda, II, 40–41.

37. Shinran, *Tannisho* 9; p. 14.

38. Ibid., 1; p. 5.

6. AUGUSTINE AND MAHAYANA BUDDHISM

1. Augustine, *On Christian Doctrine*, trans. D. W. Robertson, Jr. (Indianapolis: Bobbs-Merrill Educational Publishing, 1958). All references will be to this translation unless otherwise noted. On the role of signs in Augustine's thought, see R. A. Markus, "St. Augustine on Signs," in *Augustine: A Collection of Critical Essays*, ed. R. A. Markus, Modern Studies in Philosophy (Garden City, NY: Anchor Books, Doubleday & Co., 1972), 61–91; and B. Darrell Jackson, "The Theory of Signs in St. Augustine's *De Doctrina Christiana*," in Markus, *Augustine: A Collection*, 92–147.

2. On the identification of wisdom and happiness as an orienting theme in the thought of Augustine, see Etienne Gilson, *The Christian Philosophy of Saint Augustine*, trans. L. E. M. Lynch (London: Victor Gollancz, 1961), 3–10.

3. Sermon 52, 16 (*Patrologia Latina* 38, 360).

4. Carl Bielefeldt, *Dogen's Manuals of Zen Meditation* (Berkeley, CA: University of California Press, 1988), 166.

5. In *On the Teacher*, Augustine transforms Plato's theory of learning as recollection into a Christian theory of knowledge from the divine illumination of Christ. See Eugene TeSelle, *Augustine the Theologian* (New York: Herder & Herder, 1970), 92–106.

6. *The Awakening of Faith: Attributed to Ashvaghosha*, trans., with commentary, by Yoshito S. Hakeda (New York and London: Columbia University Press, 1967), 87, 88.

7. G. R. Evans, *Augustine on Evil* (Cambridge, England: Cambridge University Press, 1982), 54.

8. Augustine, *Confessions* 13:15. See Robert J. O'Connell, *St. Augustine's Confessions: The Odyssey of Soul* (Cambridge, MA: Harvard University Press, 1969; reprint, New York: Fordham University Press, 1989), 163.

9. See Sallie B. King, *Buddha Nature* (Albany, NY: State University of New York Press, 1991).

10. Augustine, *On the Teacher*, 8–9; Evans, 54.

11. On the role of eros in Augustine, see Romano Guardini, *The Conversion of Augustine*, trans. Elinor Briefs (Westminster, MD: Newman Press, 1960), 57–66.

12. Augustine, *Confessions* 1.1, trans. R. S. Pine-Coffin (Harmondsworth: Penguin Books, 1961), 21. All translations will be from this edition unless otherwise noted. See also Augustine, *Confessions*, trans. Henry Chadwick (Oxford: Oxford University Press, 1992).

13. Hans Urs von Balthasar, *The Glory of the Lord: A Theological Aesthetics, Vol. II: Studies in Theological Style: Clerical Styles*, trans. Andrew Louth, et al. (San Francisco: Ignatius Press, 1984), 95.

14. Michael Pye, *Skilful Means: A Concept in Mahayana Buddhism* (London: Duckworth, 1978), 4.

15. On the context of this work in Augustine's life and thought, see Peter Brown, *Augustine of Hippo: A Biography* (Berkeley: University of California Press, 1967), 1–181; and TeSelle.

16. On Augustine's "epistemology of evil," see Evans, 29–36.

17. Yoshifumi Ueda, "The Mahayana Structure of Shinran's Thought," Part II, *Eastern Buddhist*, New Series 17/2(1984):32.

18. Augustine, *Confessions* 13.40; p. 248. References in the text of this section will be to this work.

19. Augustine, *The Trinity*, trans. Edmund Hill (Brooklyn, NY: New City Press, 1991), Books 9–10, pp. 270–99.

20. Ibid., 8.5.10; pp. 251–52.

21. O'Connell, 186.

22. Ibid., 178.

23. Augustine, *On Free Will* 2.54, trans. John H. S. Burleigh, *Augustine: Earlier Writings*, Library of Christian Classics (Philadelphia: Westminster Press, 1953), 168–69.

24. Balthasar, 2:162.

25. Gilson, 3–10.

26. Masao Abe, *Zen and Western Thought*, ed. William R. LaFleur (Honolulu: University of Hawaii Press, 1985), 132.

27. O'Connell, 73.

28. Ibid., 99–100.

29. For Augustine's view of the work of redemption, see Augustine, *The Trinity*, 4.3–4; pp. 162–70.

30. Augustine, *The Trinity*, 4.4.20, trans. Hill, p. 167.

31. Paul Henry, *La vision d'Ostie. Sa place dans la vie et l'oeuvre de S. Augustin* (Paris: J. Vrin, 1938).

32. O'Connell, 23–25.

33. Gilson, 8.

34. On this period of Augustine's life, see F. Van der Meer, *Augustine the Bishop*, trans. Brian Battershaw and G. R. Lamb (London and New York: Sheed & Ward, 1961).

35. Masao Abe, "Kenosis and Emptiness," in *Buddhist Emptiness and Christian Trinity: Essays and Explorations*, eds. Roger Corless and Paul F. Knitter (New York and Mahwah, NJ: Paulist Press, 1990), 22.

36. Pelagius, *Letter to Demetrias*, trans. J. Patout Burns, *Theological Anthropology*, *Sources of Early Christian Thought* (Philadelphia: Fortress, 1981), 39-55.

37. Augustine, *The Spirit and the Letter*, in *Augustine: Later Works*, trans. John Burnaby (Philadelphia: Westminster, 1955), 195–250.

38. Ibid. 54.31; p. 238.

39. Augustine, *On the Grace of Christ, and on Original Sin*, trans. Peter Holmes and Robert Wallis, in *Saint Augustin: Anti-Pelagian Writings*, ed. Philip Schaff, *A Select Library of the Nicene and Post-Nicene Fathers*, Vol. V (Grand Rapids, MI: Eerdmans Publishing Co., 1887; reprint, 1980), 214–55.

40. Taitetsu Unno, "Afterword," in Shinran, *Tannisho: A Shin Buddhist Classic*, trans. Taitetsu Unno (Honolulu: Buddhist Study Center Press, 1984), 45.

41. D. T. Suzuki, *Shin Buddhism* (New York: Harper & Row, 1970), 36, 40–41.

42. *Amitayur-Dhyana* Sutra 17, trans. J. Takakusu, in *Buddhist Mahayana Texts*, Sacred Books of the East, vol. 49 (Oxford: Clarendon Press; reprint, New York: Dover Publications, 1969), Part II, 178.

43. Augustine, *The Trinity*, 4.1.4; pp. 154–55.

INTRODUCTION

1. Masao Abe, *Zen and Western Thought*, ed. William R. LaFleur (Honolulu: University of Hawaii Press, 1985), 231–40.

2. For an exploration of the modern notions of identity, see Charles Taylor, *Sources of the Self: The Making of Modern Identity* (Cambridge, MA: Harvard University Press, 1989).

7. THE ENGAGED BUDDHISM OF THICH NHAT HANH

3. Thich Nhat Hanh, *Vietnam: Lotus in a Sea of Fire* (New York: Hill and Wang, 1967), 4. "Thich" is the new family name that all Vietnamese Buddhist monks accept at their ordination in place of their own. It is the shortened form of "Thich-ca," Vietnamese for "Shakya," the family name of the Buddha. See Thich Nhat Hanh, *Zen Keys*, trans. Albert and Jean Low, Introduction by Philip Kapleau (Garden City, NY: Anchor Books, 1974), 1.

4. Ibid.

5. Thich Nhat Hanh, *Peace Is Every Step: The Path of Mindfulness in Everyday Life*, ed. Arnold Kotler (New York: Bantam Books, 1991), "Editor's Introduction," x.

6. Thich Nhat Hanh, *Being Peace*, ed. Arnold Kotler (Berkeley, CA: Parallax Press, 1987), 85.

7. Ibid., 86.

8. Ibid.

9. Thich Nhat Hanh, *The Moon Bamboo*, trans. Vo-Dinh Mai and Mobi Ho (Berkeley, CA: Parallax Press, 1989); *The Pine Gate: Stories by Thich Nhat Hanh*, trans. Vo-Dinh Mai and Mobi Ho (Fredonia, NY: White Pine Press, 1988); *Interbeing: Commentaries on the Tiep Hien Precepts*, ed. Fred Eppsteiner (Berkeley, CA: Parallax Press, 1987); *Present Moment Wonderful Moment: Mindfulness Verses for Daily Living*, trans. Annabel Laity (Berkeley, CA: Parallax Press, 1990); *The Miracle of Mindfulness: A Manual on Meditation*, trans. Mobi Ho (rev. ed.; Boston: Beacon Press, 1987); *The Sun My Heart: From Mindfulness to Insight Contemplation*, trans. Anh Huong Nguyen et al. (Berkeley, CA: Parallax Press, 1988); *Zen Panels: Poems*, trans. Teo Savory (Greensboro, North Carolina: Unicorn Press, 1976); *The Heart of Understanding: Commentaries on the Prajnaparamita Heart Sutra*, ed. Peter Levitt (Berkeley, CA: Parallax Press, 1988); *Transformation and Healing: The Sutra on the Four Establishments of Mindfulness* (Berkeley, CA: Parallax Press, 1990); *Breathe! You Are Alive: Sutra on Full Awareness of Breathing (Anapanasatisutta)*, trans. Annabel Laity (Berkeley, CA: Parallax Press, 1988); *Our Appointment with Life: The Buddha's Teaching on Living in the Present: Translation and Commentary on The Sutra on Knowing the Better Way to Live Alone (Bhaddekaratta Sutta)*, trans. Annabel Laity (Berkeley, CA: Parallax Press, 1990); *Old Path White Clouds: Walking in the Footsteps of the Buddha*, trans. Mobi Ho (Berkeley, CA: Parallax Press, 1991); "Please Call Me by My True Names," and "The Individual, Society, and Nature," in *The Path of Compassion: Writings on Socially Engaged Buddhism*, ed. Fred Eppsteiner (2nd rev. ed.; Berkeley, CA: Parallax Press, 1988).

10. Thich Nhat Hanh, *The Path of Return Continues the Journey*, trans. Vo-Dinh (New York: Hoa Binh Press, 1972), 10. All references will be to this edition.

11. Nhat Hanh, *The Moon Bamboo*, 7–8. All references to this short story and the following will be to this edition.

12. Daniel Berrigan and Thich Nhat Hanh, *The Raft Is Not the Shore; Conversations toward a Buddhist/Christian Awareness* (Boston: Beacon Press, 1975), 6–7.

13. Nhat Hanh, *The Sun My Heart*, 33.

14. Ibid., 32.

15. Nhat Hanh, *Being Peace*, 3.

16. Ibid., 5.

17. Ibid., 21.

18. Nhat Hanh, *Our Appointment with Life*, 35.

19. Ibid., 12–13.

20. Ibid., 25.

21. Nhat Hanh, *Breathe! You Are Alive*, 39.

22. Ibid., 9.

23. Ibid., 22.

24. Nhat Hanh, *Transformation and Healing*, 130–31.

25. Nhat Hanh, *Breathe! You Are Alive*, 29.

26. Ibid.

27. Ibid.

28. Ibid., 31.

29. Nhat Hanh, *Heart of Understanding*, 3.

30. Ibid.

31. Ibid., 4.

32. Ibid., 32.

33. Ibid., 9.

34. Ibid., 15.
35. Ibid., 17.
36. Ibid.
37. Ibid., 19.
38. Ibid., 21.
39. Ibid.
40. Ibid., 27.
41. Ibid., 28.
42. Ibid., 31–32.
43. Ibid., 33.
44. Ibid., 36.
45. Ibid., 44.
46. Ibid., 41.
47. Ibid., 42.
48. Ibid., 47.
49. Ibid., 50.
50. Nhat Hanh, *The Sun My Heart*, 116.
51. Nhat Hanh, *Heart of Understanding*, 52.
52. Nhat Hanh, *Being Peace*, 69–70.
53. Nhat Hanh, *The Sun My Heart*, 122.
54. Ibid., 124.
55. Ibid., 125.
56. Nhat Hanh, "Call Me by My True Names," 36; Berrigan and Nhat Hanh, *Raft Is Not the Shore*, 122.
57. Berrigan and Nhat Hanh, *Raft Is Not the Shore*, 124.
58. Nhat Hanh, "Call Me by My True Names," 37.
59. Nhat Hanh, *Being Peace*, 79.
60. Nhat Hanh, "Individual, Society, and Nature," 44.
61. Berrigan and Nhat Hanh, *Raft Is Not the Shore*, 111, 88.
62. Ibid., 86–87.
63. Ibid., 119.
64. Nhat Hanh, "Call Me by My True Names," 38.
65. Ibid., 39.
66. Nhat Hanh, *Interbeing*, 15.
67. Ibid., 17.
68. Ibid., 18.
69. Ibid., 27.
70. Ibid., 30.
71. Ibid., 34.
72. Ibid., 35.
73. Ibid., 40.
74. Ibid., 42.
75. Ibid., 46.
76. Ibid., 49.
77. Ibid., 56.
78. Ibid., 57.
79. Ibid., 58.
80. Ibid., 61.

8. GUSTAVO GUTIÉRREZ AND THICH NHAT HANH

1. For the presentation of the dissertation and the discussion that followed, see Gustavo Gutiérrez, *The Truth Shall Make You Free: Confrontations*, trans. Matthew J. O'Connell (Maryknoll, NY: Orbis Books, 1990). On the context of Gutiérrez's life and thought, see Curt Cadorette, *From the Heart of the People: The Theology of Gustavo Gutiérrez* (Oak Park, IL: Meyer-Stone Books, 1988); and Robert McAfee Brown, *Gustavo Gutiérrez: An Introduction to Liberation Theology* (Maryknoll, NY: Orbis Books, 1990). On the broader movement of liberation theology, see Rebecca S. Chopp, *The Praxis of Suffering: An Interpretation of Liberation and Political Theologies* (Maryknoll, NY: Orbis Books, 1986); Roger Haight, *An Alternative Vision: An Interpretation of Liberation Theology* (New York: Paulist Press, 1985); and Arthur F. McGovern, *Marxism: An American Christian Perspective* (Maryknoll, NY: Orbis Books, 1980).

2. Gustavo Gutiérrez, *The Power of the Poor in History*, trans. Robert R. Barr (Maryknoll, NY: Orbis Books, 1983), 20.

3. Gustavo Gutiérrez, *A Theology of Liberation: History, Politics and Salvation*, trans. and ed. Caridad Inda and John Eagleson (Maryknoll, NY: Orbis Books, 1973), 234–35.

4. See Karl Mannheim, *Ideology and Utopia: An Introduction to the Sociology of Knowledge*, trans. Louis Wirth and Edward Shils (New York: Harcourt, Brace & World, 1936); and Paul Ricoeur, *Lectures on Ideology and Utopia*, ed. George H. Taylor (New York: Columbia University Press, 1986).

5. Gustavo Gutiérrez, *On Job: God-Talk and the Suffering of the Innocent*, trans. Matthew J. O'Connell (Maryknoll, NY: Orbis Books, 1987), 102.

6. Thich Nhat Hanh, *The Path of Return Continues the Journey*, trans. Vo-Dinh Mai (New York: Hoa Binh Press, 1972), 24–25.

7. Thich Nhat Hanh, *The Moon Bamboo*, trans. Vo-Dinh Mai and Mobi Ho (Berkeley, CA: Parallax Press, 1989), 40.

8. Thich Nhat Hanh, *Interbeing: Commentaries on the Tiep Hien Precepts*, ed. Fred Eppsteiner (Berkeley, CA: Parallax Press, 1987), 34.

9. Gustavo Gutiérrez, *The God of Life*, trans. Matthew J. O'Connell (Maryknoll, NY: Orbis Books, 1991), 69-75.

10. Gutiérrez, *Theology of Liberation*, 234–38.

11. Thich Nhat Hanh, *Zen Keys*, trans. Albert and Jean Low (Garden City, NY: Anchor Books, 1974), 149.

12. Ibid., 150.

13. Ibid.

14. Thich Nhat Hanh, "The Individual, Society, and Nature," in *The Path of Compassion: Writings on Socially Engaged Buddhism*, ed. Fred Eppsteiner (2nd ed., rev.; Berkeley, CA: Parallax Press, 1988), 42.

15. Ibid.

16. Gutiérrez, *Power of the Poor*, 21.

17. Ibid., xii.

18. Ibid., xiii–xiv.

19. Ibid., xlv.

20. Nhat Hanh, *Zen Keys*, 31, 45.

21. Ibid., 47.

22. Gutiérrez, *On Job*, 4.

23. Ibid., 5.

24. Ibid., 54.

25. Ibid.

26. Ibid., 55.

27. Ibid., 10.

28. Ibid., 15.

29. Nhat Hanh, *Interbeing*, 27–31.

30. Gutiérrez, *On Job*, 22–23.

31. Ibid., 16.

32. Nhat Hanh, *Moon Bamboo*, 77.

33. Gutiérrez, *On Job*, 31.

34. Ibid., 65.

35. Ibid.

36. César Vallejo, *Obra poética completa* (Lima: Mosca Azul, 1974), 423; quoted by Gutiérrez, *On Job*, 65.

37. Gutiérrez, *On Job*, 66.

38. Thich Nhat Hanh, *Being Peace*, ed. Arnold Kotler (Berkeley, CA: Parallax Press, 1987), 3.

39. Gutiérrez, *On Job*, 68–69.

40. Ibid., 69.

41. Ibid., 72.

42. Ibid.

43. Ibid., 75.

44. Ibid., 77.

45. Ibid.

46. Nhat Hanh, *Heart of Understanding*, 36.

47. Gutiérrez, *On Job*, 83.

48. Ibid., 85.

49. Ibid., 86.

50. Ibid., 87.

51. Ibid., 88–89.

52. Gutiérrez, *Truth Shall Make You Free*, 17.

53. Gutiérrez, *On Job*, 96.

54. Gutiérrez, *God of Life*, 1.

55. Ibid., 16.

56. Ibid., 48–55.

57. Nhat Hanh, "Individual, Society, and Nature," 41.

58. Nhat Hanh, *Heart of Understanding*, 22.

59. Ibid., 23.

60. Gutiérrez, *God of Life*, 77.

61. Ibid., 49–56.

62. Ibid., 69–73.

63. Nhat Hanh, *Heart of Understanding*, 28–29.

64. Thich Nhat Hanh, *Peace Is Every Step: The Path of Mindfulness in Everyday Life*, ed. Arnold Kotler (New York: Bantam Books, 1991), 101–2.

65. Thich Nhat Hanh, *The Sun My Heart: From Mindfulness to Insight Contemplation*, trans. Anh Huong Nguyen et al. (Berkeley, CA: Parallax Press, 1988), 36.

66. Nhat Hanh, *Peace Is Every Step*, 102.

67. Ibid., 103.

68. Gutiérrez, *Theology of Liberation*, 275.

69. Ibid.

70. Ibid., 276.

71. Pope John Paul II, quoted by Gutiérrez, *God of Life*, 89.

72. Gutiérrez, *God of Life*, 90.

73. Gutiérrez, *Theology of Liberation*, ix.

74. Nhat Hanh, *Peace Is Every Step*, 98.

75. Nhat Hanh, *Being Peace*, 62.

76. Nhat Hanh, *Peace Is Every Step*, 98.

77. Thich Nhat Hanh, *The Cry of Vietnam*, trans. Thich Nhat Hanh and Helen Coutant (Santa Barbara, CA: Unicorn Press, 1968), 14, 37.

78. Nhat Hanh, *Path of Return*, 24.

79. Gustavo Gutiérrez, *We Drink from Our Own Wells: The Spiritual Journey of a People*, trans. Matthew O'Connell (Maryknoll, NY: Orbis Books), 109.

80. Ibid., 110.

81. Nhat Hanh, *Peace Is Every Step*, ix.

82. Gutiérrez, *God of Life*, 118.

83. Nhat Hanh, *Peace Is Every Step*, 37.

84. Ibid., 38.

85. Gutiérrez, *We Drink from Our Own Wells*, 111.

86. Nhat Hanh, *Zen Keys*, 112.

87. Ibid.

88. Gutiérrez, *God of Life*, 84.

89. Ibid., 85.

90. Nhat Hanh, *Zen Keys*, 73.

91. Ibid., 76.

EPILOGUE

1. "Dialogues, East and West: Conversations between Paul Tillich and Hisamatsu Shin'ichi," *Eastern Buddhist*, New Series 6/2(1973):106.

2. Ibid., 107.

3. Ibid.

4. Ibid., 106–9.

5. Augustine, Sermon 52, 16; *Patrologia Latina* 38, 360.

6. Gadjin Nagao, "The Buddha's Life as Parable," *Eastern Buddhist*, New Series 24/2(1991):12.

Select Bibliography

Abe, Masao. "Dogen on Buddha Nature." *Eastern Buddhist*, New Series 4(1971):28–71.

———. "Dogen's View of Time and Space." *Eastern Buddhist*, New Series 21/2(1988):1–35.

———. "Kenosis and Emptiness." In *Buddhist Emptiness and Christian Trinity: Essays and Explorations*. Eds. Roger Corless and Paul F. Knitter. New York and Mahwah, NJ: Paulist Press, 1990.

———. "Kenotic God and Dynamic Sunyata." In *The Emptying God: A Buddhist-Jewish-Christian Conversation*. Ed. John B. Cobb, Jr., and Christopher Ives. Maryknoll, NY: Orbis Books, 1990.

———. *A Study of Dogen*. Ed. Steven Heine. Albany, NY: State University of New York Press, 1992.

———. *Zen and Western Thought*. Ed. William R. LaFleur. Honolulu: University of Hawaii Press, 1985.

Ashvaghosha. *The Buddhacarita or, The Acts of the Buddha*. Part I: Sanskrit Text. Ed. and trans. E. H. Johnston. Lahore: University of the Punjab, 1937. Reprint, New Delhi, India: Oriental Books Reprint Corp., 1972; Part II: "The Buddha's Mission and Last Journey: *Buddhacarita*, xv to xxviii." Trans. E. H. Johnston. *Acta Orientalia* 15(1937):85–111, 231–51, and 253–92.

Augustine. *Confessions*. Trans. R. S. Pine-Coffin. Harmondsworth: Penguin Books, 1961.

———. *On Christian Doctrine*. Trans. D. W. Robertson, Jr. Indianapolis: Bobbs-Merrill Educational Publishing, 1958.

———. *On Free Will*. In *Augustine: Earlier Writings*, Library of Christian Classics. Trans. John H. S. Burleigh. Philadelphia: Westminster Press, 1953.

———. *On the Grace of Christ, and on Original Sin*. In *Saint Augustin: Anti-Pelagian Writings*. Trans. Peter Homes and Robert Wallis. Ed. Philip Schaff. A Select Library of the Nicene and Post-Nicene Fathers, 5. Grand Rapids, MI: Eerdmans Publishing Co., 1887. Reprint, 1980.

———. *Soliloquies*. Trans. John J. O'Meara. *An Augustine Reader*. Garden City, NY: Image Books, 1973.

———. *The Spirit and the Letter*. In *Augustine: Later Works*. Trans. John Burnaby. Philadelphia: Westminster, 1955.

———. *The Trinity*. Trans. Edmund Hill. Brooklyn, NY: New City Press, 1991.

Balthasar, Hans Urs von. *The Glory of the Lord: A Theological Aesthetics*, Vol. II: *Studies in Theological Style: Clerical Styles*. Trans. Andrew Louth, et al. San Francisco: Ignatius Press, 1984.

Berrigan, Daniel, and Thich Nhat Hanh. *The Raft Is Not the Shore: Conversations toward a Buddhist/Christian Awareness*. Boston: Beacon Press, 1975.

Betz, Hans Dieter. "Cosmogony and Ethics in the Sermon on the Mount." In *Cosmogony and Ethical Order: New Studies in Comparative Ethics*. Eds. Robin W. Lovin and Frank E. Reynolds. Chicago: University of Chicago Press, 1985.

———. *Essays on the Sermon on the Mount*. Philadelphia: Fortress, 1985.

Bielefeldt, Carl. *Dogen's Manuals of Zen Meditation*. Berkeley, CA: University of California Press, 1988.

Bloom, Alfred. *The Life of Shinran Shonin: The Journey to Self Acceptance*. Leiden: E. J. Brill, 1968.

———. *Shinran's Gospel of Pure Grace*. Association for Asian Studies Monographs, 20. Tuscon, AZ: University of Arizona Press, 1965.

Boff, Leonardo. *Passion of Christ, Passion of the World: Their Facts, Their Interpretation, and Their Meaning Yesterday and Today*. Trans. Robert R. Barr. Maryknoll, NY: Orbis Books, 1987.

Book of Serenity. Trans. Thomas Cleary. Hudson, NY: Lindisfarne Press, 1990.

Borg, Marcus J. *Jesus, A New Vision: Spirit, Culture, and the Life of Discipleship*. San Francisco: Harper & Row, 1988.

Brown, Peter. *Augustine of Hippo: A Biography*. Berkeley: University of California Press, 1967.

Brown, Raymond E. *The Birth of the Messiah: A Commentary on the Infancy Narratives in Matthew and Luke*. New York: Doubleday & Co., 1977. Reprint, Garden City, NY: Image Books, 1979.

———. *The Gospel according to John*. Anchor Bible, vols. 29–29A. Garden City, NY: Doubleday & Co., 1966, 1970.

Brown, Robert McAfee. *Gustavo Gutiérrez: An Introduction to Liberation Theology*. Maryknoll, NY: Orbis Books, 1990.

Brueggemann, Walter. "Scripture and an Ecumenical Life-Style." *Interpretation* 24 (1970): 3–19.

Bultmann, Rudolf. *The History of the Synoptic Tradition*. Trans. John Marsh. Rev. Ed. New York: Harper & Row, 1976.

Cadorette, Curt. *From the Heart of the People: The Theology of Gustavo Gutiérrez*. Oak Park, IL: Meyer-Stone Books, 1988.

Carlston, Charles E. "Proverbs, Maxims, and the Historical Jesus." *Journal of Biblical Literature* 99(1980):87–105.

Chauduri, Roma. *Ashvaghosha: Makers of Indian Literature*. New Delhi, India: Sahitya Akademi, 1988.

Ch'en, Kenneth S. *Buddhism in China: A Historical Survey*. Princeton, NJ: Princeton University Press, 1964. Paperback reprint, 1972.

Cheng-chüeh, Hung-chih. *Cultivating the Empty Field: The Silent Illumination of Zen Master Hongzhi*. Trans. Taigen Daniel Leighton with Yi Wu. San Francisco: North Point Press, 1991.

Chopp, Rebecca. *The Praxis of Suffering: An Interpretation of Liberation and Political Theologies*. Maryknoll, NY: Orbis Books, 1986.

Cleary, J. C. *Zen Dawn: Early Zen Texts from Tun Huang*. Trans. J. C. Cleary. Boston: Shambhala, 1986.

Conze, Edward. *Buddhism: Its Essence and Development*. Oxford: Bruno Cassirer, Ltd. Reprint, New York: Harper Torchbooks, 1959.

———. *Buddhist Scriptures*. Harmondsworth: Penguin, 1959.

———, et al., ed. and trans. *Buddhist Texts through the Ages*. New York: Philosophical Library, 1954. Reprint, Boston: Shambhala, 1990.

————. *Buddhist Thought in India: Three Phases of Buddhist Philosophy.* London: George Allen & Unwin, 1962. Reprint, Ann Arbor, MI: University of Michigan Press, 1967.

————. *Buddhist Wisdom Books, Containing The Diamond Sutra and The Heart Sutra.* 2nd ed. London: George Allen and Unwin, 1975. Reprint, London: Unwin Paperbacks, 1988.

————. *The Prajnaparamita Literature.* Indo-Iranian Monographs 6. The Hague, The Netherlands: Mouton & Co., 1960.

————, ed. and trans. *Selected Sayings from the Perfection of Wisdom.* 1955. Boulder, CO: Prajna Press, 1978.

Cook, Francis H. *Hua-Yen Buddhism: The Jewel Net of Indra.* University Park, PA: Pennsylvania State University Press, 1977.

Corless, Roger J. *The Vision of Buddhism: The Space under the Tree.* New York: Paragon House, 1989.

Cowell, E. B., et al. *Buddhist Mahayana Texts: The Buddha-karita of Asvaghosha, The Larger Sukhavati-vyuha, The Smaller Sukhavati-vyuha, The Vagrakkhedika, The Larger Pragna-paramita-hridaya-sutra, The Smaller Pragna-paramita-hridaya-sutra, The Amitaur-dhyana-sutra.* Trans. E. B. Cowell, F. Max Müller, and J. Takakusu. The Sacred Books of the East, Vol. 49. Ed. F. Max Müller. Oxford: Clarendon Press, 1894. Reprint, New York: Dover Publications, 1969.

Crenshaw, James L. *Old Testament Wisdom: An Introduction.* Atlanta: John Knox Press, 1981.

Crossan, John Dominic. *The Historical Jesus: The Life of a Mediterranean Jewish Peasant.* San Francisco: HarperSanFrancisco, 1991.

————. *In Parables: The Challenge of the Historical Jesus.*

Davies, W. D. *Paul and Rabbinic Judaism: Some Rabbinic Elements in Pauline Theology.* London: SPCK, 1962.

————. *The Setting of the Sermon on the Mount.* Cambridge: Cambridge University Press, 1966.

The Dhammapada: The Path of Perfection. Trans. Juan Mascaro. New York: Penguin Books, 1973.

Dodd, C. H. *The Interpretation of the Fourth Gospel.* Cambridge: Cambridge University Press, 1965.

Dogen. *Moon in a Dewdrop: Writings of Zen Master Dogen.* Ed. Kazuaki Tanahashi. San Francisco: North Point Press, 1985.

————. *A Primer of Soto Zen: Dogen's Shobogenzo Zuimonki.* Trans. Reiho Masunaga. Honolulu: University of Hawaii Press, 1971.

————. *Shobogenzo Bendowa.* Trans. Norman Waddell and Masao Abe. *Eastern Buddhist*, New Series 4/1(1971):124–57.

————. *Shobogenzo Buddha-Nature.* Trans. Norman Waddell and Masao Abe. *Eastern Buddhist*, New Series 8/2(1975):94–112.

Drummond, Richard H. *Gautama the Buddha: An Essay in Religious Understanding.* Grand Rapids, MI: William B. Eerdmans, 1974.

Dumoulin, Heinrich. *Christianity Meets Buddhism.* Trans. John C. Maraldo. LaSalle, IL: Open Court Publishing Co., 1974.

————. *Zen Buddhism: A History.* 2 vols. Trans. James W. Heisig and Paul Knitter. New York: Macmillan Publishing Co., 1988, 1990.

Edwards, Richard A. *A Theology of Q: Eschatology, Prophecy, and Wisdom.* Philadelphia: Fortress, 1976.

Eliade, Mircea, et al., eds. *The Encyclopedia of Religion*. 16 vols. New York: Macmillan, 1987.

Eliade, Mircea. *A History of Religious Ideas*. Vol. 2, *From Gautama Buddha to the Triumph of Christianity*. Trans. Willard R. Trask. Chicago: University of Chicago Press, 1982.

———. *The Myth of the Eternal Return or, Cosmos and History*. Trans. Willard R. Trask. Bollingen Series 46. Princeton, NJ: Princeton University Press, 1971.

———. *Patterns in Comparative Religion*. Trans. Rosemary Sheed. New York: Sheed & Ward, 1958. Reprint, New York: New American Library, 1963.

———. *Yoga: Immortality and Freedom*. Trans. Willard R. Trask. Bollingen Series 56. 2nd ed. Princeton, NJ: Princeton University Press, 1969.

Evans, G. R. *Augustine on Evil*. Cambridge, England: Cambridge University Press, 1982.

Fitzmyer, Joseph A. *The Gospel According to Luke*. The Anchor Bible, Vols. 28, 28a. Garden City, NY: Doubleday & Co., 1981.

———. *Luke the Theologian: Aspects of His Teaching*. New York: Paulist, 1989.

The Flower Ornament Scripture: A Translation of the Avatamsaka Sutra. Vol. I. Trans. Thomas Cleary. Boulder, CO: Shambhala, 1984.

Gilson, Etienne. *The Christian Philosophy of Saint Augustine*. Trans. L. E. M. Lynch. London: Victor Gollancz, 1961.

Gira, Denis. *Le sens de la conversion dans l'enseignement de Shinran*. Paris: Edition Maisonneuve et Larose, 1985.

Glasenapp, Helmuth von. *Buddhism: A Non-Theistic Religion*. Trans. Irmgard Schloegl. New York: George Braziller, 1966.

Grant, Robert. *Augustus to Constantine: The Rise and Triumph of Christianity in the Roman World*. San Francisco: Harper & Row, 1970. Reprint, San Francisco: Harper & Row Paperback, 1990.

Guardini, Romano. *The Conversion of Augustine*. Trans. Elinor Briefs. Westminster, MD: Newman Press, 1960.

Gutiérrez, Gustavo. *The God of Life*. Trans. Matthew J. O'Connell. Maryknoll, NY: Orbis Books, 1991.

———. *On Job: God-Talk and the Suffering of the Innocent*. Trans. Matthew J. O'Connell. Maryknoll, NY: Orbis Books, 1987.

———. *The Power of the Poor in History*. Trans. Robert R. Barr. Maryknoll, NY: Orbis Books, 1983.

———. *A Theology of Liberation: History, Politics and Salvation*. Trans. and ed. Caridad Inda and John Eagleson. Maryknoll, NY: Orbis Books, 1973.

———. *The Truth Shall Make You Free: Confrontations*. Trans. Matthew J. O'Connell. Maryknoll, NY: Orbis, 1990.

———. *We Drink from Our Own Wells: The Spiritual Journey of a People*. Trans. Matthew O'Connell. Maryknoll, NY: Orbis Books, 1984.

Haight, Roger. *An Alternative Vision: An Interpretation of Liberation Theology*. New York: Paulist Press, 1985.

Hakeda, Yoshito S., trans. *The Awakening of Faith: Attributed to Ashvaghosha*. Oriental Classics. New York: Columbia University Press, 1967.

Hathaway, Ronald F. *Hierarchy and the Definition of Order in the Letters of Pseudo-Dionysius*. The Hague: Martinus Nijhoff, 1969.

Hendrickx, Herman. *The Passion Narratives of the Synoptic Gospels*. Rev. ed. London: Geoffrey Chapman, 1984.

————. *The Sermon on the Mount*. Rev. ed. London: Geoffrey Chapman, 1984.

Henry, Paul. *La vision d'Ostie. Sa place dans la vie et l'oeuvre de S. Augustin*. Paris: J. Vrin, 1938.

The Holy Teaching of Vimalakirti: A Mahayana Scripture. Trans. Robert A.F. Thurman. University Park, PA: Pennsylvania State University Press, 1976.

Horseley, Richard A. *Jesus and the Spiral of Violence: Popular Jewish Resistance in Roman Palestine*. San Francisco: Harper & Row, 1987.

Kalupahana, J., and Indrani. *The Way of Siddhartha: A Life of the Buddha*. Boulder: Shambhala, 1982.

Kelber, Werner. *The Kingdom in Mark: A New Place and a New Time*. Philadelphia: Fortress, 1974.

Kim, Hee-Jin. *Dogen Kigen: Mystical Realist*. Rev. ed. Tuscon, AZ: University of Arizona Press, 1987.

King, Sallie B. *Buddha Nature*. Albany, NY: State University of New York Press, 1991.

Kitagawa, Joseph M., and Mark D. Cummings, eds. *Buddhism and Asian History: Religion, History, and Culture: Readings from The Encyclopedia of Religion*. Ed. Mircea Eliade. New York: Macmillan, 1989.

Kodera, Takashi James. *Dogen's Formative Years in China: An Historical Study and Annotated Translation of the Hokyo-ki*. London and Henley: Routledge & Kegan Paul, 1980.

LaFleur, William R., ed. *Dogen Studies*. Studies in East Asian Buddhism, 2. Honolulu: University of Hawaii Press, 1985.

Ling, Trevor. *The Buddha: Buddhist Civilization in India and Ceylon*. New York: Charles Scribner's Sons, 1973. Reprint, Harmondsworth, England: Penguin Books, 1976.

Louth, Andrew. *Denys the Areopagite*. Wilton, CT: Morehouse-Barlow, 1989.

McGinn, Bernard. *The Foundations of Mysticism*. Vol. I of *The Presence of God: A History of Western Christian Mysticism*. New York: Crossroad, 1991.

McGovern, Arthur F. *Marxism: An American Christian Perspective*. Maryknoll, NY: Orbis Books, 1980.

Mack, Burton L. *A Myth of Innocence: Mark and Christian Origins*. Philadelphia: Fortress, 1988.

Maida Shuichi. *The Evil Person: Essays on Shin Buddhism*. Trans. Nobuo Haneda. Los Angeles: Higashi Honganji North American Translation Center, 1989.

Markus, R. A., ed. *Augustine: A Collection of Critical Essays*. Modern Studies in Philosophy. Garden City, NY: Anchor Books, 1972.

Meier, John P. *A Marginal Jew: Rethinking the Historical Jesus*. Vol. I, *The Roots of the Problem and the Person*. Anchor Reference Library. New York: Doubleday, 1991.

————. *The Mission of Christ and His Church: Studies in Christology and Ecclesiology*. Wilmington, DE: Michael Glazier, 1990.

————. *The Vision of Matthew: Christ, Church, and Morality in the First Gospel*. New York: Paulist, 1979.

Murti, T. R. V. *The Central Philosophy of Buddhism: A Study of the Madhyamika System*. 2nd ed. London: George Allen & Unwin. Reprint, London: Unwin Paperbacks, 1980.

Nagao, Gadjin. "The Buddha's Life as Parable for Later Buddhist Thought." *Eastern Buddhist*, New Series 24/2(1991):1–32.

————. *The Foundational Standpoint of Madhyamika Philosophy*. Trans. John P. Keenan. Albany, NY: State University of New York Press, 1989.

————. "The Life of the Buddha: An Interpretation." *Eastern Buddhist*, New Series 20/2(1987):1–31.

————. *Madhyamika and Yogacara: A Study of Mahayana Philosophies*. Ed. and trans. L. S. Kawamura in collaboration with G. M. Nagao. Albany, NY: State University of New York Press, 1991.

————. "On the Theory of the Buddha-Body (*Buddha-kaya*)." *Eastern Buddhist*, New Series 6/1(1973):25–53.

Nakamura, Hajime. *Ways of Thinking of Eastern Peoples: India-China-Tibet-Japan*. Revised translation, ed. Philip P. Wiener. Honolulu: University of Hawaii Press, 1964.

The New Jerusalem Bible. New York: Doubleday, 1985.

Nhat Hanh, Thich. *Being Peace*. Ed. Arnold Kotler. New York: Bantam Books, 1987.

————. *Breathe! You Are Alive: Sutra on the Full Awareness of Breathing*. Berkeley, CA: Parallax Press, 1988.

————. *The Cry of Vietnam*. Trans. Thich Nhat Hanh and Helen Coutant. Santa Barbara, CA: Unicorn Press, 1968.

————. *The Heart of Understanding: Commentaries on the Prajnaparamita Heart Sutra*. Ed. Peter Levitt. Berkeley, CA: Parallax Press, 1990.

————. "The Individual, Society, and Nature." In *The Path of Compassion: Writings on Socially Engaged Buddhism*. Ed. Fred Eppsteiner. 2nd edition, revised. Berkeley, CA: Parallax Press, 1988.

————. *Interbeing: Commentaries on the Tiep Hien Precepts*. Ed. Fred Eppsteiner. Berkeley, CA: Parallax Press, 1987.

————. *The Miracle of Mindfulness: A Manual on Meditation*. Trans. Mobi Ho. Revised edition. Boston: Beacon Press, 1987.

————. *The Moon Bamboo*. Trans. Vo-Dinh Mai and Mobi Ho. Berkeley, CA: Parallax Press, 1989.

————. *Old Path White Clouds: Walking in the Footsteps of the Buddha*. Trans. Mobi Ho. Berkeley, CA: Parallax Press, 1991.

————. *Our Appointment with Life: The Buddha's Teaching on Living in the Present*. Trans. Annabel Laity. Berkeley, CA: Parallax Press, 1990.

————. *The Path of Return Continues the Journey*. Trans. Vo-Dinh. New York: Hoa Binh Press, 1972.

————. *Peace Is Every Step: The Path of Mindfulness in Everyday Life*. Ed. Arnold Kotler. New York: Bantam Books, 1991.

————. *The Pine Gate: Stories by Thich Nhat Hanh*. Trans. Vo-Dinh Mai and Mobi Ho. Fredonia, NY: White Pine Press, 1988.

————. "Please Call Me by My True Names." In *The Path of Compassion: Writings on Socially Engaged Buddhism*. Ed. Fred Eppsteiner. 2nd edition, revised. Berkeley, CA: Parallax Press, 1988.

————. *Present Moment Wonderful Moment: Mindfulness Verses for Daily Living*. Trans. Annabel Laity. Berkeley, CA: Parallax Press, 1990.

————. *The Sun My Heart: From Mindfulness to Insight Contemplation*. Trans. Anh Huong Nguyen, et al. Berkeley, CA: Parallax Press, 1988.

————. *Transformation and Healing: The Sutra on the Four Establishments of Mindfulness*. Berkeley, CA: Parallax Press, 1990.

————. *Vietnam: Lotus in a Sea of Fire*. New York: Hill and Wang, 1967.

————. *Zen Keys*. Trans. Albert and Jean Low. Garden City, NY: Anchor Books, 1974.

————. *Zen Panels: Poems*. Trans. Teo Savory. Greensboro, NC: Unicorn Press, 1976.

Nishitani Keiji. *Religion and Nothingness*. Trans. Jan Van Bragt. Berkeley, CA: University of California Press, 1982.

O'Connell, Robert J. *St. Augustine's Confessions: The Odyssey of Soul*. Cambridge, MA.: Harvard University Press, 1969. Reprint, New York: Fordham University Press, 1989.

Panikkar, Raimundo. *The Silence of God: The Answer of the Buddha*. Trans. Robert Barr. Maryknoll, NY: Orbis, 1989.

The Perfection of Wisdom in Eight Thousand Lines & Its Verse Summary. Trans. Edward Conze. San Francisco: Four Seasons Foundation, 1973.

Perkins, Pheme. *Resurrection: New Testament Witness and Contemporary Reflection*. Garden City, NY: Doubleday, 1984.

Perrin, Norman. *Jesus and the Language of the Kingdom: Symbol and Metaphor in New Testament Interpretation*. Philadelphia, Fortress, 1976.

————. *Rediscovering the Teaching of Jesus*. New York: Harper & Row, 1967.

————. *The Resurrection According to Matthew, Mark, and Luke*. Philadelphia: Fortress, 1977.

Pieris, Aloysius. *Love Meets Wisdom: A Christian Experience of Buddhism*. Maryknoll, NY: Orbis Books, 1988.

Pseudo-Dionysius. *The Complete Works*. Trans. Colm Luibheid et al. The Classics of Western Spirituality. New York: Paulist, 1987.

Putnam, Caroline Canfield. *Beauty in the Pseudo-Denis*. Philosophical Studies 190. Washington, DC: Catholic University of America Press, 1960.

Pye, Michael. *Skillful Means: A Concept in Mahayana Buddhism*. London: Duckworth, 1978.

Rahner, Karl. "Christianity and the Non-Christian Religions." *Theological Investigations*, Vol. V: *Later Writings*. Trans. Karl-H. Kruger. New York: Seabury Press, 1966.

————. *Foundations of Christian Faith: An Introduction to the Idea of Christianity*. Trans. William V. Dych. New York: Crossroad, 1978.

Rahula, Walpola. *What the Buddha Taught*. New York: Grove Press, 1959. Reprint, New York: Evergreen Edition, 1962.

Roques, René. *L'univers dionysien: structure hiérarchique du monde selon le pseudo-Denys*. Aubier: Editions Montaigne, 1954.

Rutledge, Denys. *Cosmic Theology: The Ecclesiastical Hierarchy of Pseudo-Denys: An Introduction*. Staten Island, NY: Alba House, 1965.

Sanders, E. P. *Jesus and Judaism*. Philadelphia: Fortress, 1985.

Sanders, Jack. *The New Testament Christological Hymns: Their Historical Religious Background*. Cambridge: Cambridge University Press, 1971.

Schillebeeckx, Edward. *Jesus: An Experiment in Christology*. Trans. Hubert Hoskins. New York: Seabury Press, 1979.

Schottroff, Luise, and Wolfgang Stegemann. *Jesus and the Hope of the Poor*. Trans. Matthew J. O'Connell. Maryknoll, NY: Orbis Books, 1986.

Schuon, Frithjof. *The Transcendent Unity of Religions*. Wheaton, IL: Theosophical Publishing House, 1984.

Senior, Don. *The Passion of Jesus in the Gospel of Mark*. Wilmington, DE: Michael Glazier, 1984.

———. *The Passion of Jesus in the Gospel of Matthew*. Wilmington, DE: Michael Glazier, 1985.

Shibayama, Zenkei. *A Flower Does Not Talk: Zen Essays*. Trans. Sumiko Kudo. Rutland, VT: Charles E. Tuttle, 1970.

———. *Zen Comments on the Mumonkan*. Trans. Sumiko Kudo. San Francisco: Harper & Row, 1974.

Shinran. *Tannisho: A Shin Buddhist Classic*. Trans. Taitetsu Unno. Honolulu, Hawaii: Buddhist Study Center Press, 1984.

Soga Ryojin. "Dharmakara Bodhisattva." In *The Buddha Eye: An Anthology of the Kyoto School*. New York: Crossroad, 1982.

Stcherbatsky, Theodore. *The Conception of Buddhist Nirvana*, 2nd ed., enlarged. Delhi: Motilal Banarsidass, 1968; reprint, 1989.

Stendahl, Krister. "Quis et Unde? An Analysis of Mt 1–2." In *Judentum, Urchristentum, Kirche*. Ed. W. Eltester. Berlin: Töpelmann, 1960.

Strecker, George. *The Sermon on the Mount: An Exegetical Commentary*. Trans. O. C. Dean. Nashville: Abingdon, 1988.

Streng, Frederick J. *Emptiness: A Study in Religious Meaning*. Nashville: Abingdon, 1967.

Stryk, Lucien. *World of the Buddha: An Introduction to Buddhist Literature*. Garden City, NY: Doubleday, 1968. Reprint, New York: Grove Press, 1982.

Suzuki, Daisetz Teitaro. *Essays in Zen Buddism, First Series*. London: Rider & Co., 1949. Reprint, New York: Grove Press, 1961.

———. *Essays in Zen Buddhism, Second Series*. Ed. Christmas Humphreys. London: Rider & Co., 1970. Reprint, New York: Samuel Weiser, 1971.

———. *Essays in Zen Buddhism, Third Series*. Ed. Christmas Humphreys. London: Rider & Co., 1970.

———. *A Miscellany on the Shin Teaching of Buddhism*. Kyoto: Shinshu Otaniha Shumusho, 1949.

———. *Mysticism: Christian and Buddhist*. London: George Allen & Unwin, 1957. Reprint, London: Unwin Paperbacks, 1979.

———. *Outline of Mahayana Buddhism*. London: Luzac and Co., 1907. Reprint, New York: Schocken Books, 1963.

———. *Shin Buddhism*. New York: Harper & Row, 1970.

———. *Studies in Zen*. Ed. Christmas Humphreys. New York: Philosophical Library, 1955. Reprint, New York: Delta Publishing Co., 1987.

———. "Transmigration." *Eastern Buddhist*, New Series 17/2(1984):1–6.

Takeuchi Yoshinori. *The Heart of Buddhism: In Search of the Timeless Spirit of Primitive Buddhism*. Ed. and trans. James W. Heisig. New York: Crossroad, 1983.

Tanaka, Kenneth K. *The Dawn of Chinese Pure Land Buddhist Doctrine: Ching-ying Hui-yüan's Commentary on the Visualization Sutra*. Albany, NY: State University of New York Press, 1990.

TeSelle, Eugene. *Augustine the Theologian*. New York: Herder & Herder, 1970.

Tillich, Paul, and Hisamatsu Shin'ichi. "Dialogues, East and West: Conversations between Paul Tillich and Hisamatsu Shin'ichi." *Eastern Buddhist*, New Series 4/2(1971):89–107; 5/2(1972):107–128; 6/2(1973):87–114.

Tuttle, Gary A. "The Sermon on the Mount: Its Wisdom Affinities and their Relation to its Structure." *Journal of the Evangelical Society* 20 (1977):213–30.

Ueda Yoshifumi. "The Mahayana Structure of Shinran's Thought," Part I, *Eastern Buddhist*, New Series 17/1(1984): 57–78; Part II, 17/2(1984):30–54.

Van der Meer, F. *Augustine the Bishop*. Trans. Brian Battershaw and G. R. Lamb. London: Sheed & Ward, 1961.

Wink, Walter. *Violence and Nonviolence in South Africa: Jesus' Third Way*. Philadelphia, PA: New Society Publishers, 1987.

Index

Other Titles in the Faith Meets Faith Series